WrestlingObserver's

PURE DYNAMITE

THE PRICE YOU PAY FOR WRESTLING STARDOM

Former "British Bulldog" Tom Billington

WITH ALISON COLEMAN

WINDING
STAIR
PRESS

National Library of Canada Cataloguing in Publication Data

Billington, Tom, 1958–
The Wrestling observer's Pure dynamite : the price you pay for wrestling stardom

ISBN 1-55366-084-6

1. Billington, Tom, 1958–   2. Wrestlers – England – Biography.
I. Coleman, Alison   II. Title.   III. Title: Pure dynamite.

GV1196.B54A3 2001   796.812'092   C2001-902116-X

Winding Stair Press
An imprint of Stewart House Publishing Inc.
Etobicoke, Ontario
www.stewarthousepub.com
Executive Vice President and Publisher: Ken Proctor
Director of Publishing and Product Acquisition: Joe March

    2   3   4   5   05   04   03   02

Book design by Counterpunch / Linda Gustafson
Photographs courtesy of Alison Coleman

This book is available at special discounts for bulk purchases by groups or organizations for sales promotions, premiums, fundraising and educational purposes. For details, contact: Peter March, Stewart House Publishing Inc., Special Sales Department, 195 Allstate Parkway, Markham, Ontario. Tel: (866) 474-3478.

Printed and bound in Canada

DEDICATIONS

To my wife, Dot, for being with me.

To my dad for believing in me.

To my coach, Ted Betley, for inspiring me.

And especially to "The Golden Ace" John Naylor.
There is life after wrestling

ACKNOWLEDGEMENTS

With special thanks to Findlay Martin at SW Publishing for his editorial direction and support throughout the writing of this book.

INTRODUCTION

Everybody, at some point in their life, must look back and wonder what they did with it. Did they do all the things they planned to do? Did they see all the places they wanted to see? I was 40 years old when I found myself in that position; not a great age, I know, for reflecting on your life's achievements, but that's because I was a wrestler, and in wrestling, depending on how dedicated you are to the job, careers don't last forever.

All I ever wanted was to be the best wrestler I could be. I wasn't interested in gimmicks, or being a great talker; I wanted to be remembered for my ability in the ring. That was my ambition. And it's true what they say about wrestling – it is a hard business, whether you're at the bottom, trying to make a name for yourself, or at the top, watching the guys at the bottom trying to knock you off your spot. You had to be on form, delivering the goods, every single night.

And when pro wrestling became big business, you more or less devoted your entire life to it. It didn't matter whether you were married, or whether you had kids, your job came first. The hours were lousy, the money was never guaranteed – in America at least – and injury was always a worrying possibility; sometimes, a terrible reality. But as you can imagine, wrestling had its advantages as well, and they more than made up for the disadvantages. For example, I travelled the world – and never paid a penny for the airfares. National television exposure turned wrestlers into celebrities – when I became a wwf World Tag Team Champion, they even put me in Playboy magazine! And when business was good, which, I'll admit, with the bigger promotions, most of the time it was, the money, and the lifestyle that came with it were great.

At the time, while you are enjoying all that fame and the fortune, you fool yourself into thinking that it's never going to end. But it does. And as hard as it is being in the wrestling business, take it from me, when you are out of it, it can be a lot harder. While I probably achieved more than a lot of wrestlers, I'm sure I lost a lot more than most too.

By the time I left the wrestling business, I'd been a World Champion, twice over, worked for three of the biggest promotions in the world, wrestled some of the biggest names in the business, and become a millionaire – on paper at least. I probably packed more into my 16 years in the ring than most people manage in a lifetime, but I walked away from it with nothing. So, at the age of 40, I found myself with nothing better to do than look back and wonder what I did achieve – and where those years all went.

There I was, one minute, a young kid, lacing up my boots ready for the biggest adventure of my life, and the next, hanging those boots up for the last time. Really, that's how fast it went. As for what happened in between, well, as I recall, it went something like this...

CHAPTER ONE

For someone born just a few miles outside Wigan, in Lancashire, becoming a wrestler should have been no big surprise. Wigan has a long history of wrestling – not professional wrestling, but catch-as-catch-can, or shoot wrestling; down on the floor. It was the coal miners who worked down the local pits who started it, and over the years, a lot of very good shoot wrestlers learned their stuff in Wigan.

But, in fact, until I was 13 years old, I had no interest in wrestling whatsoever. When I was born on December 5 1958, in Golborne, my dad, Billy Billington, was already sizing me up for my first pair of boxing gloves. He was a coal miner, but he also boxed professionally, along with his brother, Eric. My uncle Eric once beat Jim Sullivan in the amateurs; as in Jim Sullivan, who later became World Champion. So I more or less grew up in a fighting family.

Just before I was born, my granddad, who used to be a second at ringside, gave my dad a ten-pound note and said to him, "If it's a boy, I want you to call him Thomas," which was his name. My mum's name is Edna. I had two sisters, Julie, a year older than me, and Carol, five years younger than me. And a brother, Mark, 15 years younger than me.

When I was growing up, I never liked school. I was one of the smallest kids, but that didn't stop me getting into trouble, and I got caned, on average, about three or four times a week. It was for different things really, like the time a friend and myself turned on all the gas taps in the chemistry lab. But we forgot about it when we went for a quick smoke behind the back bench. The whole building could have gone up; well, that was what the Headmaster said after he caned us.

About the only thing I did like at about school was the sport; the soccer and rugby league, which I played for the Wigan Town team. And I was good at gymnastics, you know, the acrobatics. Somewhere around this time, I was probably aged 11 or 12, I started to get a reputation for being a bit of a prankster. For example, one Christmas I was in my dad's shed on his allotment and I found a doll that he'd bought as a present for my sister, Carol. I also found a tin of paint, and a brush, and decided to paint the doll blue. I once painted my Doc Marten boots bright green, got caned, and was sent home from school.

My dad was a very strict man. He'd worked as a miner which was a hard job, a horrible job, but he never swore, ever – well, except perhaps "bleeder," if he got really mad. But if I did something wrong and he caught me, he'd crack me one, straight in the face. No warning, he just did it. He broke my nose once; I can't remember what it was for, but afterward, I said to myself, as I always did, "Well Tommy, you've done it and you deserve it." I definitely never argued with him.

But when I was in trouble and he thought I was right, he did stick up for me. I was very close to my dad, and as I got older, I'd say we became more like close friends or brothers than a father and son. I wasn't kidding about the boxing gloves either. When I was very small, he used to buy me pairs of little boxing gloves and then he'd kneel down on the floor in our house and spar with me. I used to go with him to the gymnasium where he trained three or four times a week. He also boxed with my Uncle Eric and the two of them used to fight at the Liverpool stadium or at Belle Vue in Manchester. When I was about seven years old, my uncle Eric left England to live in Canada, in Edmonton, Alberta, and my dad retired from the coal mine and from boxing, and went into the construction business. When I was 12, I started to train as a boxer with a coach in Golborne called Cyril Dunne. And that made my dad happy.

At weekends, he used to take me with him to the building site, where he let me drive the hydraulic dumper trucks. He'd say, "Right Thomas," he always called me Thomas, "Go and empty that lot." So I'd be driving back and forth, loading and unloading the dumper, and when I'd finished he'd give me ten shillings. I was made up... that was a lot of money.

One weekend he took me with him to a house that he was working on, for a man called Ted Betley. What we didn't know at that time was that Ted Betley used to be a wrestler. Anyway, Ted had been watching me for a while, driving around in the truck, and eventually he came over to my dad, to find out who I was.

Ted said, "He looks a handy lad, does he wrestle?"

My dad called me over, introduced me to Ted, and asked me if I wanted to have a go at wrestling. At first I said no, I didn't want to wrestle because, well, like a lot of people, I didn't think it was real. Ted just sort of laughed and said why didn't I just come up to his gym anyway and give it a try. I still wasn't sure, but I said I'd go. It turned out that Ted used to wrestle as Doctor Death, with a mask and a long black cloak. He showed me some of his old photographs and told me about his matches. He took me to his gym, which looked a bit like an old army barracks. Two other fairly young boys were already there, practising their wrestling moves. Straight away, Ted told me to get in the ring with one of them and try to pin him. Bear in mind, they'd been training with Ted for a while and already knew a lot of wrestling moves. I didn't know any, but I could fight. So I got in the ring with the oldest one and straight away he went for me. I didn't back away though, which was what he expected me to do, and I more or less knocked him all over the ring without throwing a punch.

We were just two little kids, but we fought as hard as anybody could have done. I can't even remember how the fight ended, but when it was over, Ted told my dad to bring me back the next day. I had no idea what I was doing, but that was it. From that first day, I never felt like not going back. Every day after school my dad would drive me to Ted's gym. As I got to know him, I also got to like him. He and his wife didn't have any kids of their own and I think in a way, in his heart, we – myself, and the other lads who trained regularly – were his kids.

I trained with Ted six days a week, for three years, with only Sundays off. He was very strict. He'd stand at the side, explaining and explaining what we were supposed to do. And when we got it wrong, well, he could be short-tempered, and he'd lose patience. But he was a great trainer, as you can see for yourself from the lads he that he trained.

But he didn't just teach me how to wrestle, he gave me advice as well. "Tommy," he said. "No matter what you have to face in life, no matter how scared you are, don't ever take a step back. Always take a step forward." And he told me, "It doesn't matter how good you are, or how many people you beat, there'll always be somebody waiting round the corner who will beat you." What he said made sense, and I listened, probably for the first time in the whole of my 13 years.

By this time I was starting to look forward to leaving school, although probably not as much as school was looking forward to seeing the back of me. I never learned a thing, but, if I'm honest, that was entirely down to me. There was one lad, older and bigger than me, who lived near me, Jimmy Parrot – not his real name, but he had a big nose. He shouldered me into the road one day as I was walking past. I shouted something after him and he came for me again. I managed to grab him, and pushed him headfirst into a brick wall. His head was a bloody mess and I thought, "This is it Tommy, now you've done it." So instead of going home, I ran to the allotment and locked myself in the shed. Well, I was scared of my dad. Anyway he found out what had happened and came looking for me. When I opened the shed door, I said, innocently, "What do you want dad?"

He didn't say a word, just dragged me round to Jimmy Parrot's house, and said to the both of us, "Do you two want to carry on with this?"

Jimmy didn't say anything, but I heard his mum say, "Yeah."

So I said, "Right, let's do it."

My dad opened the back door and said, "Get in the backyard. Now." But Jimmy wouldn't come out – which wasn't surprising really, because his head was a mess. So, as far as my dad was concerned, that was the end of the matter. There were quite a few incidents like that when I was growing up. Sometimes when I look back, it seems all I ever did was fight.

But I kept on training and my wrestling kept getting better. So much so that Ted said it was time I learned to shoot wrestle. You remember when I told you about Wigan having a wrestling history. Well, Ted took me to a little gym in Wigan, Riley's Gym, where a lot of that history was supposed to have happened. It wasn't much of a gym really, more like a shed or a little hut, but in Japan Riley's Gym was known as the Snake Pit. Billy Riley, who had owned it for years, had trained a lot of shoot wrestlers there, people like Billy Robinson and Karl Gotch. There was a lot of talk about how good those two were, and I don't doubt that they were, but the truth is, neither of them became what you would call big stars in America. As a pro wrestler I ran into both of them, in America and in Japan. Karl Gotch was, well, a nice enough man, but a big-headed bastard. Whatever you had, he had twice as many. Whatever you did, he'd already done it, only better. As for Billy Robinson, well, he did make his name, and a bit of money, as a shooter in America and Japan. By the time I met him, his best days were well gone, but I'll tell you more about him later.

When I went to Riley's Gym in 1971, Billy was still there, with his son Ernie Riley, Billy Joyce, and Jack Dempsey; all grown men with years of experience, but there were no young boys. It had never been a young boys' gym. Anyway, they said to me, "Come on, we'll teach you to shoot." But they didn't make any allowances for the fact that I was just a young kid with no experience.

They kept taking me down to the mat, throwing me around, putting on double wristlocks, front facelocks, and leglocks until I screamed. I thought they were going to break my legs. Billy Riley – he was an old man by this time – he just sat on the bench and watched, not saying a word. I'll be honest with you, I was scared. By the time they'd finished with me, I could hardly stand up and I had burns all over my face and arms from where they'd dragged me across the mat.

No, I didn't think much of shoot wrestling. Although, to be honest with you, in the shooting ring, I'd say these men, in their day, were probably the best in the world. But I think Ted was upset at the way they treated me, and I only went there a couple more times. Instead he took me to another gym about a mile away to train with another ex-wrestler, Billy Chambers, who used to wrestle on TV as Jack Fallon.

Well, shoot wrestling wasn't any easier with Billy Chambers. Ted would say to me, "Tommy, whatever he does to you, don't tap out," as in don't submit. So I had to grit my teeth and hang on while Billy Chambers almost tore my knees out. I was in agony. And then after the session he'd say, as nice as pie, "Would you like some ice cream Tommy?" But, you can't learn to shoot without getting hurt and I admit I did learn a lot from Billy Chambers. Bastard.

Although I didn't really enjoy those sessions, they made me realize what I wanted to be in life. The way I see it, if somebody gets hurt in wrestling and doesn't come back, they don't want it. If they get hurt but still keep coming back, over and over again, they want it. And I wanted it. So I kept on going back to Billy Chambers and putting up with the pain, once or twice every week.

By this time, I was absolutely sure about what I wanted to do when I left school. I remember when they sent us all from school to see someone at the careers office. We all sat there and he asked us all in turn what we wanted to be. One by one they answered, "a bricklayer," "a plumber," "a welder." I just sat there.

"Thomas Billington, what about you?"

I said, "I'm going to join the professionals." They thought I meant the police or the army. But at 14, I had it in my mind what I wanted to do – I was going to become a professional wrestler. Ted Betley had been telling me for a while that he believed I had the talent to make it. My dad was behind my decision one-hundred per cent. From the first time I told him I was going to be a wrestler, he and my mum stood by me and believed I would do it. If he ever had any objections my dad never said a word, like when he could see I was getting hurt during training. He left it down to me. Every day after he finished work he drove me to Ted's gym, or to Billy Chambers' gym. And after I turned pro he drove me to the matches all over the north of England, until I was old enough to drive myself. And even then he still came with me.

Just before I left Golborne Comprehensive School one of the teachers asked me what I was planning to do. When I told him I was going to be a wrestler he laughed and said I'd never make it because I was too small. His name was Belshaw, and he was from a very famous wrestling family in Wigan. I laughed as well, because I knew I would prove him wrong.

CHAPTER TWO

When I decided to become a professional wrestler, I had no idea where it was going to take me.

It was Ted who got me into the business and made the all arrangements for my first match. And when I needed a ring name, it was Ted who came up with Dynamite Kid. Over the years, certain promoters tried to tell me the name was no good, and that I should change it, but I never did.

My first professional match was against a man called Bobby Hems, in Malvern Wells, near Birmingham. I met him before the match, we shook hands, and he looked down at me and smiled. Well, you can guess why – all he could see was a nervous, skinny kid about to make his debut. What he didn't know was how much knowledge and experience I had from the three years I'd just spent with Ted Betley.

I remember sitting in the canteen with Ted, having a cup of tea before the match and feeling very nervous. A man, who I didn't know, came in and started chatting to Ted, who pointed at me and said, "This is the Dynamite Kid. He's a wrestler, do you want his autograph?"

The bloke said, "Yeah, OK." And then quick as anything, Ted turned to me and whispered, "Tommy, can you spell Dynamite Kid?"

I said "Erm... I think so Ted." That was the first autograph I ever signed. Then I went to the dressing room to get ready for the match. I'll never forget what it felt like, standing behind the curtain, waiting to hear my name. I was terrified, not of getting in the ring, but of the people – a sold-out crowd – watching me wrestle. It's funny how, 12 years later, I stood behind the curtain at the Silverdome in Pontiac, Michigan, looking out at a crowd of 92,000 people. That was WrestleMania III, and I remember standing there, completely relaxed, cigarette in one hand, cup of coffee in the other, waiting for "Rule Britannia" to start playing before we walked down to the ring.

But on this, my first night, I looked through the curtains, thinking "What am I going to do?" Anyway, once the match started and I could think about what I was suppose to be doing, the nerves just disappeared. And Bobby Hems got a bit of a surprise, because all the things I know he was planning to do to me, I ended up doing to him. I think the match went five or six rounds, and for most of them, I didn't know what day it was because of all the screaming and whistling and clapping coming from the crowd. I won that first match, and right afterward, Bobby Hems was at least polite enough to acknowledge what I'd done out there. Actually, he couldn't believe it.

That first match was for a promoter called Jack Atherton, and I stayed with him for a few months while I got the feel of the job. The other wrestlers used to complain that the pay was rotten, but for a 16-year-old kid, it wasn't bad. Jack booked me for a few shows in Wigan, which was great because I got to wrestle some of Wigan's finest, shooters like Alan Woods and the Golden Ace, John Naylor, who also knew the pro job and could give you a fantastic match. Alan Woods, or Tiger Woods, as the magazines used to call him, was, in my opinion, one of the most underrated wrestlers in the country. He never used a gimmick, just came to the ring in his regulation black trunks, and got the job done.

John Naylor was a good friend of mine, and being from Wigan, we had a similar sense of humour. I remember one Christmas, one of the wrestlers, a big African called Honeyboy Zimba wanted a goat for his Christmas dinner. I don't know, maybe that's what they eat over there instead of turkey. Anyway, John Naylor said he could get him a goat from one from the allotments in Wigan. Zimba gave him £8 and said he would meet us at the allotments the next day to pick up the goat. Only when we got there, the bloody thing was already dead. Rigor mortis had set in. John said, "Oh Christ, what are we going to do?" Zimba was going to be there any minute, so he said to me,

"Tommy, stand it up and lean it against the shed." So I did, and just then we saw Zimba in his white Chrysler, coming down the drive. John waited until he thought Zimba could see him and then started hitting the goat over the head. As the car got closer, I gave the goat a little push and it keeled over. Zimba climbed out of the car with a big smile on his face, thinking John had just killed it for him.

A few days after Christmas, when John him how the goat was, Zimba rubbed his fat belly, and said, "Oh, fantastic, man."

After a few months I started working for Joint Promotions, which was run by Max Crabtree. His two brothers were also in the business. Brian Crabtree was a referee, well, actually, he was just a glorified idiot. After the match the villain would throw Brian off the rope, he'd do a cartwheel, land on his feet and then drop kick the villain. Prick. Shirley Crabtree, of course, was Big Daddy. The star. For the first few months I wrestled a lot of different wrestlers, no big names, but slowly, I started working my way up the card.

I was always fairly quiet in those early days when I was around the other wrestlers, and kept myself to myself in the buildings; hard to believe now, I know, but true. Wrestling all those different men, most of them older than me, some with 20 years of experience in the business, made me realize that what I'd learned in three years with Ted was more than most of them ever would. There were some bad – and I mean bad – wrestlers. And a lot of them, in spite of being bloody awful, would still try and take liberties with smaller or less experienced men.

I soon learned that you had to work a lot harder to make yourself look good against a man who gave you nothing in the ring. In other words, he was only concerned with making himself look good. I met a few of them over the years, too.

For a while, quite early on, I was Big Daddy's tag-team partner. He was the biggest draw in the country at that time, and the most popular wrestler on British television. What did I think of him? Well, I'll say it. I know he's dead, bless him, but he was a load of shit. Well, what would you think if you were a decent wrestler and someone like Big Daddy hit you with a couple of belly butts, and the people were all going "Ooooh"? Exactly.

The trouble was, Big Shirley wasn't even a nice bloke outside of the ring. Oh, he always seemed OK. You'd walk in the dressing room and he'd shake your hand and smile, and say, "Eeee Dynamite. It's good to see you." And then as soon as you'd gone out, he'd turn round to the other wrestlers, pull his face, and say, "Nothin' but a bastard." I know, because I saw him do the same to everybody.

Another thing he liked to do was team up with a little guy, like me, to wrestle tag matches. The little guy would do all the running about and take all the knocks, and, if you remember, we wrestled some big men – like King Kong Kirk and Giant Haystacks – imagine the size of them wrestling someone the size of me. When one of those fat bastards dropped an elbow, you knew about it. Anyway, I'd always end up getting my head kicked in, I'd manage to crawl across the ring and make the tag, and collapse in the corner. Then Big Shirley would get in, hit them with his big belly, and win the match.

After a year or so, the competition got a lot better. I started wrestling Mark "Rollerball" Rocco, who later wrestled as Black Tiger in Japan. We had some fantastic matches. Like me, Rocco was a hard-hitter; he followed everything through and never held anything back. We put a hundred per cent into those matches – none of the high-flying stuff at that time – just hard, solid bouts that always excited the crowd.

I wrestled Marty Jones, who also went to Japan, but I think he was better known in the UK. Marty also trained with Ted Betley for a while. All the time I was wrestling these people, I was learning from them. I carried on training at Ted's in the afternoons and wrestling at night. On Sundays, my day off, I used to help Ted with a grocery business that he owned, packing potatoes for him. You see, Ted never charged me a penny to train with him.

I finally got a shot at a championship belt, the British Lightweight title held by Jimmy Breaks. That match was televised from the Guildhall in Preston in front of 5,000 people. Five thousand. In England today, you're lucky if you can get 350 people in the building. Jimmy Breaks was, in my opinion, a good little wrestler – I think he held that title eight times in total – but like a lot of wrestlers he could be a bit, well, two-faced. In other words, you had to be on your guard. Anyway, I beat him for the title that night, which made me, at 18 years old, the youngest British Lightweight champion. Ted came along to watch, and after the match he said to me, "Tommy, the world's your oyster now. If you want it, take it." I didn't really understand what he meant then, but that night was the greatest moment of my career, up to that point.

Just a few months later I challenged and beat Bobby Ryan for the European Welterweight title, right on his own doorstep in Stoke-on-Trent. Now I had two championship belts. Max Crabtree was happy, the arenas were doing good business, although that was something he liked to keep to himself, because apart from the very top names, like Big Daddy and Kendo Nagasaki, the pay wasn't that good. Even Bert Royal and Vic Faulkner, who were far better wrestlers, and did draw business, even they were only on about £18 a night.

I can remember wrestling a match on a card in Lincoln in 1975. Tony St. Clair had just become the champion. Mark Rocco was on the bill, as well as the African wrestler Honeyboy Zimba. He was supposed to be wrestling King Ben, only King Ben didn't turn up. He probably took one look at the line up and went home. You see Zimba, who was a big clumsy bastard, didn't care whether he hurt you or not, and nobody liked wrestling him.

Anyway, this night in Lincoln, Max Crabtree was a match short and a wrestler spare. He told Tony St. Clair that he'd have to do a double, because King Ben had no-showed. Tony said, "Who with?" "Zimba."

"No chance."

So Max asked Rocco, but he wouldn't do it either. In the end there was only me left to ask. I was 16, and I'd been in the ring barely six months. Max came up to me and said, "Keeed, I need a favour. Will you wrestle Zimba?"

I was getting paid about £8 a night at that time, so, as you would expect, I said, "How much for, Max?"

Max said, "Tell you what. If you wrestle Zimba, I'll give you King Ben's pay packet."

I said "OK, I'll do it."

We were the last match on the card that night, and normally before then all the other wrestlers would have gone home. But this night, they stayed to watch the last match – well, to watch Honeyboy Zimba break me in half. I didn't win the match – it wasn't even close – but when I walked past those other pricks on my way back to the dressing room to pick up my extra pay packet, I had a big smile on my face. Until I opened it and found £10 inside. I'll give Max Crabtree some credit, he always took care of himself.

There was one incident when a German wrestler got involved in a dispute with all three of the Crabtrees. What it was about, I couldn't tell you, but he ended up jamming Big Shirley's arm in the door and nearly broke it, he grabbed Brian and nailed him straight in the face, while Max ran off and locked himself in the toilet.

In fact, Max Crabtree and money were the two main reasons why I left the UK and went to Canada.

In the spring of 1978, I held the British and European titles, and I was wrestling hard, seven nights a week, to defend them. I wrestled a very good match against Rocco in Cleethorpes – well, we always had a good match – but on this night it was being watched by Bruce Hart, a Canadian wrestler who was in the UK on a six-week tour. Bruce came to see me after the match, introduced himself and asked if I wanted to go back to Canada with him for a few weeks to work for his dad, Stu Hart, who had his own promotion. He told me I would get a free car, a free apartment, and $400 per week.

I didn't know anything about wrestling outside of the UK. I'd never heard of Stu Hart, or his Stampede Wrestling promotion. But I liked the sound of what he was offering. As usual, I called Ted to ask his advice. Straight away he said it was a great opportunity for me, and I decided there and then I would go. Until I told Max Crabtree.

He shook his head and said, "Keeed, you're the champion. If you go, you can' t come back under the same circumstances."

"What do you mean, Max?" I said.

"You'll have to forfeit the belts before you go."

I said, "But Max, I'll only be away for six weeks."

"It doesn't matter; if you go, you lose the belts. And those Canadian bastards will murder you. But I'll tell you what, if you stay, I'll give you a pay rise."

He wouldn't say how much, but he told me not to worry, and that he'd sort it all out. And I cancelled my plans to go to Canada.

Now at that time I was getting paid £12 a night. A few nights later I was in Leicester. After the match, Max handed me my pay packet, which contained my rise. When I counted it, he'd paid me £13, and that included expenses. I thought he must have made a mistake, so I said, "I'm not being funny, Max, but what's this?"

He just said, "You're only a young lad. That's a lot of money for you."

That same night, I rang Ted and asked him to call Stu Hart to see if he would reschedule the Calgary trip. "No problem," Stu had told him, or so Ted thought. He'd even pay for my return plane ticket. So it was arranged that I'd fly out at the end of April and come back around the middle of June. And, after that incident with Max and the £1 pay rise, I also decided it was the last time anybody would do me, financially or otherwise.

My last match in England was in Chester, just a few days before I left. I was wrestling Rocco. Ted was there, and my dad, as usual, and this time he'd brought my cousin, Davey Boy Smith to watch the show. He would have been 13 or 14 years old at that time, and he'd just started training at Ted's gym. Even back then, I could see he how looked up to me, saw what I'd achieved, and wanted the same for himself. I left for Calgary, Alberta, Canada, on April 27 1978, with £20 in my pocket. My dad came to see me off at the airport. I said, "Bye Dad. See you in June." Well things didn't go exactly as I planned, and I didn't see him in June. But when I left England that day, I really had no idea it would be 13 years before I'd be back.

CHAPTER THREE

So there I was, one week the British and European Champion, the next, a complete unknown in Calgary. It felt like I was starting all over again.

I did like Canada; being up the mountains, the scenery and everything – I'd never seen anything like it. Apart from Bruce, I didn't know anybody, and for a while at first, I felt like a stranger, which I suppose I was. But some things were not so different from home. I was still playing stooge to wrestlers with not much ability, and the crowds were not as big as they could have been. Don't get me wrong, Stampede Wrestling was doing better business than a lot of other territories. But when I arrived, it wasn't great business, and in my opinion, that was down to two things: management and money.

Stu Hart was the owner, or the promoter, but most of the time it was his sons who seemed to be in control; too many chiefs and not enough Indians. In the ring, they were what I would call glorified. Nice people, very generous and kind, but as wrestlers, completely glorified. And if I'm honest, apart from Bret and Owen, I didn't rate any of them. As amateurs maybe, but not as pro wrestlers.

Anyway, there I was, 19 years old, and a stranger in Calgary. I flew in on the Thursday, and was told to be at the Victoria Pavilion the next day for my first match with Stampede Promotions. I walked into the dressing room, and the first person I ran into was the promoter, Stu Hart. He just looked me up and down, started prodding me like a piece of meat, and then said, "Ehhhhhh, you're a skinny little bastard."

Those were the first words Stu Hart ever said to me. But you know, that "skinny little bastard" ended up making more money for Stu Hart than any other wrestler in Stampede, including Archie "The Stomper" Gouldie and Abdullah the Butcher. That's true. Stu Hart said it himself.

But on that first Friday night, I still had it all to do. It was a television taping which would go out on TV the next day. My first opponent was

The Cuban Assassin. He was Cuban, but because he'd wrestled quite a lot in Germany, we were familiar with each other's style. We wrestled hard, had a good match, and I beat him. I don't recall exactly how many people were in the building that night, but it wasn't a lot. It wasn't a lot most weeks. The trouble was, Stu couldn't afford to bring big names into the territory, at least not on a regular basis, because he didn't make enough money to pay their guarantee. So most of the matches were made around the Harts, mainly Bruce, Keith, Smith and Bret, and while there weren't a lot of other big names around, well, the Harts were the big names, which meant they could be as glorified as they wanted.

I did like Calgary, but it took me a while to get used to it. It was a lot colder, and being up in the mountains, the air was thinner, which meant, at first, I was out of breath a lot more than I would have been in England. All the things Bruce Hart had promised when I met him in England; the car, the apartment, the $400 a week... a load of bollocks. There was no car, there was no apartment, and I got paid $350 a week. I found out later that when Ted Betley had been calling Stu to make arrangements for me, he'd really been speaking to one of Stu's sons impersonating their dad.

So at first I stayed with Wayne Hart, who didn't wrestle, but was a referee for Stampede. And that worked out OK until he turned round one day and told me I owed him a lot of rent and that it was time I moved out. The original six weeks I was supposed to do had stretched to more like three or four months. And although I was growing to like Canada, I think at that moment, after the lies about the money and the other promises that were broken, I was ready to pack up and go home. I still had my return plane ticket. But the Harts really didn't want me to leave. So we smoothed things over, and I stayed on with Wayne until I could afford a place of my own.

Stu and Helen were very good to me and always made me welcome at their house. I'm not sure what the kids thought of me, but I know what I thought of them. Smith was the eldest and a terrible wrestler.

Bruce, well, Bruce managed to beat more or less all his opponents without too much trouble, which I suppose, made him a great wrestler. We got along well enough at first, and I'll give him credit, he was responsible for bringing me to Calgary. But there was a bit of friction between us which turned into something more serious a few years on. Keith, who was really a fireman, had a similar wrestling ability, and like Bruce, was very good at keeping a clean sheet.

Ross was one of the youngest Hart boys. He spent a bit of time in the UK, and I think he worked behind the scenes at Stampede; a nice enough lad, but a bloody awful wrestler.

Dean, who died a few years ago, didn't wrestle at all as far I remember, and he was different to the rest of the Harts. He once asked Jim Neidhart if he could borrow his Cadillac for the day. Jim said OK. But when he came back to get his car, it wasn't there, Dean had sold it. I suppose deep down Dean was OK, he just couldn't help some of the things he did.

Bret was really just starting out as a pro wrestler when I first came to Calgary. And although we had our differences in the early days, I did like Bret and probably got along with him better than any of his brothers.

Owen, who died in 1999, at this time was just a kid, maybe about 13 years old. When he got a little bit older, he started training and eventually went into the business. Of all the Harts, I think Bret and Owen definitely had the most ability, which was fairly obvious when you see where their careers went.

When I first started with Stampede, I was always the good guy in the ring. Being just a young kid and everything, it was the obvious thing to do. That changed a few months later when Dick Steinborn came into the territory and took over the book for Stu. There was one guy I was wrestling at that time, I can't even remember his name, but every night he threw me round that ring like a sack of shit. Up, down, bang, bang, bang, and every time he threw me, the crowd would go, "Ooooh." Then after the match one night, Dick came up to me and said, "Tom, you're taking too many good bumps. The crowd is too sympathetic. I'd rather you took the same bumps and had the crowd cheering."

So I had a change of heart. I was wrestling a tag match with Bruce, and at one point he got himself into trouble in the middle of the ring. When he finally got close enough to tag me, I bent down to tie my bootlace and pretended I hadn't seen him. I pulled that stunt on him a few times, although at first I did apologize on the microphone for letting him down and said it wouldn't happen again.

Anyway, a week later we tagged up for another match. As usual, Bruce was struggling, only this time when he tried to make the tag, I just smacked him in the mouth. Well, that was it; the crowd went wild. After the match, I had to have security escort me back to the dressing room, because the people were so angry. They were screaming and spitting and throwing things at me; I knew at that point there was no going back. To tell you the truth, I preferred being the villain – I enjoyed it. If I could get the crowd riled to near-riot level, I'd do it. Because angry or not, those people definitely got their money's worth, and a match they could talk about for a long time.

The highlight of the wrestling year in Calgary was Stampede Week, which took place in the middle of July. It was a big occasion, with all kinds of shows and attractions going on all across the city, and a great atmosphere. The best thing about Stampede Week for us was that some of the big American names would come into the territory, a tradition that had gone on for years.

Back in 1969 Dory Funk Jr. was the NWA World Heavyweight Champion, and he came to Calgary for Stampede Week, with plans to wrestle Archie "The Stomper" Gouldie, at that time the Stampede North American Champion and one of the promotion's biggest draws. But the week before the big championship match, they held a "winner of this match to face the World Champion," as in Dory Funk Jr. Well, that match came down to Archie Gouldie, and a fellow countryman of mine, Billy Robinson, who I mentioned earlier.

Billy Robinson was supposedly giving Archie a bit of a hard time, well, he gave most wrestlers a hard time. In fact, knowing Billy, he was probably giving Archie nothing, if you see what I mean. I don't know what happened, but all of a sudden, in the middle of the match, Archie rolled out of the ring, grabbed his stuff and left. Just like that. Which left Billy Robinson to face Dory Funk Jr. for the World Heavyweight title. That, in my opinion, was where Billy Robinson got one of his biggest breaks, and after that he did OK for himself in America and Japan.

In 1978, Stampede Week was still a big occasion for wrestling. Stu always hired the Corral, an ice hockey stadium which held about five or six thousand people. He brought in people like André the Giant, occasionally, Abdullah the Butcher, as well as the midgets, and a few women wrestlers. That year we also had the NWA World Heavyweight Champion Harley Race and NWA Junior World Heavyweight Champion Nelson Royal.

Now at that time, I didn't know anything about Harley Race, or his track record in the business. The first time I really met him, we were in a car on our way to the next match, for example, in Edmonton. Harley Race was driving, as usual. He always drove, whether he'd had been drinking or not. Nelson Royal was next to him in the front, and I was in the back with Bret.

I was saying something to Bret, but because of my accent, which, at that time, was still a strong Wigan accent, Harley Race turned to Nelson Royal and said, "You know, I can't understand a fucking word that Limey bastard's saying."

So I shouted back – I was only 19 – "That's OK Yank, because I can fucking understand you, which means I must be cleverer than you."

Harley slammed the brakes on so hard, we were nearly catapulted into the front seat. The car screeched to a halt and Harley climbed out, looking really angry. He ripped the back door open, leaned his head inside and just said, "Get out."

All I could hear was Bret saying, "Tom, don't go out." Well I didn't know Harley had a rep, but it didn't matter anyway, because in my opinion, win, lose, or draw, you have to make the attempt. So I got out. And eventually, Bret got out. The three of us stood there, by the side of the road, in the middle of nowhere. Then, Harley Race, who had been drinking and driving, grabbed us both in a side headlock and said, "I don't see why we should fight, boys, do you?" He was crushing our heads so tight, we couldn't speak, but as he started to slacken his grip, I stuck a boot out behind him, tripped him up, and put him flat on his backside. Luckily for us, he saw the funny side of it and the three of us ended up laughing. Years later, Harley Race – "The King" – and myself became very close friends. We did get into a lot of trouble, in and out of the ring, and he was on the wrong end of some of my worst pranks, but, as Dionne Warwick once sang, "That's what friends are for."

Stampede Week was also when I got to meet the great Lou Thesz. He was in Calgary as the special guest referee for the World Championship match. I never actually saw him wrestle, and when I met him in 1978, he must have been in his sixties, but he was still in good shape. I only spoke to him a couple of times that week, but I thought he was a great bloke.

I wrestled Nelson Royal for the NWA World Junior Heavyweight title every night. We went round the Stampede loop, through Edmonton, Regina, Saskatoon, Medicine Hat, and Yellowknife, and finishing in Calgary on the Friday. We wrestled for nearly an hour every night – no separate rounds like they had in England – and every night I got disqualified, usually for throwing him over the top rope, which, in Canada meant an automatic DQ.

Then on the last night, Keith Hart wrestled Nelson Royal in the Corral. I watched that match, which ended in a one-hour draw, and I couldn't believe it. A fireman made a one-hour draw with the World Champion.

But apart from that, Stampede Week was a big occasion and for a fairly unknown wrestler like me, a chance to get yourself noticed. Which was exactly what happened. A German promoter called Schober came to Calgary that year. He watched my matches with Nelson Royal and afterward asked me if I wanted to go to Germany for the Oktober-fest, a six-week tournament, later in the year. He spoke to Stu who eventually he said it was OK, and I was surprised to learn that Bruce and Keith would be going as well. I didn't find out why until a few years later.

I spent a lot of my spare time over at Stu Hart's house, or I should say, the Hart mansion, which looked more like the Addams Family house. Mostly I'd be training down in the basement gym, which everybody liked to call The Dungeon. It wasn't very big; it had a wrestling mat, like the ones you have in amateur wrestling, a few dumbbells and a bench press. In a way it was a bit like Riley's gym in England. Personally, I never saw the point of giving a gym a name, like the Snake Pit, or The Dungeon, but I suppose it came about because of the screams that used to come out of it.

If we weren't working the loop, I'd train at Stu's house maybe five or six days a week. A lot of wrestlers were training down there, not at the same time because it wasn't big enough, but all day there'd be people coming and going, in and out of Stu's house. All the Harts trained there as well as Jim Neidhart, Junkyard Dog, Hercules Ayala, and a few years later, a young Chris Benoit and Brian Pillman. There was a couple of Japanese wrestlers as well, Kazuo Sakurada and Mr. Hito, whose real name was Hadachi.

Bret's mum, Helen, was a great lady, always very good to me, very polite, and on many occasions she would ask me over for Sunday dinner. Occasionally Stu would lend me one of his cadillacs – he owned a fleet of about 20 – and I'd drive up to Edmonton to visit my Uncle Eric. Stu was good to me as well.

And as I got to know them over those first few months, they got to know me. One day, Bruce and Keith asked me to go skiing with them at a ski resort in Banff, a few miles west of Calgary. Now, as you would imagine, I'd never been skiing before in my life. All I had on were my jeans and a little T-shirt, but they told me, "No, you'll be fine like that Tom. The sun will be shining at the top of the mountains you know."

So I went. The slope we were going on was about a mile down. They fastened my skis on and we got the chairlift up to the top. I don't think they put the skis on properly because as soon as I set off, one fell off and dragged along behind, because it was still tied to my foot. Well, with only one ski on, I couldn't stay up, and I just fell and rolled, fell and rolled ... so many times that I lost count.

Eventually, about halfway down the slope, I hit a tree or a bush. I'd had enough, so I took the skis off and walked the rest of the way to the bottom. All I had on was this T-shirt – well, more like a vest – and it was about -30 degrees. I finally got to the bottom and went for a coffee to try and warm up. But by this time I was so cold, I couldn't stop shaking. Ten minutes later, those two bastards walked in, smirking and grinning. I never said a word, but I thought to myself, "They've done me here."

Well, a few months later, I'd been working out with Bruce down in The Dungeon, and we both went for a shower. They had this great big shower room with shower heads all round the wall. Bruce was in there, shampooing his head, and I was thinking about that skiing trip. So I turned the cold water off. Bruce hit the roof, screaming and shouting that the hot water was scalding him. I said, innocently, "Sorry Bruce. I must have hit the wrong tap." I'm sure he still has the marks on his head from the blisters.

A couple of weeks after that, I was wrestling Keith in the Pavilion. I slammed him as hard as I could, then said, under my breath, "Don't move." I climbed to the top, dropped a knee on his head, and accidentally loosened a couple of his teeth. He came looking for me in the dressing room afterward, a bit upset, saying, "What the hell was that supposed to be, Tom?"

"Keith," I said, all innocent. "Just a minute lad, I did tell you not to move. I had it all weighed up – you must have flinched." After that, no matter who he was wrestling, Keith Hart always wore a gumshield. I don't suppose either of them made a connection, but I knew I'd reached a point where other wrestlers would definitely think twice before trying it on with me.

One wrestler who I did get along with and who I always rated as a great character in the ring was my old friend Jim Neidhart. Jim was from Anaheim, California and played football for the Oakland Raiders. He came to Stampede the same year as me, long before he became Bret's partner in The Hart Foundation. His first match was against me, the Dynamite Kid. It was only a little spot show in Lethbridge or Regina, but he managed to fuck it up grand style.

In our profession, whether you're in America, England, Japan, Germany, wherever, you always put a headlock on with your left arm. Everything is left, left arms, left legs – you're trained to think left. The only place you don't think left is in Mexico, where you do everything on the right.

Anyway, on this night, Jim put me in a right-hand headlock, which meant I had no leverage to push him off onto the ropes. So there I was stuck in a headlock wondering what to do. Eventually I did manage to push him off, but he hit the referee with his shoulder – Jim was about 280lbs – and the referee went down. Jim managed to hit the referee not once, not twice, but three times, and then got himself disqualified.

Afterward I said, "Jim lad. You're not ready for this yet." But he got there in the end, and what a great character; I still think the world of him.

I was working really hard for Stampede, wrestling The Cuban Assassin and Norman Frederick Charles III. Just after Stampede Week, I wrestled him in the main event of a contest for the British Commonwealth title. They'd just introduced that belt, so after beating Norman Frederick Charles, I became the first British Commonwealth Champion. I defended the title for the next few months, and eventually it was Charles who took it off me.

By this time it was October and I was due to fly out to Germany for the Oktoberfest in Hanover. Keith couldn't go, so the first year I went with Smith, and the year after I took Bruce. I found out a few years later that the Harts had only gone along because Stu insisted they were part of the deal. Apparently he had told Schober, "If you want Dynamite, you have to take Smith and Bruce as well." In 1981 when I went to Japan to wrestle for Antonio Inoki and NJPW, Stu made sure that Bret was part of that deal as well.

Anyway, the Oktoberfest was a good chance to stop off back home in Golborne for a few days to see my mum and dad. While I was there I had a call from my old friend Marty Jones. He wanted me to wrestle him in Croydon, on a one-night-only basis, for a television match. Well, as I was only passing through I said, "Fine. I'll do it."

Also on the card that night were a couple of Japanese wrestlers billed as Sammy Lee and Kwik Kick Lee, who were wrestling Mark Rocco and Giant Haystacks. I'd never heard of them, but I found out that Sammy Lee's real name was Satoru Sayama, and his friend was Akira Maeda. What I didn't know then was that Sammy Lee, or Sayama, would be the man behind the mask of the first – and in my opinion the best – Tiger Mask, and the two of us would have some of the greatest matches of our entire lives.

But that night in Croydon, they were a couple of nobodies. I was in the dressing room and Max Crabtree was watching Sayama get ready, shaking his head and saying, "What the fucking hell has Karl Gotch sent me?" Sayama was only a small man, but when he got in that ring, well, the crowd, and even Max Crabtree, couldn't believe what they were seeing. Sayama was fantastic.

Eventually I made it to Hanover, Germany for the Oktoberfest. Most of the time in Germany I wrestled in tag matches with Bruce or Smith. Now I always thought Smith had some strange ideas, but the year that he came to Germany, right at the end of the tournament, he lost it completely.

One of the traditions over there was to have a big parade after the matches, when all the wrestlers' names would be called and one by one they'd go down to the ring to wave to the crowd.

The announcer started calling our names, "DYNAMITE KID," and I walked down to the ring, waving and smiling at the crowd, while they were cheering and clapping. Then it was, "SMITH HART." I don't know what Smith was thinking that night, but he came down the aisle with his boots on the wrong feet, which made him look bowlegged. He had a towel stuffed down the front of his trunks, and he'd shaved his long moustache into a little moustache, exactly like Adolf Hitler's. Then he climbed in the ring, stood in the middle, and gave a Nazi salute. The crowd just went silent. There wasn't a sound. And Smith was fired on the spot.

The second year when I went with Bruce, there were a few American wrestlers there; Junkyard Dog, The Samoans, Afa and Sika, and Michael Hayes who later became one of the Freebirds. There were a couple of English wrestlers there besides me, and some Germans. Most of them were OK, but one German who I didn't like was Axel Ditta. Although Schober was the promoter, Ditta seemed to be the man in control of the matches. He was always shooting his mouth off about how great he was, and putting the other wrestlers down.

I was told that he'd once pulled a gun on an English wrestler, and said to him, "There is only one shooter here tonight." The wrestler, who in fact was a good shooter, was so scared that he lost control of himself and had to change his trunks. Another year Ditta had tried the same trick with the French Canadian Bob Dellasurra, who wrestled as The UFO. But when he pointed the gun, Bob just said, very calmly, "Well pull the fucking trigger then." Ditta hadn't realized that Afa and Sika, The

Samoans, were standing either side of him. So if he had pulled the trigger, he'd have been dead as well. Axel Ditta was a big hero with the home crowd, everybody else thought he was a no-good, two-faced, big-headed bastard. Well, by this stage of my career, the pranks had become a little bit more serious, and before I left Germany, I decided to cook up something special for Axel Ditta.

While I was in Hanover I stayed at the home of a friend of mine. When he was out at work, I went out to the shops, and bought some ready-made pastry. I rolled it out and put it in a big bowl. I'd also bought a can of dog food which I emptied into the pie. I seasoned it – salt, pepper, some herbs, and a few other, erm, ingredients – and put the crust on top. I got a knife, cut three little holes in the lid, so it looked nice, and baked it.

It was the last night of the tour, and as usual, there was a parade after the matches. And on the last night, the fans always brought presents for the wrestlers – it might be 100DM or it might be a cake or a leg-of-lamb – but they all brought something to place on the timekeeper's table, ready for the big parade. I got to the building early with the pie, which was labelled "To Axel Ditta," and put it on the table.

At the end of the night, we did our parade around the ring, and the ring announcer gave all the presents out. Axel Ditta had a big smile on his face as he picked up his pie, and for a minute I thought to myself, "Bloody hell, what have I done?" But it was too late, although I did tell some of the wrestlers, "Whatever you do, don't eat the pie."

The next year, the day before the Oktoberfest, my Lufthansa air ticket was cancelled without any explanation. I think someone must have told Axel Ditta about the pie.

Anyway, when I got back to Calgary after that first Oktoberfest, the first thing Stu Hart told me was that his son Bret was the new British Commonwealth Champion. He said, "I want you to wrestle him for the belt next week." Which was OK by me, but I don't think Bret was too thrilled about it.

CHAPTER FOUR

When I first arrived in Canada, Bret Hart was just learning the ropes as a professional wrestler. He had a good amateur record at school, right up to the provincial level, but like a lot of amateur wrestlers, he found it hard to make the switch to pro wrestling.

Some time during 1978, Bret had tagged with his older brother Smith and they'd gone down to Puerto Rico for a few weeks to work for Carlos Colon. They even held the Caribbean Tag Team belts for a while, but Bret didn't stay long, because he couldn't stand the place. When I asked him how it was, he just said, "Terrible. It was like being in jail." The money was no good and the promoters down there didn't take much care of their wrestlers. He hated it.

When Bret came back he carried on working down in Stu's gym, where he was being trained by Hadachi, and Sakurada, who had once wrestled as a tag team. Hadachi could be very short-tempered and was a bit of a bully in the dressing room, as in, taking advantage of smaller wrestlers. As a wrestler though, I'd say he knew his way around the ring. That much I will give him credit for. Sakurada was OK; also a good wrestler who had worked for Inoki.

Anyway, these two were down there in the gym "bump training" Bret Hart, as in training him to take a bump – which actually you can only learn by getting in the ring and taking a bump. And they'd been doing that for three or four months when I got involved.

Now Stu's gym didn't have a ring or any ropes, it was just a basement room with four walls and an amateur wrestling mat. So I said to Bret, "Throw me into that wall over there. When I run back at you, I want you to leapfrog over me while I run under. And when I come back the other way, give me an arm-drag."

Bret just stood there, looking at me a bit blank, and said, "I can't do that."

"Why not?"

"Because all my friends from school will be watching me on television, and if I start doing leapfrogs and arm-drags, they're going to laugh at me."

I said, "Why's that?"

"Because I was an amateur wrestler at school, and I don't do things like that."

I said, "I know you were an amateur, but you can't just stay on the floor, you know. You've got to do this."

Well, he took a bit of persuading, but eventually he did it. He even started to use some of my moves in the ring.

When I got back from the Oktoberfest, Bret had beaten Norman Frederick Charles III to become the British Commonwealth Champion, and Stu wanted me to wrestle him for the belt the following week. That was OK with me, but I knew straight away that Bret didn't want to wrestle me. He went to his dad and told him that he didn't want to wrestle me. Part of the reason, he said, was that I still wrestled the English style, which was different from the American style. But another part of it was that, well, he just didn't want to get in the ring with me. I didn't care either way. I said, "Fine. Get yourself another opponent." But Stu wasn't having it; we were going to wrestle.

We had our first match at the Friday night TV tapings at the Pavilion in Calgary. A few minutes in and I knew it wasn't looking good because Bret was wrestling stiff as a brush. I tried a few different moves to loosen him up and get him going, but he was rigid, and looked awkward. So I thought, "Right." I got him in the corner, smashed him with a forearm and broke his nose. And it did the trick – he wasn't rigid any more. We wrestled to a double disqualification or a double count out, I don't remember which, but after the match he came marching into the dressing room, his nose a bloody mess, and he was really mad. He was ready to have a go, but Hadachi and Sakurada held him back.

The crowd enjoyed those matches. And six months later Bret even thanked me for what I did. Seriously. We became very good friends, had some great matches and some good laughs.

But by the summer of 1979, my life had changed a lot more than I'd expected it to. Part of it was that the business was changing, and wrestlers had to change with it. In England I'd never used steroids. I don't know if any of the other wrestlers were using them, but if they did, I never knew. I was just a kid. All that changed the first time I went to Germany and met Sylvester Ritter, or Junkyard Dog.

I liked Junkyard Dog, and to be honest, what he lacked as a wrestler, he made up for as a talker – not the best, but definitely not the worst. And like a lot of wrestlers, he could talk business into the building. Anyway, the point of this story is that Junkyard Dog was the first person to give me drugs of any kind, and they were steroids: dianabol pills. I would imagine at that time, quite a lot of the wrestlers were taking them. And within just a few years, nearly everybody was taking them; you had to if you wanted any work.

It wasn't just steroids. The second year I was in Calgary, I was wrestling Nelson Royal again for Stampede Week. Jake Roberts had just joined the territory, and he asked me one night, "How long are you gonna wrestle tonight, Tom?"

I said, "As long as possible." I was a lot younger than Royal, but he had more experience than me. Jake handed something to me. "Here's some help. Take it. The only thing is, it will make your mouth dry." It was a Yellow Jacket – amphetamine – speed – whatever you want to call it. Just this one little pill. So I took it and I went nearly an hour with Nelson Royal. I felt great. So that was how I got into taking drugs. Not massive amounts at first, but over the years, it became a habit, just like smoking, and eventually, the side effects did start to show.

That Stampede Week was when I nearly became the youngest NWA Junior Heavyweight Champion ever. I was definitely up for it that week. Stu spoke to Leroy McGuirk, the NWA promoter in Louisiana, who didn't have a problem with me getting the belt. We'd even chilled the champagne. But Nelson Royal had other ideas. "Don't take it personally Tom," he said. "I think you're a great wrestler, but I'm not going to lose this belt to you." It turned out that he and Leroy McGuirk weren't seeing eye to eye, which meant if Leroy was OK about the idea of me being the champion, Nelson wasn't. But I didn't take it personally. And it didn't make any difference to our matches that week. We wrestled hard and filled the buildings all round the Stampede loop.

Abdullah the Butcher was in the territory for a few days. Normally he would wrestle for Stu on a one-night-only basis, when they would fly him in and fly him back out the same night. Abdullah always drew big crowds, and his matches were always very bloody and violent. Anyway, on this occasion, he was in the territory for a whole week. I can't remember who he wrestled the first night, but the poor bastard was getting ripped to shreds, as usual, when who should come down to the ring to make the save, but Bret Hart. He pulled off one of his cowboy boots and nailed Abdullah across the head with the heel of it. And because of that, Bret Hart, a novice wrestler, also got the rematch against Abdullah the Butcher.

Business was picking up in Calgary. I finally moved out of Wayne Hart's apartment because I had enough money to buy a place of my own; a duplex with four apartments. It was good to have my own home.

Bruce Hart, Stampede's creative genius, brought the idea of penalty cards back from Germany. If a wrestler did an illegal move the referee gave him a yellow card, then a red card, and finally, a black card, which meant you were disqualified. I lost count of how many black cards I was given, but, all credit to Bruce, the crowds did seem to take to the idea.

I was doing more television interviews now, probably because people were finally beginning to understand my accent. At first, they couldn't understand what I was saying, and it confused a lot of Canadians. After a while I started using an American accent and as time went on, the interviews got easier.

Wrestling went out on television every Saturday at 4PM, just like it did in England with Kent Walton and "World of Sport." The Hart Hour, everyone used to call it, and it has to be said, the Harts didn't lose many matches.

There were times though when they would try to play one wrestler off against another. For example, when we did TV on a Friday night, one Hart, for example, Bruce, would say something to one wrestler, while Smith or Ross, would say something else to another wrestler, and as you can imagine, it caused a lot of confusion in the ring. I'm not saying that the Harts weren't a close family, because most of the time they were. But there was some jealousy, and in-fighting, even with their dad, Stu.

One time they brought a wrestler in from Georgia, a big black guy called Charles Bouffont. So they put him on with me. He hadn't been in the business very long, which was obvious once we got in the ring and started wrestling. I got a few early shots in, kicks and elbows, and then I grabbed his head and ran it along the top rope, you know, to burn it. I let go and he just stood there, looked at me, and laughed, as if it was nothing. I thought to myself, "He's trying to show me up here." So I kicked him hard in the stomach, and as he fell, his jaw caught my boot, which knocked him a bit senseless. I covered him and got the pin.

When I got back to the dressing room, Smith Hart, who was friendly with Bouffant and obviously had big plans for Charles, was going nuts. He screamed, "What the goddam hell were you playing at out there?"

I just said, "Oh bugger off Smith, he was a waste of time."

So Smith went off to find his dad. "Stu," he said – they all call their dad Stu – "What the hell does Dynamite think he's doing?"

Stu just said, "Eehh, well, what can you do?" Like, he couldn't have cared less. He turned round and as he did, Smith, his eldest son, kicked him right in the balls from behind. He did that to his own dad.

In spite of what everybody thought, or the image they tried to put across, I don't think the Hart boys were that intimidated by their dad. They'd say things or do things to him that you wouldn't expect a person to say to their father, and then they'd just laugh. Funnily enough, Stu always called his kids "little bastards." And I know why.

Later that year, 1979, out of the blue, Hadachi asked me if I wanted to wrestle in Japan. It sounded like a good idea, and a good opportunity, but as always, I asked, "How much for?"

He told me it was $1,000 for ten days. "But," he said. "Don't forget you will be on television. And when the other promoters see you, they will want you."

So I said I'd do it. I was going to wrestle for a promotion called the International Wrestling Enterprise, or the IWE, for Yoshihara. I didn't know anybody in Japan, although there were some Americans on the tour, but none of them knew me. So when I got there, I felt like a stranger again, completely on my own, and I hated it.

My first match was against Isamu Terenishi. The match was televised and we wrestled to a 30-minute draw. I also wrestled Fighting Hara, who was the Junior Heavyweight Champion, and a big star for the IWE. He was Japanese and we, as in myself, Hadachi and Sakurada, had trained him in Calgary a few months before that.

We had to travel by coach to all the different places, which meant we had to sit squashed up on that coach for fourteen hours, with our cases piled on top of us. There was no hotel. At that point I felt as if I'd made a really big mistake coming to Japan. Later on the tour I met some American wrestlers: Ox Baker, Haystacks Calhoun, The Samoans, Alex Smirnoff and André the Giant. Now I was a bit surprised to see him there because just a few weeks before that, in Calgary during Stampede Week, André had said, "I will never wrestle in Japan for another promoter. I wrestle only for Inoki." So when I got to Japan and saw André in the IWE ring, I said, "What are you doing Boss?" He called everybody Boss, and we all called it him back.

He said, "A favour for Inoki."

The crowds weren't very good, except when André was there, and then it picked up, but there again we weren't wrestling in the Sumo Palace or the Tokyo Dome. They were just little halls with a few hundred people. But the funniest thing about Japan was the crowds. It didn't matter what I did in the ring – a suplex, or a flying head-butt – the people just sat there in silence. When the match was over they just applauded quietly, as if they were just being polite.

I've got a good idea why they didn't clap or cheer, it was probably the great American team that they had. Inoue or Terenishi would go to throw Haystacks Calhoun into the corner post and he'd give them nothing. Ox Baker was that clumsy and useless, a big heavy bastard, and his timing was that bad, he'd go for a leg-drop and land his arse right on their faces instead of across their neck. So the Japanese crowds must have wondered what they were watching.

At that time, I think there were still some bad feelings about westerners, or at least, Americans. If a foreigner went up to a Japanese stranger, man or woman, they'd turn their backs on you and walk away. That's true. Things did change over the years as Japan became more westernized, but back then, on my first visit, I hated it. I hated the whole ten days that I was there.

I couldn't speak any Japanese, I had no idea how much 1000 Yen was, and I was too scared to go and buy any food by myself in case I didn't have enough money. As I sat in Narita Airport waiting to catch a plane back to Canada I decided I would never go back to Japan again.

Anyway, a few months later, it turned out that Calgary was going to be part of an overseas tour for New Japan Pro Wrestling, and they were bringing a Japanese television crew with them. Inoki, Shinma, Sakaguchi, Tiger Jeet Singh and Tatsumi Fujinami were going to be there, and somewhere along the way, Hadachi had told Bret Hart that he would definitely be wrestling Fujinami, who, at that time, was the NJPW WWF Junior Heavyweight Champion. But a week before they arrived, Hadachi had to tell Bret there was a change of plan. He said, "They want Dynamite to wrestle Fujinami." Well, for me, that was great, but Bret wasn't happy about it. As usual, off he went to Stu, asking him to do something about it, but Stu couldn't. This one was out of his hands.

That night, Stan Hansen wrestled Antonio Inoki, Tiger Jeet Singh wrestled Sakaguchi and I wrestled Tatsumi "The Dragon" Fujinami. And what a fantastic match it was. I was leg-dragging him, snap suplexing him, then I went up on the top rope for a flying head-butt, only for him to hit me with a drop-kick in mid-air. Well, that was the end of the match because he drop-kicked me right out of the ring. And when he came out after me, the match ended in a double count out – a draw. I know he was disappointed not to have won, because he was the champion, but as Stu pointed out to him, "You are only here for one night. Dynamite will still be here next week." It was probably one of the best matches I'd ever had up until then, and the crowd definitely enjoyed it.

They took their TV tapes back to Japan, and the people over there must have enjoyed the match as well, because the next thing I know, Shinma, who I understood to be a sort of foreman for Inoki, called me and asked me to come to Japan to wrestle Fujinami for NJPW. Well, after what happened with the IWE, I wasn't sure I wanted to go back, but I asked, "How much for?"

Shinma said they'd pay me $1,000 a week more than IWE, which was more or less double. I thought about it for two minutes, and said "OK, I'll go." Well, business is business. And this time it was different. First class hotel, first class train – that was the bullet train, no crowding – and you were just treated altogether better by the promoters.

I went on TV many times over there wrestling Fujinami. He was a little bit older than me, a bit heavier than me and he had more experience than me, but the matches were always very close. We both wrestled hard – I mean when you hit you hit, when you kicked you kicked. That was the big difference between America and Japan. They did not fuck about in that ring. And I gave Fujinami a run for his money; up, down, up, down, bouncing him from one corner to another, I never let up. And I would say I was in better condition than him, because after nearly every match he'd be dripping with sweat and gasping for breath, and he'd say, "Dynamite, always, you blow me up." That's true. And although I would say Fujinami wrestled hard, I did meet some Japanese opponents who wrestled a lot harder, who I'll tell you about later.

I was there nearly six weeks, and in that time I got to wrestle, usually as part of a tag match, Riki Choshu, Fujiwara, Kido, Sakaguchi, Kimura. I also met Takada, and Maeda – who I knew from England a year or so earlier. They were what the Japanese called young boys, or green boys. They probably weren't even that young, but what it meant was they were right at the bottom of the ladder. You'd see them during the matches, crouched down on the floor around the ring, watching. Now you remember me telling you about Karl Gotch, who trained at Riley's gym and was working as the top wrestling coach for Inoki. The promotion would send all its young boys to the NJPW dojo in Tokyo to be trained by him.

I never wrestled Inoki in a singles match but I did some six-man tags with Steve Kiern and Stan Hansen against Inoki, Fujinami and Kengo Kimura. It was a hundred times better than the IWE, and as the crowds got to know me and my style, I began to enjoy Japan. I also preferred their aggressive style. In Japan they'd rather go in and kick the bloody hell out of you, and they'd rather break your nose or your jaw. In England, they'd rather not get hurt at all. And you can't blame them I suppose if they're only earning a tenner a night. But the Japanese attitude to wrestling suited me perfectly.

After that six weeks it was back to Canada and the Stampede loop. I had some great matches against Bret, very strong and very physical, where we'd both end up with a mouthful of blood or a black eye. We were trying new moves that a lot of people had never seen before, and both trying to look the best in the ring. For example, one night during a match Bret went to suplex me onto the rope. I hooked the rope with my right leg so that he was straining. He tried to suplex me again, but I kept my leg round the rope. Then suddenly I let go and suplexed him straight up in the air. I was on my back on the top rope and we both went over like a catapult right out onto the concrete. The result was a double count out, but that move had the people up off their seats. It was great for business, and I know that many times there were lines of people around the buildings waiting to see those matches.

I wrestled a lot of tag matches too. For a while I was Junkyard Dog's partner. I did all the wrestling; he just went in on his hands and knees and did the head-butting. I did the same thing with Giant Haystacks when he came over to Calgary. They renamed him the Loch Ness Monster and we wrestled Bret and Keith when they had the Stampede Tag Team belts. Haystacks had to go home after two weeks though, after he ate too many strawberries and came out in a rash.

In the summer of 1980 I teamed up with a wrestler called Kasavubu, a big black guy from Ohio whose real name was Jimmy Banks. He was a good friend of mine. Duke Myers was another tag partner, a 300-pounder who I also I sent over to Japan. Bret would tag with Bruce or Keith, and they were good matches too, but a pattern was setting in. Whenever we wrestled in tag matches, Bret and myself did more or less all the work for our team. And over the years, however you want to remember it, that never really changed.

It was around this time that I got myself a manager, John Foley. He was another ex-Riley's wrestler, who'd been to Japan, just like Karl Gotch and Billy Robinson. I liked Karl, well not that much, but I did have respect for what he'd done for wrestling. Billy Robinson, I never really knew, because I only met him once in Chicago. But I hit it off with John Foley straight away.

I was definitely making a name outside the territory because the promoter Leroy McGuirk called me up from Louisiana. He also got his booker, Bill Watts, to call Stu. "I want Dynamite," he said.

Stu said, "You can't have him, because I'll lose too much money." Meaning there would be less people coming into the building. Not long after that Nick Gulas, a promoter from Tennessee rang me and said, "Tom, if you come down to wrestle in Memphis, I'll pay you $600 a week."

So I said yes, but I didn't tell Stu. The only trouble was I didn't have a visa to work in the States. Gulas said, "Don't you worry about that. Just get yourself down here and then we'll sort your visa out."

I'd heard that Nick Gulas had a reputation for being a bullshitter. So I said, "I'm not being funny Nick, but you'll have to send me the visa first." Well he didn't. The prick was obviously going to let me work without one, which could have got me in a lot of trouble.

A lot of territories were asking for me, but Stu always said no. Which must have meant, financially, I was worth something to him. Takings had definitely gone up since I came to Stampede. I'm not saying that was entirely down to me, but Stu did say one time that I'd made more money for him than Abdullah and Archie ever did. So, no, he didn't want to let me go anywhere else. Except NJPW, and that was only on the condition that Bret came along as well. There was another condition, but I didn't find out what that was until a few years later.

Meanwhile, I had some news from England. My dad rang to tell me that my little cousin, Davey Boy Smith, who had been trained by my former coach Ted Betley, had finally turned pro. What's more, he was wrestling for Joint Promotions alongside my former tag-team partner, Shirley Crabtree. And Big Daddy was still doing his belly butts, winning the matches and getting all the glory, while Davey Boy Smith was the skinny little kid getting his head kicked in.

It seemed as if he was following in my footsteps, and I'll be honest, I was pleased for him. I told my dad if I could help him in his career, I would. And I meant it.

CHAPTER FIVE

It was coming up for three years since I'd left England. Did I miss it? I'll be honest, apart from not seeing my family as much I'd have liked, no, I didn't. I managed to get home about once a year, and at 22, I'd seen more of the world than most people back home could only dream of; Canada, Germany, Japan, even Hawaii on a couple of occasions. And going to all those places gave me a lot of experience as a wrestler; as long as you keep getting in the ring, you keep learning.

The first time I went to Hawaii was in 1981, when I went with Bruce and Keith Hart to wrestle for Peter Maivia's Mid Pacific Promotions. I flew straight in from a five week tour of Japan, where, as I often did because I was a heel over there, I had shaved my head. Peter Maivia took one look and said, "That's too short for a babyface," and made me wrestle in a mask.

Hawaii was where I first met a very good friend of mine, Tonga, who later wrestled as King Tonga, then Haku, and later still, as one half of The Islanders tag team. There was a mix of wrestlers in Hawaii; Giant Haystacks was over from England, Peter Maivia's son, Rocky Johnson was wrestling, as well as King Curtis Iaukea and the Steigers, Kurt and Karl. Anyway, I'd only been on the island a few hours when I got a call from Stu. "Kid, will you come home?"

I said, "I'm not being funny Stu, but I've only just got here. What's the problem?"

The problem was Stu had brought the English wrestler Steve Wright into the territory for a few weeks, and nobody would wrestle him; not one of them. Like me, Steve had been trained by Ted Betley, and by a lot of other people who could shoot wrestle. So he knew the job, top to bottom, and now he was being a bastard with everybody, trying to cripple them. I was having trouble with my knee at that time, I'd torn a cartilage in Japan, and could have done with resting it a bit. But, as usual, I said, "OK Stu. I'll do it."

And two days later I was back in Calgary. I went to see Steve, who I knew quite well from wrestling in England, and said, "Steve. Look. My knee's bad. Just, you know, take care of me a bit will you?"

He slapped me on the back and said, "Don't you worry Tommy, I will."

So that was that. I thought maybe we'd go in and do a short match, say ten minutes, because of my leg. Instead, we had a 30-minute draw, and all the way through it, Steve ripped the hell out of my knee. I wrestled him every night for about 30 minutes all that week he was there, and every night, he did the same thing, went straight for my leg. But, that's wrestling. It was nothing personal, and after the matches, we were still good friends.

I went back to Hawaii on my own later that year, again, for Peter Maivia. We were wrestling in a big building not far from Pearl Harbour. I would say, full, it could hold about 15,000 people. We had 600. We toured round the islands, Maui, Oahu, but none of them really did any business. At the end of the week Peter said to me, "Come on brah," which is brother in Hawaiian. "I'll buy you a beer." He bought me a great big jug of beer and then handed me an envelope which had my paycheque inside. But before I opened it, he stopped me and said, "Don't worry. It will be better next week."

Well, I opened it, and inside was $25. That was my pay for the whole week, for maybe four or five matches. "Don't worry," Peter said. So I didn't. I flew back to Calgary the next day. Don't get me wrong, I liked Hawaii, and I still have some good friends out there, but that was it, I never wrestled there again.

Back on the Stampede circuit, most of the time I was still going head-to-head with Bret, and we were coming up with some really exciting stuff. The first cage match I ever did was with Bret for Stampede. In Calgary we used a wire-mesh cage instead of steel bars, which I preferred because it was more flexible and could do a lot more damage when you rubbed your opponent's face into it.

We also did a few ladder matches, which added another dimension to our feud. The first one was at the Pavilion, which was taped for the next day's television. The ladder was up in the middle of the ring, with the belt – the British Commonwealth belt – hanging just above. At one point I got Bret in a headlock, he shot me off into the ropes, and I came back with a flying head-butt. Then he moved, or dropped, and I head-butted the ladder.

It was a great weapon, and by the end of that match both our heads were pouring with blood, and we were crawling round the ring; more or less selling on our knees. The place was full and for the last ten minutes of that match the crowd couldn't stay on their seats. I managed to reach the ladder first and started climbing up for the belt, but then Bret got up and drop kicked the ladder sideways. I was nearly at the top, and as it tipped over, I was catapulted off, bollocks first, onto the top rope, which got a great reaction from the crowd.

And as one feud with Bret finished, I'd start another one with Bruce, and then Keith, and then back to Bret again. I remember talking to Stu one day, and telling him about my cousin back in England, Davey Boy Smith and how he was coming along. Stu was interested. He knew Ted had trained him and that he'd had some matches with Giant Haystacks and Big Daddy. Stampede was doing OK, business-wise and he was always looking out for new faces. So I rang Davey Boy Smith and said, "Dave, how would you like to come out to Calgary?"

And as you would imagine, straight away, he said, "Yeah, when?"

I said, "Make it for next month then you won't mess up Max Crabtree's schedule."

Stu paid for his air ticket, and when he first arrived in Canada, he moved in with me. Most people assumed, in later years, that because we were first cousins, we'd been close friends from the start. But he was five years younger than me, just a kid when I left England. I'd trained in Ted's gym with him, at most, a handful of times, so, no, at first, I didn't know Davey Boy Smith at all.

But for the first few months in Stampede, I wrestled him; Dynamite Kid versus Davey Boy Smith. He was the babyface, I was the heel, which straight away caused a bit of a problem for the Harts. One night Bret came round to my apartment – at that time he had his own place just a couple of blocks away from me – with a worried look on his face and he said, "Tom, this is a really bad idea you know."

I said, "What do you mean Bret?"

"We can't have Davey sharing an apartment with you when you're wrestling him every Friday night on TV. Everyone will see what's going on."

Well, having him move in with me hadn't been my choice anyway, so I shouted, "Dave! Pack your bags. You're moving in with Bret."

Not long afterward, Davey Boy Smith was back, knocking on my door, wanting a favour. He said, "Tommy, I want to be big like these other wrestlers." Bear in mind when he first left England to come to Canada he looked like a matchstick.

I said, "Well, you need some steroids."

"Yeh, but I don't know nobody." That was how he talked then, before he got his American accent.

"Well, er…em, Dave, I'll give you a couple of shots right now if you want, just to start you off, but don't tell anybody."

I drew the stuff up, a thick white liquid, and then I gave him two injections, one in each arse cheek. I told him, "This is Winstrol V water-based steroid. I'm giving you 2CCs in one cheek and 2CCs in the other." So, off he went, I imagine, feeling very pleased with himself.

The next day we had to go to Edmonton, about 200 miles away from Calgary. We used to travel around the loop in an old van, and on this day I made sure I got in the van before Davey. Well, I had to let everybody in on the joke. Then Davey turned up and got in the van, all quiet and shy, as he was back then, and we set off. We'd only been on the road five minutes when somebody, it might have been Bruce, started going, "Mooooo." Somebody else went, "Miaaow." Davey Boy Smith just sat there, wondering what was going on. The rest of us were falling about laughing, until finally, somebody said, "Davey, you daft bastard, did you not know he injected you with milk?"

So that was that. A few months later he started going out with Stu's youngest daughter, Diana, and quite soon afterward, he married her. All in all, I would say Davey Boy Smith had a great time in Calgary. The Harts took care of him, I took care of him. When he first came over, he would only have been 17 or 18, and looked like a puff of wind would blow him away. I made him look like a million dollars in the ring during those first matches, at the expense of myself, because I took all the bumps, all the backdrops, all the back suplexes. But I didn't care. The people enjoyed the matches, and to me, that was all that mattered.

He even became a champion for the first time because of me. I was due to go out to Japan for Inoki, and at the time I had a World Championship belt. It wasn't an official World title, but one that the Harts had come up with after Nelson Royal had kept hold of the NWA Championship belt during Stampede Week.

The Harts knew I was going to be away on tour for four or five weeks, and they knew that the belt would be left undefended. But they didn't think Davey Boy Smith was up to being the champion. I was wrestling him the night before I was flying out to Tokyo, and just before the match, Bruce said to me, "Just make sure you beat him and leave the belt at home."

I thought about it and said, "OK."

We went in the ring, and I tell you, I made the bastard work that night. I bounced him round all four corners, threw him out of the ring, suplexed him in the ring, but then he dropped behind me, back suplexed me, went into a bridge and beat me, one, two... three. That was it. He was the champion. And nobody was more surprised than Davey Boy Smith.

As you can imagine, back in the dressing room, the Harts, especially Bruce, were like raging bulls. I just said, "Bruce, I'm going away. You need to use the belt." The truth was, I didn't need to have done it, but I knew it would give Davey Boy Smith's career a good boost. So yes, I looked after my cousin, set him up in Canada, took him to Japan, got him into the WWF, and when I look back, I wonder what made him do the things he did.

That same night, there was a knock at the dressing room door. When I opened it, there was this little kid, maybe 12 or 13 years old standing there. I knew his face because he was always at the Stampede shows. He was a nice enough kid, and he told me he was working out – he showed me his muscles – and he said, "When I'm older, I want to be a wrestler, exactly like you."

I said, "OK, very good." I'm sure a lot of young kids who watched wrestling had ideas about becoming wrestlers. But I had to hand it to that young kid. His name was Chris Benoit, and when he grew up, he became a terrific wrestler.

It had been nearly a year since I'd wrestled for New Japan. That second time in Japan had been so different to the first time with the IWE, so much better. So when Shinma called me up early in 1981 and asked if I could make it for a tour in the spring, I said yes straight away. I arrived in Tokyo on March 31 and went into a straight four-week run; Tokyo, Osaka, Nagoya, Yokohama. All the usual places, all sold out. By this time, my little friend from England, Sammy Lee, or Satoru Sayama, was a regular on the New Japan cards.

The promoters had some big plans for him. On the last night of the tour, which was at the Sumo Palace in Tokyo, they were relaunching him as a new character, Tiger Mask. And although in my opinion, it was one of the best gimmicks New Japan ever came up with, on that first night, it looked like a load of shit.

You see, Shinma, or whoever was supposed to make sure Sayama's Tiger Mask outfit was ready, forgot one thing, the most important thing – the mask. So, on this night, I'd already gone to the ring, and as usual, I was swearing at the crowd, kicking the ropes, and waiting for Sayama, or Tiger Mask, to come out. And when he did, well, I didn't know what to think. The mask was the worst I'd ever seen. It was completely flat to his head, it had no ears, and looked like it had been crayoned on. Worst of all, as he came running down to the ring, the crowd started chanting "SA-YA-MA."

In Japan before the matches, you've probably seen the little ceremony that they have when the Japanese girls come into the ring and present flowers to the wrestlers. Well Sayama climbed into the ring, and I started pelting him with the flowers, like I always did, but I could see he was upset. He had his hands up to his face and looked as if he was going to cry. Well, I'll be honest, he looked like a prick, but it didn't make any difference to me, we still had a match to wrestle.

I said to him, quietly, so nobody could see, "What's the matter?"

He mumbled something like, "The mask." And put his head down.

So I said, under my breath, "I know. It's the shits."

I had some sympathy for him, but there was nothing he could do about it, so I just said, "Oh shut up and let's get on with it."

And we did. We had a great match that night, which probably went about 15 minutes, and the crowd were just going crazy. You have to remember, what I was doing with Sayama was all new stuff for me as well. I'd just about got used to the American style of wrestling, although I could still use a lot of European stuff in my matches, and here was Sayama, just back from Mexico where he'd learned all the fast, high-flying moves, and I had to adapt again.

For example, I'd pull him to the turnbuckle, and as he came out of it I'd put him in a back-breaker on my shoulder. From that, he'd land straight on his feet, I'd turn around and, bump, he'd arm-drag me straight through the ropes. So I'd be picking myself up from the floor outside the ring, meanwhile, he'd hit the opposite ropes and was running back as if he was going to dive out at me. Sometimes he did, sometimes he just caught the top or the middle rope and swung himself back into the ring. I never really knew, so the timing had to be bang on. Those matches moved so fast, if you weren't sharp enough, well, somebody could get caught out and hurt.

I remember one time when Sayama dived through the ropes so fast I did catch him, but the force of the dive sent us right over the guardrail and into the crowd. I took the brunt of it – in fact I took all the skin off my back. I can remember lying there in this tangle of feet, and my back felt as if it was on fire. Then all the young boys who'd been crouched around the ring came rushing over and put a load of wet towels on my back. But I still enjoyed the match, and I know the crowd did.

So with Sayama, I had to pick up his style very quickly. Our matches were very different to the ones I'd had with Tatsumi Fujinami, but there again, Fujinami had also spent time in Mexico and Florida and Germany when he was younger. So he had adapted to the European style and mixed it with the Japanese style.

But, for what ever reason, it did work between us. Sayama was the flyer. I let him do all his high spots; he'd jump and I'd catch. Then I'd get him in the ring and kick the shit out of him – and the people loved it. As usual, I took all the bad bumps. Basically, I took all the wear and tear in those matches with Tiger Mask. We'd both be aching and paining afterward – me, I'm sure, more than him – and looking back, I'm sure it was those matches that were the start of all the injuries I had a few years later.

It wasn't just the wrestling styles that were different in Japan, the crowds were different as well. I was going to wrestle a tag match in Sapporo one night with Stan Hansen. Just before we went on, the referee, Peter Takahashi, came to the dressing room. He said, "Tonight you wrestle Choshu."

I said, "So what?"

"He is third babyface in this company."

"Very good. I'll tell you what I'm going to do to the third babyface of this company Peter. I'm going to slam him upside down in the corner post and drop an elbow right on his bollocks."

He shook his head and started waving his hands about. "No, Tom, you can't do that,"

I said, "Why not?"

He said. "The people will laugh."

Now, anywhere else in the world, kicking your opponent in the balls would really get the crowd against you, you know, as in "Ooh, the bastard." In Japan they'd just laugh, which I thought was really strange. But they liked strong matches, I mean hard physical matches, where the wrestlers connected. All those matches I had with Choshu, who was a hard-hitter, Sayama, Kimura; if you look close enough there was no wind between the shots. Don't get me wrong, they paid us well to do that. But like I said before, the price I paid in the long-run was a lot higher.

All the time I was in Japan, I was picking up a bit more of the language and the way of life over there. I'd heard people talk about the Monkey House. I didn't know what it was, but before I finished that tour, I found out. Right at the start, Peter Takahashi said to me, "In the ring, the Japanese are the nice people. You and the other foreigners, you are no good. Understand?"

So I said "Yeah, OK."

And he said, "So you must do whatever you want."

I said, "What do you mean?"

"Go to the ring, but on the way, you slap, kick, punch – whatever you want – to the fans."

So I thought about this and said, "All right." I think I was wrestling Yoshiaki Yatsu this night. He used to be an Olympic wrestler, and he used a lot of submission moves; front facelocks and toeholds; and he could hit a bit hard as well. Anyway, I set off for the ring, and as I walked out from behind the curtains, the fans were leaning over the barrier, calling out and patting me on the back. Well, one young lad slapped me a little bit too hard. So I remembered what Peter had said, I turned round, grabbed him – he was just a kid – and dragged him over the barrier.

I ripped all his clothes off, knocked him to the floor, and kicked him in the mush. Then I left him lying there in his underpants and carried on walking to the ring, while the rest of the fans were going nuts. I got in the ring, as usual, spotted the Mafia men on the front row, with their smart suits and dark glasses – nice enough people as long as you didn't bother them – and waited for Yatsu to come in.

We wrestled a good match, not what you would call fast-paced, but a good solid fight. But when it was finished, before I got back to the dressing room, I could see the police were waiting for me. I think they must have turned up while I was in the ring, but I imagine Inoki or Shinma said, "Please can you wait until he's finished his match before you arrest him." Well, they couldn't really come down to the ring and arrest me in the middle of it. There was a lot of shouting and arguing in Japanese, then one of the policemen said to me, "You play monkey, you go to Monkey House."

So they arrested me, took me down to the police cells and left me all by myself. None of them spoke much English, and I sat there wondering what was going to happen. I don't know if I'd been set up exactly, although I had a good idea at the time that I was, but I'd just thought, I'll do it anyway, get a bit of time off, something to eat, and bollocks to it. Well I'm not being funny, but I got an apple, a bit of rice and some green tea. And after three days, somebody, probably Inoki, paid to get me out. And, I still got my guarantee, even though I missed two nights of wrestling.

When I got out, the story was all over the newspapers, making me out to be this terrible person. So, you can imagine what that did for business. All I'm saying is whatever the company paid to get me out, they definitely got their money back.

When I got back from Japan, Davey was round straight away wanting to know all about it. He wanted to know what the money was like, what the chances were for him. Well I knew he wasn't ready for Japan, not yet. I said, "Don't be in such a big hurry. When you're ready to go to Japan, I'll take you with me."

Anyway, a few months after that he rang me up and said, "Tommy, I'm going to Japan. I've got one night with New Japan."

I said "Dave. Don't do it. Wait till I go over again and I'll get you a good deal."

But he didn't listen. He went out there for a week, wrestled one match against The Cobra, and had to wear a mask. At first the people thought it was me and were chanting "KI-DO, KI-DO," and then he took the mask off. They paid him $1,000, and when he got back, feeling all clever with himself, I said, "You stupid prick. I could have got you twice as much." When I eventually did take him to Japan with me, I did get him a good deal, and he was happy with it, until he found out that it was less money than me.

But apart from that, I had better things to think about than Davey Boy Smith being a stupid bastard. A short-tempered bastard called Dave Shults had just come into the territory. Dave, or Doctor D. as he was known, was from Tennessee, and he could be a bit funny with the other wrestlers. Most of them were scared of him because he was handy and could take care of himself. If anyone messed up a spot and ended up hurting him, even a little bit, he'd put them away right after the match. So a lot of wrestlers didn't want to get in the ring with him.

We were in Medicine Hat, Alberta, doing a spot show. In the middle of the match I accidentally caught Dave on the side of the face with a knee-drop or something. We carried on wrestling, but I could tell he was mad. After the match he came storming into the dressing room and said, "Tahmmy," that was how he talked, "If you wanna play them kind of fuckin' games, I'll play them right back." Then he turned round and walked out. Everybody else sat there, not saying anything, pretending to look the other way, so I got up and walked after him, straight into his dressing room. I heard somebody say, "Ooooh, Shults is going to do Dynamite now."

I said, "What's wrong with you? Look, accidents do happen Dave. What's the crack here altogether? You get a little fucking love tap and you're upset over that? A man of your size?"

Well, I think Dave Shults was a bit surprised by this. He just stared at me, like he couldn't believe what he was hearing, and then he said, "Tahmmy, we're friends. You're right. Anybody can make a mistake."

I just said, "Thank you." And I walked out. It was just as Ted had always told me, win, lose or draw, you never step back, always forward.

Anyway, not too long after that he was in a cage match with Leo Burke. Just before the match, Dave had said to me, "Tahmmy, if something goes wrong out there, I want you to give me a hand."

I said, "OK Doc."

Well, something did go wrong for Dave, and Leo Burke had him on his back and was about to pin him. So I ran up the aisle, climbed right to the top of the cage and from 20 feet up, without stopping to think, I dove off with a flying kneedrop. Bloody hell, it was a long way down. Before I landed, Leo rolled out of the way, and I ended up dropping the knee from 20 feet – straight into Dave Shults' ribs. I thought, "Oh Christ." Then, easy as anything, Leo Burke rolled back and pinned him one, two, three. But you know what? Dave Shults, who would have knocked the shit out of anybody else in a second if they'd done that to him, never said a word.

And it was only back in the dressing room that I realized how dangerous that 20 foot knee-drop could have been. I'd never done anything like that before. But once I had done it, I started doing other risky moves. I just didn't think; it was whatever came to me at the time. For example, I was the first man to take another man and suplex him off the top turnbuckle.

The very first time I did it was to a Japanese wrestler called Masa Fuji. I didn't plan to do it. I just found myself up there on the top with Fuji, and the idea just came to me that a suplex from there would be a great way to finish. It was an incredible move that first time, and the whole crowd, thousands of people, went "Ohhh." Like they couldn't believe it. I know a lot of wrestlers do that move now, and other things that I'm sure are a lot riskier, but that one, the superplex – I did it first.

New Japan called Stu up again at the end of that year to see if I was available for a tour at the start of 1982. Stu came to an agreement with New Japan: they could have me, as long as they took Bret as part of the deal. What I didn't know at that time was that Stu also negotiated himself a booking fee from New Japan to compensate him for what he lost in takings at home.

Personally, I didn't care whether Bret came or not. We were getting along fine; our matches, in my opinion, were some of the best that the Canadian fans had seen in a long time. Plus we'd met a couple of girls out in Regina, Saskatchewan, and as it happened, they were sisters, Julie and Michelle. So, no, it didn't bother me having Bret along, in fact we were having a great time, and between us, we got up to a few pranks as well.

We were in Sapporo one night, me, Bret, Freddie Blassie, and Rick McGraw, who you might remember as Quick Draw McGraw. Peter Takahashi was there as well. Peter used to act as the translator for the Americans who couldn't speak any Japanese, for example, when they went out to a restaurant, he'd order the food for them. Anyway, after we'd been for something to eat, Peter and Fred went back to their hotel room, while we stayed and had a few more drinks with Rick. He was hitting the sake, strong Japanese wine, and by the end of the night he was well out of it.

We got back to the hotel, got Rick's kimono from his room, and got him to dress up as a Sumo wrestler, wearing nothing but the kimono wrapped round his arse. I found a wheelbarrow and we stuck Rick in it. There was nobody on reception, so one of us, probably me, rang Peter and Freddie in their rooms.

I said, "Fred, there's something wrong."

It must have been about 1AM and Fred was half asleep. He said, "Dynamite? Is that you?"

"Yeh, it's me. But you'd better come down. Rick's acting funny. I think he might try and do something stupid."

"What do you mean?"

I said, "I'm telling you he's off his head."

Fred said, "OK, I'll be right down."

I rang Peter, told him the same story, and then we pushed the wheelbarrow, with Rick in it, into the lift and sent it up to the sixth floor where we knew Fred and Peter would be waiting to get the lift down. And when the lift doors opened all they would see was Rick in the wheelbarrow, wearing a diaper, and with a big stupid grin on his face. Next day, he couldn't remember a thing.

On that tour in December 1981, we wrestled some tag matches against Tiger Mask and Kuniaki Kobyashi, and I had a lot of singles with Tiger Mask, with Bret as my manager.

There was one Japanese wrestler called Hoshino who always wanted to be the big hero in the ring – well the little prick was only five-foot-four anyway. We wrestled a singles match one night, and all the way through he kept trying it on with me, so in the end, I just opened up on him. Which he didn't like. He had me in a corner, he stuck a grovit on me, and said, under his breath, "You shoot." A grovit is a front facelock, an old Wigan move anyway, but when it's put on you properly, forget it. He would have learned how to put a grovit on from Karl Gotch, I'm sure. But one thing that I learned from the short time I was at Riley's Gym, was how to get out of one. I reached across for his left elbow and wrenched hard. It took him by surprise, and nearly took one of his fingers off.

The next night, me and Bret were wrestling Tiger Mask and Oshino in a tag match, Before we went to the ring, Sayama came to me and said, "Tommy, no trouble tonight, please."

Anyway, Tiger Mask started the match off with Bret, and after a few minutes they both went for the tag at the same time. As Oshino turned round and saw that I was in the ring, he went straight back and made another quick tag. He definitely didn't want a part of me that night.

It was around this time that Tatsumi Fujinami moved up to the Heavyweight division and vacated the NJPW WWF Junior title. So now there were a few of us, myself, Tiger Mask, Kobayashi, Kimura, and a few Mexican wrestlers, all in contention for the belt.

To be honest, Fujinami could have moved up a long time ago, but when he went, in my opinion, it was because the company had much bigger plans for Tiger Mask. He was doing great business for them and you know it was a shame that New Japan never really gave Sayama the credit he deserved for bringing that business in. But, on New Year's Day 1982, he did become the NJPW WWF Junior Heavyweight Champion, courtesy of the Dynamite Kid.

CHAPTER SIX

New Japan Pro Wrestling, was in my opinion, one of the smartest wrestling promotions at that time. They had the best wrestlers, the best storylines and the hardest matches. At that time. There were some things they did that I didn't agree with; for example, Antonio Inoki always wrestling the main event. I'll be honest, some of those matches were a bit of an anticlimax after, say, Sayama or The Cobra. But, Inoki was the promoter, so he could do what he liked.

In 1982, when I was on tour with New Japan, I can remember travelling by coach with the other wrestlers going to the next venue, and they always had TV on the coach. We used to watch some of the matches from All Japan Pro Wrestling, which was New Japan's nearest rival, and we'd all sit there laughing because at the time, All Japan was a joke. Well, a couple of years later, things did change a little bit, and for a while the All Japan wrestlers were the ones doing the laughing. But I would say, in 1982, Inoki was the number one promoter in Japan.

But, even the best promotions can make mistakes, and New Japan made a big one when it sent a team of wrestlers on a tour of the Middle East in the spring of 1982. Apart from Inoki, Sakaguchi, Sayama, or Tiger Mask, and a few other Japanese wrestlers, there was myself and Bret, Dick Murdoch, Bad News, and a couple of German wrestlers.

We were booked for a ten-day tour around Dubai and Abu Dhabi, but on the way we had to make an unscheduled stopover in Karachi, Pakistan because of a sandstorm. We were stuck there for two days, and it was bloody awful. Everywhere looked dirty, and all along the side of the street there were big canopies, with cans of food underneath. Every can was covered in flies, great big bluebottles, and there were gangs of beggars outside the hotel and following you everywhere.

We finally made it to Dubai, although, to be honest, I only just made it on that tour. I was recovering from knee surgery for a torn cartilage, and when Shinma called me to book me for the tour, I wasn't sure whether I was up to it. The one concession that Shinma made was that I wouldn't have to wrestle Tiger Mask, so Bret was brought in for that one.

I wrestled Osamu Kido instead, which gave me a fairly easy schedule; no aerials, just side headlocks, a couple of reversals, so I could rest the knee a bit. Bret Hart versus Tiger Mask? Well, those matches were OK, but I would say not as lively as the ones I'd had with him.

But apart from that, the reason why New Japan made a mistake coming to Dubai was that it didn't do any business. In fact, they had to cut the tour short, from ten days to two. Part of the reason was that it hadn't been organized very well. An Arab promoter called Azeem was supposed to sort all that out, but there was no media coverage, no interviews, no publicity, nothing.

Also, and this was just my own opinion, the wrestlers spent too much time together, socially, at the hotel. The Japanese, the Germans, the Americans, all eating and drinking together, sunbathing round the swimming pool together; well, we didn't exactly look like a bunch of men who were ready to knock the shit out of each other. And to the fans, things like that mattered. In Japan, you would never see the Japanese wrestlers and the American wrestlers together other outside the arena.

So, the day before we left, we all went to see Shinma to pick up our wages. All the wrestlers would line up outside the office and go in one by one; that way nobody else could see how much you were paid, and vice versa. When it was my turn, I went in and Shinma gave me a cheque for half the original guarantee.

I said, "Er...em, what's this? Where's the rest of it?"

Shinma said, "That's it. Only two days work. Business has been very bad."

"I'm not being funny Shinma, but my guarantee was $5,000."

He just shook his head. So I said, "OK. Very good. But this is my last tour for New Japan."

Anyway, after I said that, the little prick stopped me and said, "Wait, wait. OK." And he paid me the rest of the money for ten days work in full.

But we had a few laughs while we were there, mainly at the expense of the promoter, Mr. Azeem. He became the subject for some of Bret's best works of art. Bret Hart is a very good artist, and he could draw cartoon pictures of just about any of the wrestlers. Some of them were very funny. He drew one of me, with a cigarette hanging out of my mouth, playing a set of drums, and it looked just like me. Some wrestlers got a bit upset when Bret drew them.

Azeem didn't like Bret's pictures much, because every day Bret drew a new picture of Azeem and pinned it to his hotel room door, so it was the first thing he saw when he came out of his hotel room every morning. He drew Azeem sitting next to a sheep, with his arm round it and big smile on his face; on another one he was lying underneath a camel giving it a...well, you get the picture. And every day, Azeem ripped them down off the door.

Being stuck in that hotel for a few days, well, we had to make the most of it. So we ate, we drank, we went to the shows in the hotel, and generally had a good time. Everything we had, we put on the bill, which I always signed, K. Azeem, Room 418. So, by the time we checked out, Azeem's hotel bill was a fairly long sheet of paper. We'd checked out before him, but we stood outside and watched through the window while he kept staring at his bill and shaking his head.

After a long flight back to Calgary, it was more or less straight back to work. The first few months of the year were always hard for Stu, and as far as I could make out, it was mainly because of a French Canadian wrestler called Leo Burke.

I never figured out what the crack was with Leo, but every winter, he came into the Stampede territory from out east, and took over as the head booker. And for a few months, he was more or less running Stampede. He always brought his own team of French Canadian wrestlers with him, booked all their matches, and then in the spring, they'd leave.

The rest of the year, Leo and his men wrestled for Emile Duprée who ran the Atlantic Grand Prix Wrestling promotion in Moncton, out in the French quarters, near Nova Scotia. But come the next winter, they'd be back in Calgary again. All the television interviews would be full of French-speaking Canadians and to be honest, I thought it sounded bloody awful.

It wasn't even as if Leo made a lot of money for Stampede; he wasn't a draw and didn't make any real difference to business. But what I didn't agree with was the fact that when he was in Calgary with his own wrestlers, there wasn't enough work for all of Stu's wrestlers, and he had to let a lot of them go. Just like that, they were out of a job. And when the French Canadians went back to Moncton in the spring, Stu had to start rehiring for Stampede all over again, which also meant building up new characters from scratch, which is never easy.

Like I said, Leo wasn't a great wrestler. He was a serious wrestler, with no real character. One of the Harts, it might have been Bruce or Stu, came up with the idea of a mixed tag match; half of it wrestling and the other half boxing. Whoever got the most pinfalls or ten counts combined would be the winner.

So it was Bret Hart and the Dynamite Kid against Leo Burke and Hubert Gallant, another French Canadian. For the first 30-minutes we wrestled, and I would say we definitely had the edge over them. The second half didn't go quite so well for us, mainly because Bret Hart couldn't box. I can still see him now, standing on the apron, with his boxing gloves on, and his head down because he was laughing so much – he was one of the worst for laughing in the ring – laughing at me in the ring, swinging away at Leo Burke. But, when I landed one – I landed one.

For a while, Stu had been sending TV tapes of the wrestling to a promoter in Antigua, down in the Caribbean. It might have been Smith's idea, because he knew a lot of people down there. Anyway, with the tapes being shown on TV, interest was starting to grow, and that summer, Stu booked us all on a tour of Antigua and Monserrat.

I was in Japan with Bret right up until the day before the tour started, so we flew into Vancouver from Japan, carried straight on to Calgary, had a few hours at home to get some fresh gear together, and then caught a flight to Toronto, Miami and then Antigua. As you can imagine, we were both completely knackered.

I liked Antigua. I spent a whole day shark fishing with John; we caught ourselves a barracuda and a king fish, and really, I just enjoyed the pace of life there. But there was bad news for Stu. He'd left Smith to look after the money side of things and it seemed that when the tour was over, Smith took off to Puerto Rico with the takings. When he came back, the money had disappeared. So instead of giving me a cheque for the tour, Stu had to pay me in instalments, a hundred dollars at a time over the next few weeks.

I'd only been back in Calgary a couple of weeks when I had a call from Shinma. He told me that New Japan was doing a show at Madison Square Garden in New York City, and they wanted me to wrestle Tiger Mask. I'd never been to New York before, but, it sounded like a good deal. Shinma promised me $1,000 just for the one match. I flew from Calgary, to Portland, to Atlanta and landed at La Guardia Airport in New York, for the first time, on my own, and took a cab to the Ramada Inn in the middle of New York City.

Shinma was there, Inoki, Sakaguchi, and of course, Sayama. The card was being promoted by what was then the World Wide Wrestling Federation, run by Vince McMahon Sr. I met him, just the once, and I remember him smoking a cigar, shaking my hand, you know, a polite man – I think most people considered him a great man – and he had a lot of respect from the wrestlers.

His son, Vince McMahon Jr. was commentating at ringside that night, I think, alongside Jesse Ventura. You have to remember that the promotion at that time was big, but not as big as it became a few years on when it moved into all the other little territories in America and Canada, and took all their top men.

It was a sold out crowd at Madison Square Garden that night, not just the arena where the matches were being held, but the floor below where they had the matches shown on a giant screen. My match against Tiger Mask was only short, but it was 12 minutes of fast, non-stop action, which I think the people enjoyed. In the dressing room after the match Shinma came looking for me to pay me. He gave me a cheque for $500.

I said, "You told me $1,000. Where's the rest?" After what happened in Dubai, I couldn't believe he would try to rip me off again.

He said "That is good. One night, $500."

I said, "Fine. But this time Shinma, finished. No money, no more wrestling."

And I meant it. This time Shinma didn't try to stop me, and so as far as I was concerned that was it, I'd finished with New Japan.

I didn't hear from Shinma again until about a month later when the little prick turned up at a spot show in Calgary. He opened the dressing room door and stuck his head round. As soon as I saw his face I said, "What do you want you bastard?"

He got all defensive, smiling and waving his hand for me to come over. He said, "Big mistake, big mistake." He put his hand in his pocket and pulled out the other $500.

I took it off him and said, "You're right. It was a big mistake."

So now we were straight, and a few weeks later I went back to wrestle for New Japan. But he must have pulled that same trick on me about three times, and then a few weeks later he'd come back to me and say there had been a mistake, which, to me, meant he was trying to blame somebody else, like Inoki or Sakaguchi, although he never actually mentioned them by name.

So I did go back to New Japan, and every time I went back, I was getting a bigger name, although that wasn't always for my wrestling. I remember being over there in 1982, when I was with Dave Shults, Bad News Allen, and a guy called Mike Davis, who we called Jackson, because he was from Jacksonville in Florida.

Mike Davis was OK, but I had a mind to set him up for a bit of a laugh. So I went to a a a pharmacy, in Tokyo – bear in mind I could only speak a little bit of Japanese at that time, and I didn't know the Japanese word for constipation. So I stood there at the counter, groaning, going, "Ohhh," and pointing to my arse. The chemist thought I had diarrhea, so I said, "No, no, that's what I need." He got the idea eventually and gave me some laxative tablets, about 20 of these little pink pills.

Dave, and Bad News were both in on this one. At that time Bad News had some sores on his arms, from rope burns or mat burns, and he said he thought the ring was infected. So I pretended that these little pink pills were like antibiotics, to stop you catching anything, and I gave some to Bad News. Dave said he wanted some and I pretended that I was going to take some as well. So then Mike Davis said, "In that case, you'd better give me some if there's an infection in the ring." So I gave him ten.

Well I didn't know he would take them all, but later that night, they kicked in. I know he ran out of wrestling trunks, and 24-hours later he was still suffering.

So me and Dave Shults decided to take him out for a drink, to try and take his mind off it. He was going a bit heavy on the sake, and by the end of the night, we had to take him back to his hotel room. We lay him on his bed, then Dave disappeared and came back with a tube of hair remover. He poured it all over Jackson's hair, and then I found a plastic shower cap and stuck that on top of his head. The next morning when he woke up, his hair had dropped off, not completely, but in chunks. So what with the laxatives and the hair remover, I would say Mike Davis left Japan feeling a bit lighter than when he came.

Back home, things were moving on the home front in Calgary: I was about to get married. Bret was already married to Julie; in fact they'd got married in secret about a month before I did, but they hadn't told anybody, not even the family. When I got married to Michelle, Julie's sister, we did the same, just went off, got married, and then told everybody afterward. But there was one problem, and that was that I was still living in Canada on a temporary working visa. To get landed immigrant status, I would have to spend so many weeks or months out of the country.

I got in touch with a promoter down in Portland, Oregon, called Don Owens. I knew him through another wrestler, Buddy Rose, who I'd met in Japan. Portland was the closest territory to Calgary, about 700 miles away. After six months I could apply for landed immigrant papers and more or less do anything I wanted in Canada – except for two things:s I couldn't vote and I couldn't claim welfare payments.

So I had to commute in and out of Portland every week or so for the next few months to keep the Canadian authorities happy. I still wrestled for Stu, but I also did some matches for Don. And as it turned out, I enjoyed it in Portland. It was different to Calgary and on the whole the wrestlers were better qualified. That was where I first met Curt Hennig, and in 1982 he was as skinny as a matchstick. But Curt was good and he wrestled hard. Billy Jack Haynes was there. I knew him from Calgary because I'd helped to train him in Stu's gym. Billy was 31 years old and he was a fighter, I mean he could use himself. I found that out when I had to wrestle him for the West Coast Championship a year later.

Johnny Smith came out to Calgary that year. His real name was John Hindley and he was the nephew of Ted Betley. It was the Harts who named him Johnny Smith so they could introduce him as Davey Boy Smith's brother, also a babyface. We had some good matches in Calgary, tag matches and some singles matches. One that I remember went down very well with the crowd was a chain match, where we were joined by a ten-foot chain and you had to touch all four turnbuckles to win.

We were both cut to buggery, bleeding everywhere, but at one point I'd managed to touch three cornerposts and was nearly at the fourth. What I didn't realize was that the chain had got stuck between my legs. Just as I reached out, Johnny yanked the chain across my knackers so hard, I did a somersault and missed the post. So I was holding onto my bollocks while Johnny ran round, dragging me on the chain, and touched the four posts.

In April 1983 I kept my promise and took Davey Boy Smith to Japan with me for a six-week tour. We wrestled singles and tag matches, but to be honest, I preferred the tag. I think the people preferred them, because we didn't need rest holds, and, because you had chance to get your breath on the apron, when you were in the ring, you could wrestle a lot harder and faster.

Our first tag match was against Kobayashi and Terenishi at the Korakuan Hall, and this was the first time we'd ever wrestled as a tag team. How did it work out? Well, I'll be honest with you, I did all the thinking for our team, from the first match we ever did together, to the last.

For example, if we were both in the ring together to double team somebody, he'd get one arm, I'd get the other arm and we'd throw the Japanese wrestler to the other rope. I would say "Double tackle," under my breath, so nobody could see, but that was why our moves always went so smoothly, and why the timing always looked so good. It's like I said before, the timing is everything, but when there's two of you, it was even more important, and somebody had to take the lead.

Even the clothesline – which I know caught a lot of people out, even though I'd warned them before the match – I timed it just right. Before we went in the ring, I would say to them, "It's up to you. If you don't go down, I'm throwing it."

So Davey Boy Smith and myself had our timing off to perfection – most of the time. And as a tag team, I think the Japanese people enjoyed our matches because they were exciting. And because we were foreigners, we were the bad guys or the heels, which was more fun for us too.

Somehow, I managed another trip to the Monkey House, and because I didn't want him to feel left out, I took Davey Boy Smith with me. Part of it, if I'm honest, was the effects of steroids. I was taking them everyday. It wasn't just me, at that time I would say most wrestlers were taking them. But, while steroids made you look the part, they made you aggressive and short-tempered as well.

So, out we came for our match, me and Davey, to wrestle Tiger Mask and Kengo Kimura. As usual, the fans, mainly young kids, were slapping our backs and shouting. One of them was thumping me really hard on my back, and suddenly, I just snapped. I turned round and grabbed him, he was probably about 16 or 17, and yanked him out of his seat into the aisle. Then Davey Boy Smith picked him up in a press slam and threw him straight into the wall at the back. As he went down, I kicked him in the ribs.

When we went back to the dressing room after the match there was a big commotion. Somebody had called the police and they'd come to arrest us. But before they took us away, two of the older wrestlers came into the dressing room, dragging behind them the young lad who we'd beaten up. He was crying, on his hands and knees on the floor. He kept bowing to us and saying "Sumimasen, sumimasen," which is Japanese for excuse me.

Well, we didn't know what to make of this, because really, they were rougher on him than we were. But, we still got a couple of days in the cells – the Monkey House. Fair enough, we didn't lose any money, and when we got out, the papers were full of the story, giving us a bad name. Well just like the last time, for the next few weeks, the arenas were full of people wanting to see us.

Sometimes I found it hard to understand the Japanese people. For example, I remember watching the news, with English subtitles, on the hotel TV one day. There was a story about a little boy who'd been run over in the middle of Tokyo. It seemed what had happened was, the little kid's dad had taken him with him to the pechinko hall – pechinko is a gambling game, like roulette but with little silver balls – and the dad had been so wrapped up in the game, he didn't notice his little boy wander off outside and into the traffic, which in Tokyo, is just crazy. So, he got run over, killed straight away, and he was five years old.

I felt so sorry for that little kid, but what I thought was strange was that it seemed as if the dad wasn't that upset about what had happened. Later that night I was talking to Peter Takahashi and I asked him if he'd seen the story on the news. He just shrugged and said he had. It was like it didn't matter. I know deep down it did matter, to Peter and to that little boy's dad, it's just that in Japan, they never let it show.

But, apart from that, we had a great tour. For his first tour, Davey Boy Smith was well pleased with it – apart from being in prison – because he had got over with the fans nearly straight away. But when he found out he was getting paid less than me, a $1,000 a week less than me, he soon changed his tune.

Eventually, he went to Shinma and said, "How come I don't get the same money as Dynamite?"

Shinma told him, "You are only young boy." Which, as far as the Japanese were concerned, he was.

But apart from that, I would say Dynamite Kid and Davey Boy Smith went down well with the wrestling fans in Japan. They hated us, which was great. But what didn't go down well with the fans was Tiger Mask Sayama walking out on New Japan at the end of 1983.

I think I know why he left. For two years he had worked his backside off as Tiger Mask, but was never appreciated for it. We wrestled one night on TV, maybe in Osaka or Sapporo, and the live TV ratings doubled. But the credit always went to Inoki against Stan Hansen or Fujinami against Choshu Riki. And they never put him on top of the bill, even though his matches, in my opinion, were more exciting than Inoki's.

Even Shohei "Giant" Baba, bless him, when he knew he was getting too old, he put himself in the middle of the card and let the younger wrestlers take the main event, which, is really the way it should be. So no, I wasn't really that surprised when Tiger Mask went. But I was disappointed, because I knew I'd never have an opponent like him again.

CHAPTER SEVEN

Sayama had been so successful as Tiger Mask, everybody wanted to wrestle him. And on the two or three occasions when I quit New Japan over Shinma not paying me, the others hadn't wasted any time moving in.

Mark Rocco, who I wrestled many times in England, had already wrestled in Japan for the IWE under his own name, Mark "Rollerball" Rocco. From there he'd moved to New Japan, still using the same name. I imagine that was through him knowing Sayama from all the matches they had in England, and also through Karl Gotch who got Sayama into Joint Promotions in the first place. But really, Mark Rocco's biggest break in Japan came about through a very good friend of mine, Bad News Allen, who later became known as Bad News Brown.

Bad News had wrestled in Japan for many years and was very well known to the fans. But at the end of one tour in 1982, Shinma said to him, "Bad News, on the next tour, you come back and wrestle in a mask. You will be Black Tiger and wrestle Tiger Mask."

Well, Bad News knew that was a bad idea because he was too well known, and the fans would never buy him in a mask. So he more or less told Shinma, "No. Bollocks to that. I'm not doing it." Which was where Mark Rocco came in, because they asked him to be Black Tiger instead. They gave him the exact same outfit as Tiger Mask, except it was black, and the two of them had some great matches.

During the six-week tour, Rocco would wrestle a lot of different Japanese wrestlers, some of them very good, and he would beat them every single night. Then on the last night of the tour, he'd wrestle Tiger Mask for the World Championship, but never managed to beat him for it.

One time, when Sayama had been out injured and the belt was vacant, Rocco did become the champion by beating Gran Hamada in the final match of a championship tournament. But he was only the champion for a couple of weeks because as soon as Tiger Mask was back in the ring, he lost the belt to him.

We were good friends, Rocco and me, we still are, but I know he wasn't happy about me going back to New Japan. And I could understand that, because I was taking the limelight.

Every time I went back to Japan, I was using more dangerous moves and taking more risks. It was what the people came to expect. Sometimes – and this happened to me a couple of times – you'd get right up on the top turnbuckle to dive onto your opponent, and then realize he was way out of position. In America, or even in England, you might get away with climbing down and saving yourself from getting hurt. But not in Japan.

Once the crowd sees you go up, they start getting excited, because they know you're going to do something risky. But if you climbed back down, they'd laugh. Just like they did if you kicked somebody in the balls. So, unless you wanted everybody in the building laughing at you, once you'd got yourself up there, you had to follow it through – the head-butt or the splash – and if you missed it, well, tough, you got hurt.

One thing I did learn to do in Japan was pace myself. The first few times I'd gone over there, I was doing quite a bit of damage to the Japanese wrestlers in the first few matches, throwing them over the ropes and into the steel barriers, all at top speed, and the promoters were getting a bit worried. The referee said to me at the start of one tour, "Dynamite, please, we've got six weeks. Our boys are getting hurt. More easy please." So after three or four years I could pace myself in the ring without taking anything away from the matches.

But, whether it was the constant pounding on my back from all the suplexes and the piledrivers, or whether it was the steroids, or a combination of both, at the age of 25, my back was starting to give me some serious pain. Sometimes my ribs, my kidneys, my whole body, just ached. But I never thought of cutting the high-risk moves out. Never. They were what the people had paid to see.

I think the men in suits who always sat on the front row enjoyed my matches, because on a couple of occasions, they took me, and some of the other wrestlers, for a night out. I'd heard a lot of things about the

Japanese Mafia, some good, some not so good. For example, I heard that if somebody in their family – their brother or even one of their kids – did something wrong, they'd cut their finger off. I also heard that they controlled all the taxi cabs in Japan, and that the taxi drivers were Mafia employees.

I know it sounds unbelievable, talking about the Mafia, because to most people they are something you see in the movies. But they were real, so were the Mafia wars. We were in Sapporo one night, and after the matches, all the wrestlers were told to go back to the hotel and stay inside, because for the past few nights, the Mafia had been shooting each other on the streets. Oh, they were real.

And they always turned up at the matches, always in ringside seats – not that they'd paid for them. I was in the Sumo Palace in Tokyo one night, getting ready to go to the ring, and I remember seeing Antonio Inoki talking to one of the Mafia men. They were speaking in Japanese, so I don't know what they were saying, but at the end of it, Inoki bowed and the man slapped him hard across the face, right in front of all the other Japanese wrestlers. Inoki said "Domo arigato." Well, I knew what that meant. Inoki, who is a big name in Japan, had just thanked the Mafia man for slapping him across the face. That's true.

Personally, I thought they were very nice people, especially when they took us out on the town. They didn't take everybody. I remember one time there was myself, Davey Boy, Bad News Allen, the Samoans, Afa and Sika, and some of the Japanese wrestlers. They took us to restaurants, strip clubs, even live sex shows where the audience could join in. Some people did. One wrestler – no names, but he was hung like a horse – stripped off and frightened the women away. But, no, as far as I was concerned, the Japanese Mafia were very nice people. And as long as you didn't cross them, they were OK with you.

And they did enjoy their wrestling, especially when the Americans were there. Hulk Hogan was a big draw for New Japan. He had been coming over for quite a few years that I knew of, first from the AWA, and later, from the WWF. And like I said, he was making a lot of money for Inoki, no doubt about it. Maybe too much money. It reached a point where Vince McMahon didn't want to let him go, because while Hogan was in Japan, the WWF was losing money. New Japan had an agreement with the WWF, where they could book the top names for the big shows. One time, Inoki asked Vince for Hogan, Dick Murdoch and Adrian Adonis. He sent the money, and Vince sent Murdoch, and Adonis – but no Hogan. He sent Greg Valentine instead. In the end, I think Inoki decided Vince was asking too much money, because not long after that, he cancelled the arrangement.

A couple of times I wrestled on the same card as Hogan, and I have to say he was popular with the fans. They used to chant "Hulk, Hulk, Hulk," and I'll give him credit, he leg-dropped a lot of top Japanese wrestlers. But the Japanese always went easy on the top people like Hulk Hogan and Dusty Rhodes. With others they'd go straight through them, but they took care of the big American names – well, they had to, because otherwise, the promoters knew they wouldn't come back.

For me, everything changed in New Japan when Sayama quit. I didn't know how the promoter would replace somebody like him. I wasn't sure they could. But to be honest, at that time, I was enjoying myself so much in Portland, Oregon, waiting for my immigrant visa, I can't say I gave it a lot of thought.

I was wrestling a lot of six man tag matches as part of a team called The Clan, which was myself, Rip Oliver and the Cuban Assassin. Our opponents were Curt Hennig, Buddy Rose and Billy Jack Haynes, and I had a lot of singles matches against all of them. One night we wrestled a straight tag, which was myself and the Cuban Assassin against Curt and Rip Oliver.

We had a hard match, and at one point I threw Curt out of the ring and suplexed him on the concrete. I got back in the ring and Curt got up, but while his back was turned, the Cuban Assassin sneaked up and cracked him from behind. Curt went down and stayed down, so they brought a stretcher to ringside, while I sat on the top rope, smiling and acting casual. As usual, the crowd was getting angry, swearing at me and throwing things – Curt was a big favourite you see – but I didn't care. They lifted Curt onto the stretcher and started carrying him out. So, when I jumped on to the stretcher, and my knee caught him, by accident, right across his throat, it nearly caused a riot.

Somewhere towards the end of 1983, I beat Curt Hennig for the West Coast Championship belt. I went to Eugene in Oregon, where Don Owens' brother, Elton, was in charge. He took one look at the belt and said, "Jesus Christ, what the hell are you doing with that thing round your waist?"

I said, "I'm the Champion. What do you think?"

He shook his head and said, "Harley Race is coming next week, and he wants to wrestle Billy Jack Haynes."

Which meant that before Harley came, Billy Jack Haynes, who I told you about before, had to wrestle me for the belt. Now with Billy, I'll give him credit, he might have been a bit loose upstairs, but if he knew you and he liked you, he'd do anything for you. But in the ring, he could be a real bastard. We had a hard match which somehow I lost, but at the end I was still standing up straight, while Billy was leaning over the ropes gasping for breath. So, for a joke I said, "Referee, I want five more."

The referee went to Billy and said, "You want five more?"

I heard Billy say, "Fuck that," under his breath. He couldn't stand up.

But I got on with Billy Jack. In fact, in all the years I wrestled, I could count on one hand the wrestlers who, in my opinion, were the hardest men. And by that I mean, they could take care of themselves, in or out of the ring. Billy Jack Haynes was definitely one of them.

The last time I'd seen Harley Race was during Stampede Week in 1979, and it was great to see him again. He hadn't changed, he was still a bit of a nutcase, still liked his drink, and he still had his gun. Harley always carried a gun, a little .38 Special.

We were sat in the bar after the matches one night and he shouted over to Don Owens' son, "Open that window you little sonofabitch," a bit like John Wayne, in fact he reminded me a lot of John Wayne. So he opened the window, and Harley held his empty beer can up to the window, pulled out his gun and pulled the trigger. I'll tell you, he scared everybody in that room to death.

After Harley Race left Portland, I didn't see him again until about a year later, when we were both in Japan. That's how it was for a lot of wrestlers. Your paths might cross, just for a week or two in a certain territory, and then you might not see each other again for years. But it never made any difference to Harley Race and me; we became good, very close friends. I'd say he was one of the best I had in the business.

Business wasn't bad in Portland, but in some of the smaller towns in Oregon, like Salem and Eugene, where wrestling wasn't shown on television, it was bad. Sandy Barr, who was Jesse Barr's dad, used to promote Salem, and I know he barely made enough money to get by. The only time he made anything was once a year when all the big names came in, like Harley Race and André the Giant, and then they'd do great business. Sold out every night. Sandy would be so excited about making all this money, after he'd paid the big names, he gave the rest of it to us, the wrestlers who were there every week. All year long he'd be scraping by, and when he did make some money, he gave it away. He was a very good, kind-hearted man, a great man, especially for a promoter.

Portland wasn't too far from Calgary, and sometimes I brought my wife, Michelle, down for a few days. And when I had a few days off, I'd fly back to Calgary. I was getting ready to fly back to Portland one day when she started crying. She was expecting our first baby at this time, so I asked her what was wrong. She said, "When you come back to Calgary and I have this baby, everybody will call it a steroid baby."

I must admit, by that stage I was a lot bigger. It was only looking back that I realized how much bigger. But I said to her, "Don't be stupid. Everything will be OK." As it turned out, when she was born, my little girl, Bronwyne, was OK. In fact, she was brilliant.

Stampede was working Al Tomko's old Vancouver territory after he'd more or less run it into the ground. Well, Tomko had no idea anyway. He used to wrestle in an army uniform and put himself on the top of the bill, but he was a waste of time. They'd tried bringing people in from outside Vancouver, from Portland, and one or two other promotions – Buddy Rose, Rip Oliver, Rowdy Roddy Piper – they all spent some time up there, but it never made money, until Stampede started running shows there.

For the first six months or so, Stu just sent video tapes of Stampede wrestling to be shown on TV all along the west coast. It took time to build the characters up, but after that first six months, we were ready to move in and run some shows. As it turned out, some of Stampede's biggest crowds were in Vancouver, and I would say Stu Hart turned that business around.

The wrestlers did their bit as well. Stu had a business partner in Vancouver who also happened to be Brian Adams' manager – the singer, not the wrestler. He owned a radio station called C-FOX. So we, as in myself, Bret, and the other Harts, used to go to the studio, give an interview, plug the matches, and then say, "And don't forget people, we always rock with the Fox."

Really, what Stu was doing was a small-time version of what Vince McMahon did with the WWF TV shows. He knew that television was the only way to bump business up. And that was one of the reasons why Stampede did so well in Vancouver.

Like Billy Jack Haynes, Bad News Allen was one of those four or five wrestlers who I considered to be the hardest men in wrestling. He was definitely bad news. Don't get me wrong, he was a good friend, but once he got you in the ring, it was as if he didn't know you. I've had a lot of hard matches in my career, but the matches I had with Bad News were something else.

His real name was Allen Coage, and later on, in the WWF, he wrestled as Bad News Brown. I already knew Bad News from Japan, where he was always good for the crowds because he was so vicious. He'd started going bald so he shaved all his hair off to make himself look even meaner. And I never saw his opponents give him an arm-drag or a backdrop, he was always completely in command of his matches.

The first few months he was with Stampede, Bad News was wrestling Bret. Now I don't know whether Bret got careless or was trying to be clever, but every time he threw an uppercut, instead of going across his chest, he was banging him in the face. Bad News put up with this a few times, but then, all of a sudden, he snapped. He threw Bret on the floor, called him a bastard, and started throttling him.

That was it. Bret was terrified of him and wouldn't get in the ring with him again. Nobody else would get it in the ring with him either, so it ended up being me, the Dynamite Kid against Bad News Allen, because like I said before, I never ducked out of a match, against anybody. Not even a no-holds-barred streetfight with Bad News.

I knew Bad News was a fighter and he knew I could take care of myself, so before we ever got in the ring, we understood each other. The streetfights always sold out, guaranteed, because they were so violent. We did one at the Calgary Pavilion that got completely out of hand, and after one incident where Bad News hit me with a broken bottle, the Alberta Athletic Commission barred Stampede from the building for a month. So we moved to another building on an Indian reservation about 15-miles away. Stu had an old Greyhound bus and he used it to pick up the fans outside the Pavilion and drive them to the match.

The climax to one series of matches between me and Bad News was a cage match in Vancouver. We'd wrestled a normal match, a taped fist match, both televised, and now this, a cage match, so we were hoping for a good turn out. I can't remember the name of the arena, but it was a big building, and right next door to it was another arena. On the day of the cage match, we found out that a rock concert was booked to play at the building next door to us. When we got there, the car park was full. I said, "Bloody hell News, we're knackered here." We thought they'd all come to see the band. But we were wrong. Those 10,000 people had come to see the wrestling.

There was no way that Bad News Allen was going to lose a cage match in front of 10,000 people. He told me he wouldn't. So they brought my friend, Rip Oliver, in from Portland to give me a hand. We hammered each other all round that cage, smashing each other's faces into the mesh. In the middle of the match Rip threw me a knuckle-duster, but I missed it and Bad News caught it, and rattled me over the head with it. There was so much blood flowing in that match – bear in mind it was a no pinfall, no submission, fight to the end match – that the referee had to stop it.

Violence was a main feature of all our matches, and I could guarantee we'd both end up hurt. If Bad News picked something up to hit you with, a plank of wood, a chair, or a bottle, you had to move fast, because he would hit you. He didn't care. Before the match he'd say, "When I bring that two-by-four down on your head, you'd better move, because I will hit you."

He wasn't kidding. I was sprawled against the apron and I saw him lift this bloody great plank of wood over his head, he had a crazy look in his eyes, and I just managed to roll out of the way as it came crashing down next to me. He definitely would have hit me.

I'll tell you one thing about Bad News Allen – he never bled during a match. At least not intentionally. And if you look at his head you won't see many scars on it. I know he looked like he was cut during the matches, but that was because I would lean over him and let my blood run onto his head, so the people would think he was cut. But I got along OK with Bad News, unlike all the other wrestlers, even those in the WWF, who were scared of him. And between us, we did some great business for Stampede Wrestling.

There was a time in Calgary when, for one reason or another, there were no heavyweights in the territory to challenge the Stampede North American Champion Killer Khan, and he was a big man. So one night Bruce said to me, "Killer's leaving Calgary next week. We want you to go for the belt."

To be honest, I thought this was a bad idea, a mistake, because even with the steroids I was taking, Killer Khan was a lot bigger than me. He was massive. Bruce said, "Just let him keep hitting you, let him throw you out of the ring. When he's tired, you can backdrop him."

So I did. I backdropped him right out of the ring, which should have been an automatic disqualification for me, but the referee didn't see it. So, for a while, I was the Stampede North American Champion. A heavyweight. I'll be honest, I was into serious stuff with the steroids. I was taking at least 6 CCs of testosterone – 3 CCs in each arse cheek – every day, which could make you feel very bad. And I went from about 180lbs to 225lbs.

It wasn't just in Calgary. I always took steroids with me when I went to Japan, and although I won't mention their names, some of the boys – or men – over there took steroids off my hands as well. Don't get me wrong, they worked out hard, everyday. They might have been doing 1,000 squats a day. Might. But if you look at their legs, you can see some of those boys had a bit of help.

By the time me and Davey Boy Smith went back to Japan, Sayama had been gone quite a few months, and the promoters were pushing a new face, and a new character, The Cobra, alias the wrestler George Takano. He wasn't really a new wrestler, he'd spent a couple of years in Mexico, and from there had come into Stampede, wrestling as The Cobra. I can even remember the first match I had with him in Lethbridge, Alberta.

I'll be honest, the first time we met, I didn't think much of George Takano as a wrestler or as a person. Coming straight from Mexico, I think he thought he could try it on with me in the ring. That first night, I let it go. But I slept on it. And the next night, in Red Deer, he got in the ring, and I kicked the shit out of him, in a working fashion. And in the space of that one match, I'd say we came to an understanding. After the match I thanked him, you know, being polite, and he thanked me, also being polite. And after that, everything was fine between us. In fact when we met up again in Japan, we became good friends.

So I think New Japan had big plans for Georgie Takano, The Cobra, who was a very good athlete, and a good character. But, like I said before, characters have to built up slowly, which was something New Japan was very good at. There were always loads of young boys around, learning, training, and waiting to come in. They were just kids really, but they'd run around for you, carrying your bags, getting your cigarettes, whatever you asked them to do they'd do it. And they used to spend hours watching the wrestling, which, I suppose, was how they learned.

I remember one of the young boys. He'd been at ringside during one of my matches, crouched down in front of the apron, where they always sat. After the matches were finished, I called him over. His name was Keichi Yamada, and he was a very serious little guy, but he came over to me and he bowed, as they do, a couple of times. I said to him, "You. Speak little English?"

He bowed and said, "Yes Kid-san." Which was like calling me Mr. Kid.

His hair was cut in a short back and sides; I mean a very short, square cut back and sides. So I said to him, "Your name in England – English name – Frankie."

He looked at me with big wide eyes. "Oh."

I said, "Franken – stein."

He said, "Oh. Arigato gozayamas," or "thank-you very much." He thought it was great. Well, a few years later he grew that short back and sides right out, and as Jushin Liger, he was a fantastic wrestler. But he was a nice lad, very polite and respectful, very serious; well those young boys had to be, because if they made a mistake in the ring, the coach used to hit them with a big bamboo cane.

We were back in Tokyo on New Year's Day 1984 to wrestle in a tournament for the vacant NJPW WWF title. Apart from myself and Davey Boy, there was Mark Rocco, The Cobra, Kobayashi, Kido, and a few others, including a Mexican wrestler called Babeface, all taking part. The tournament was going to run over five or six weeks, and for every match you wrestled, you scored points, depending on whether you won, lost or drew. At the end of the six weeks, the wrestler with the most points would be the champion.

The wrestling magazines covered the tournament matches, and every week they printed all the scores, so toward the end, it got very exciting for the fans. I had matches with Rocco, which were fantastic, Cobra, and Kobayashi, who I remember really hated my piledriver. Most of the Japanese wrestlers were scared of it. They used to say to me, "Oh Dy-na-mite. Piledriver. Very dangerous." That was because I'd pick them up and then jump up in the air before piledriving them. I did take care of them, but it was still a dangerous move. The more dangerous the better, as far as the fans were concerned.

I'd go up on the top rope, for example against The Cobra, and once I was up there, he'd do a spinkick. Where did I go? Straight back, onto the concrete. Or I'd have Kobayashi up against the top rope, ready to suplex him. Where did that suplex finish? Not in the ring, but out on the concrete, both of us. The trouble was, after you'd done those moves a few times, while they never lost their danger for the wrestlers, they maybe lost a little bit of excitement for the fans. So then you had to come up with something different and even more dangerous.

I had to wrestle Davey Boy Smith in Sapporo a couple of weeks before the final. We'd been wrestling each other in Calgary for nearly three years, so we knew each other's style and what we were supposed to be doing in the ring better than anybody. We wrestled a good hard match, which I won.

And then the week before the final we were in Nagoya where I wrestled Cobra, and he beat me, one, two, three. And on account of that result, the three of us, myself, Cobra and Davey Boy Smith, all ended up on equal points, which meant we had to wrestle a three-way contest to decide the winner and World Champion.

For the final night of the tournament, we were in the Budokan Hall in Tokyo. First match on was Cobra against Davey Boy Smith, which I think ended as a count out or a disqualification. George went back to the dressing room, while Davey stayed in to wrestle me. As soon as I got in the ring I could see he was knackered, sweating and sucking air in. I slapped a headlock on him and I heard him say, under his breath, "Tommy, I'm fucked." Now I've never taken liberties in the ring, even with people I don't like. So fucked or not, Davey got a great match that night, and after 15 minutes, I beat him with a suplex over the top rope, taking us both over, only I managed to crawl back into the ring and win the match.

I caught my back on the corner of the apron as I landed, and was in a lot of pain. But now I had to wrestle The Cobra, George Takano, who'd been sat on his backside enjoying a fifteen-minute rest. And this one was for the World Championship belt. Cobra waded in right from the bell. I was tired and sore, but he came at me hard, kicking me and cracking me, really laying into me. I thought, "Right." I kicked him back, so hard he had to back into the turnbuckle, and then I hit him with one of my favourite combinations; two drop kicks, a nip up, and a middle finger to the crowd. They went wild.

Cobra was beating me good, and I let him keep hitting me – that never bothered me anyway – he leapfrogged me, and then tried to give me a backdrop with his feet. But quick as anything I dropped to my knees, hooked his legs and went for the pin before he kicked me off. The crowd were off their feet, and I had my arm in the air, but Peter Takahashi said, "No, only two." Cobra started to get up. You've seen the back suplexes they do in Japan – like a jackknife. He barely got to his feet before I grabbed his arm, threw it around my neck, put my arms around his waist and took him straight up in the air and slammed him down hard, right on the back of his neck. And this time he didn't move as I waited for the three count. That was it. I was the World Champion.

Now, as special as a World Championship belt is, especially in Japan, I always believed the quality of the match was what really mattered – much more than winning it. But to the Japanese, being the was a big deal. So when Peter Takahashi came to me in the dressing room after the match, he was being very serious when he said, "Kid-san. You take the belt home. We trust you. Take care of it. Don't wrestle anybody for it. Then you bring it back."

I know why he was worried. A few years earlier somebody, maybe one of the Guerrerros had won a belt in Japan, gone to Mexico or America, and never brought it back. So I suppose they thought the same thing could happen again. But not with me. I said, "Don't worry Peter. I'll take care of it."

I went back for another tour in July, but knew deep down that things weren't the same in New Japan without Tiger Mask. And probably never would be. Don't get me wrong, there were some great junior heavyweight wrestlers in that company, including Georgie Takano, but in my opinion, they were no replacement for Sayama. And they couldn't put somebody else into the Tiger Mask costume because Giant Shohei Baba, who owned All Japan Pro Wrestling, had already paid to use the gimmick for his own promotion. Which probably had a lot to do with that little prick Hadachi turning up in Calgary a few weeks later with a briefcase full of money. He opened the briefcase and I could see it was a lot of money, $15-, maybe $20,000 dollars. I said, "What's this?"

There were just the three of us in the room. He looked at Davey Boy Smith, then he looked at me and said, "Please. Baba wants you to wrestle for him."

CHAPTER EIGHT

We weren't the first wrestlers to switch promotions in Japan; and we wouldn't be the last. A few years before we jumped, Abdullah the Butcher, who at that time was probably the top heel in All Japan, appeared on a New Japan card. That same year, Stan Hansen jumped from New Japan to All Japan. But it was after we made the switch, that I would say rivalry between the two promotions began to heat up.

As always in wrestling, it came down to money. Baba was building his promotion up to compete with New Japan, and he was prepared to pay for the wrestlers who could do the job. So when Hadachi opened that briefcase and offered us the money, I said "Yeah," straight away.

The deal was this. Baba would pay us $20,000 each, up front; $10,000 straight away if we signed a contract, and $10,000 when we got to Japan. After that we'd be paid $6,200 for every week of the tour – which was $1,000 a week more than Inoki was paying us. Not only that, Baba would let us pick the tours we wanted to do; we could have done the lot.

So I signed the contract, and although he was scared shitless about what we were doing, Davey Boy Smith signed his. Our first tour for All Japan would be in November, at the annual tag-team tournament, but there was one problem – officially, I was still the World Champion for New Japan. And they were expecting me to give George Takano a rematch for the title when we went back. So for the next few weeks we had to keep everything quiet; we didn't tell anybody.

We flew to Tokyo, the idea being that we'd lie low for a week in a secret location to keep us out of the way and, I imagine, make our appearance for All Japan a bigger surprise. Baba sent someone to meet us at the airport and they took us to a hotel somewhere in Tokyo.

Hadachi was waiting for us at the hotel, with enough money to see us through the week, 50,000 Yen for me, and 50,000 Yen for Davey. But

Hadachi wouldn't give it to us all at once; he dished it out, a little bit every day. And he stayed at the hotel, I imagine to make sure we didn't do anything stupid.

I decided not to be ignorant about the World Championship belt that I still had. I packed it in a box, put a note in which said, "Thank you very much, Dynamite Kid" and sent back to the New Japan office in Tokyo. I didn't have to; I could have kept it. I know a lot of other wrestlers would have kept it. But I thought sending it back it was the polite thing to do. Plus, I could now say I'd retired undefeated.

On our first day with All Japan, we turned up at the hotel where all the other American wrestlers were staying for the new tour. And as we walked through the door, who should we see but Baba, sitting at one side of a table in the lounge, smoking one of his big cigars, and, on the other side of the table, Seiji Sakaguchi. They were obviously talking about us.

Well, I'll be honest, I wasn't expecting that, but I carried on walking, looking casual. And Davey Boy Smith, who was nearly filling his pants, hid behind me – hid, as if he thought Sakaguchi wouldn't see him.

He said, "Tommy, we're going to get in trouble."

I told him to shut up. We'd made the jump, signed the contract, I'd sent the belt back. That was it. If Sakaguchi had bad words to say about us, I could say a few bad words back. But Sakaguchi didn't say anything. In fact, he didn't even look at us, because he was in serious discussion with Baba. We found out later that they'd come to some sort of agreement, because somehow, probably because of that belt, we were officially still tied to New Japan.

I imagine Baba gave Inoki some financial compensation, and he agreed to blackout any media coverage, because New Japan didn't want anybody to find out what we'd done. At least not yet. That didn't bother me, because we were getting paid. And I didn't feel guilty about what we'd done, because I know for a fact that any wrestler in the same position, offered the same deal, would have done exactly the same.

I heard that Sakaguchi took it very badly. It was about six months later when I saw him in Madison Square Garden in New York; the first time I'd seen him since we'd left New Japan. He put his hand out, shook my hand, and said, "No hard feelings." That was it. And a few years after that I ran into Antonio Inoki at Tokyo Airport. I shouted to him, "Antonio." He turned round, saw me and gave me a big smile. We shook hands, and that was that. And I was glad I had the chance to do that. Inoki, Sakaguchi, Fujinami, Choshu; these were men who I liked and respected, and who I like to think respected me. In the end everything was OK between us.

But not in 1984. As part of the media blackout, our first match was filmed but never shown on TV. Which was a shame because it was a great match; myself and Davey Boy Smith against Terry and Dory Funk Jr. in the Korakean Hall in Tokyo. It ended in a double countout, with me and Terry outside the ring; I was trying to crawl back in the ring, but Terry kept hold of my leg and wouldn't let me get in. As wrestlers, the Funks were fantastic, and in my opinion, probably had the greatest wrestling brains in the ring.

That was the first time I'd met Terry Funk, in the hotel in Tokyo. I remember the first words he ever said to me.

"Dynamite, I think I've got a job for you. Can you speak Russian?"

Straight away I said, "Yeah. Nastrovia."

He said, "OK, I think you've got the job." Then he started telling me how he was a very good friend of Sylvester Stallone, who, at that time, was making another Rocky film with Dolph Lungdren. Stallone was looking for somebody who could speak Russian. "And he wants somebody who can box," said Terry, "I think you're the man."

So I said, "OK, when is it?"

"In a few months Dynamite. I'll let you know."

Six months later, the film came out at the cinema, and the next time I saw him I said, "Terry, what happened? How come I didn't get the part with Sylvester Stallone?"

He said, "Well Dyno," he always called me Dyno. "There's been a bit of a mistake."

"What do you mean Terry, a mistake?"

"You're too short."

We had some great laughs over the years, mainly because Terry was always messing about and acting the loony. And he is one of the greatest wrestlers I've ever been in the ring with. All the years I wrestled, I took pride in giving every single opponent a good match. It didn't matter how pathetic or useless they were, I never let anybody look bad. Never. But you know what, Terry was better at it better than me.

He took the weakest chops and the worst clotheslines, then he'd bounce round the ring, and flop about on his back like a fish out of water. He could wrestle a broomstick and made it look like a million dollars. That's how good he was. I remember a match he had with the Native American, Steve Gatorwolf. He was a waste of time; always bullshitting about how great he was, and then just before the match he'd get so nervous he couldn't speak. Against Terry Funk, he got in the ring and froze. He couldn't move. And when he finally managed a feeble tomahawk chop, Terry looked as if he'd been hit with a sledgehammer. He was fantastic. And, he was a terrible joker. Nearly as bad as me. But I couldn't think of a better way to kick off a tour than a tag match with the Funks, televised or not.

Meanwhile, Sayama, who hadn't wrestled in nearly a year since he left New Japan, appeared on a card at the Korakean Hall, wrestling for a new promotion called the UWF. I'd known about this for a while because he called me while I was still with New Japan to tell me about it.

"It's a different promotion," he said, "No backdrops, we don't hit the ropes. Just shooting style."

What he really wanted was for me to join the UWF with him, so I said I'd think about it, and I did, but I decided not to go. I thought to myself, these men, Sayama, Maeda, Takada, if they go ahead with it, what happens if it goes wrong and nobody turns up? In my opinion, with that style of wrestling, it was a gamble. So I decided to stay put with Inoki. Sayama called me a few times after that, trying to make me to change my mind, and I think he was a bit upset that I said no.

And the bad feeling that I had about it, was proved correct, because the UWF – the first UWF – did close down. Which was a real shame, because they were all very good wrestlers, all hard-workers – I'd known Nobuhiko Takada since he was a young boy, and in my opinion he was always trying to do more than he could. But he had a big heart and I admired him for that.

Anyway, with all the hassle of switching promotions behind us, we finished our first tour for Baba thinking we'd done the right thing. The fans enjoyed our matches; they got their money's worth and so did Baba. And of course Hadachi took all the credit for bringing us to All Japan. Baba's wife, Motoko, who always went to the matches, thanked him personally, because, and I don't mind saying it, we were a good tag team. But going to All Japan was nothing to do with Hadachi. It was Baba's money that got us there, nothing and nobody else. But it was time to head home to Calgary. To another load of trouble. Stu Hart was mad, probably madder than I'd ever seen him.

"What the fuck did you two think you were doing going to All Japan?"

So I told him. "Well Stu that's my prerogative," which he probably didn't understand, "Plus I'm on $1,000 a week more, plus I've done my time for all those Japanese wrestlers in New Japan, plus I've got a sched-ule – I can pick any tour I want."

He said, "Well you just cost me, you little bastard."

That was when he told me that Inoki had been paying him, about $10,000 a tour, to let us go to Japan. It was news to me, but I could understand why he was so mad. I was mad – I thought we should have had a share. Bret was even more upset. He was upset because I went without him.

As things turned out, Bret Hart didn't have time to sit around feeling sorry for himself, the WWF was in town. George Scott, who at that time was Vince McMahon's right-hand man, turned up at the Pavilion to see the Friday night TV taping. He took one look at me – bear in mind, I'd just come back from Japan, where I'd start out clean-shaven – including my head – but after four weeks, looked more like Robinson Crusoe – and he said, "You'll have to shave that lot off you know." He watched the matches – I was wrestling Bret – and afterward he asked us both if we would go to New York for a WWF TV taping. It sounded great, because even then, in 1984, the WWF was on a much bigger scale than Stampede – we were about to make ourselves some serious money.

We had to go to Poughkeepsie, in upstate New York, where, at that time, the WWF did most of its TV tapings. I walked into the dressing room, and the first person I spotted was my old friend Sylvester Ritter, The Junkyard Dog. He took one look at me, and if he could have, he would have turned white. I walked straight up to him and said, "Right you bastard, where's my money?"

The last time I'd seen Junkyard must have been four or five years ago in Calgary. Back then he was Big Daddy Ritter and we were tag partners. He decided that we should have matching ring gowns, and said he knew a place in Calgary where he could get them made. So I gave him $1,000 and the last thing he said to me was that they'd be ready the next Monday. Monday came; no word from Junkyard Dog. I went round to his apartment, but it was empty, literally. He'd cleared out. I went down to the shop where the gowns were being made, and found it closed down. Junkyard Dog had gone, and taken my $1,000 with him. I thought that was it – until I walked into the dressing room in Poughkeepsie. Well, he was full of apologies and excuses, and promises that he was going to pay me back, which he did, eventually, although I should have charged him interest. But to tell you the truth, I was glad to see Junkyard Dog again.

But apart from that, our first appearance for the WWF went OK. And luckily for us, the place was sold out. I knew the wrestlers were paid according to business on the night, and as I looked around I thought to myself, "We'll be alright here." We wrestled a tag match, then singles matches against a couple of job boys. We got changed and waited for our windfall. Arnold Skaaland was in charge of the money and paying the wrestlers. He handed us our pay, $25 each. I looked at it and I said, "I'm not being funny Arnold, but where's the rest of it?"

He said, "That's it. $25 apiece."

There had to be a mistake. I said, "You mean we've travelled 3,000 miles to wrestle for $25? Arnold, we didn't bring much money with us."

I kept on at him until in the end he said, "What it is Dynamite, is this. You're getting the publicity. Do you know how many people will see you wrestle on TV?" Which didn't make me feel any better because $25 for two matches was, to me, still a rip off. And worse than that, the job boys were getting $200. So that night, me and Bret had to find a cheap hotel before making it back to Calgary with about $5 between us.

The next day I went straight to Stu and told him to call Vince McMahon. "You can tell him we are *never* going back again." I meant it. I didn't care because I still had Japan, and I could wrestle for Baba all year if I wanted to. But George Scott called again and asked us back to do a few spot shows, which are small house shows, on the New York loop. And he told us that we'd get more money for a house show – at least a proportion of what was in the building on the night. So me and Bret did go back, and for a week of spot shows on the New York loop, we made about $5,000.

That year saw massive changes to wrestling in the United States. Vince McMahon Sr. had died and his son, Vince Jr., was running the WWF. And he had big plans for the company, like a coast-to-coast monopoly on the wrestling business. They took all the top names from the different territories, places like Portland, Minneapolis, Louisiana, put the television in, and took over the business. Stampede Wrestling was no different, and when Vince McMahon made Stu an offer, he took it.

When Stu told us that Stampede was closing, it didn't mean a lot to me. I knew I was OK because I had Japan, but I did feel sorry for the other wrestlers who were suddenly out of work. Vince didn't want them all. He signed Bret up straight away, and Jim Neidhart shortly afterward, and I knew he wanted to bring me in as well. The problem with the WWF was that the money was never guaranteed, and I had a mortgage to pay and a family to look after. In Japan, I knew exactly how much I could earn. On the other hand, the WWF was already the biggest promotion in America and about to get even bigger. So when they called again from the WWF to arrange a meeting, I said I was interested. And, because I knew we were a good tag team, I told them about my cousin, Davey Boy Smith.

They flew us to Toronto for a meeting with Vince McMahon and George Scott. We were in a press-conference room at the Howard Johnson Hotel by the airport where we sat and talked for about half an hour. Vince was friendly, and what he seemed most interested in was the fact that me and Davey Boy Smith were first cousins and that we were British. It was during that meeting that he came up with the idea of the British Bulldogs.

He laughed and said: "Well, you look like a pair of bulldogs."

And if I think about it, what with the steroids, and our mean-looking faces, I suppose we did. Anyway, after the small talk, Vince got serious. He said, "Well what do you think? Do you want to come along or not?"

I looked at Davey and said, "What do you want to do?" Well as I expected, he never even opened his mouth, so I said to Vince, "OK. We'll give it a try."

That was really the first time I met Vince McMahon. I met him many times after that, usually after I'd done something wrong, or he mistakenly thought I'd done something wrong. For example, somebody shaved some bald patches in George Scott's son's hair while he was asleep, and although it could have been any one of twenty wrestlers who'd done it, George thought it was me.

We might have an afternoon match in New York City, and an evening match in Hartford Connecticut, about 50-miles away. There'd be a message for me at the hotel saying "Call in at the Stamford office on your way to Hartford. Vince wants to see you." But even if he was mad, Vince never let it show. He never raised his voice. We'd be in his office, sitting in front of his desk, with Davey Boy trying to hide behind me, and Vince would say, calmly, "Tom, I know it was you that did it."

And I'd look at him, all innocent, and say, "Vince, there were twenty other wrestlers in that dressing room. How come you always blame the Bulldogs?" But he was right. Most of the time it was me, but I couldn't admit it then or he would have fired me.

But anyway, on that first night as the British Bulldogs, at a TV taping in Poughkeepsie, we set out to be on our best behaviour. We were wearing our brand new Union Jack outfits and if I say so myself, we looked great. Pat Patterson was the road agent in charge on this night, and when it was time for our match he said to us, "Boys, pur-leese, when you get in that ring I want you to bark like a couple of bulldogs." So we did. We ran down the aisle, climbed through the ropes, and crawled round the ring on all fours, and shouted, "Bowsie wowsie, bowsie wowsie." The audience saw the funny side of it, but for some reason, Pat Patterson didn't. In fact, I'll be honest, we nearly got fired on our first night.

It was George Scott who asked us to sign a contract during one TV pre-taping. He handed me a piece of paper, which he said was a five-year contract and asked me to sign it there and then. What it meant was no more Japan, no working for anybody except the WWF. So I said no, and gave him the contract back. I know the majority of wrestlers were under a contract of some kind, but not the Bulldogs. I needed to know that I had Japan as an option if I wanted it. So we never signed one.

For a while, we had the best of both worlds; in between bookings for the WWF, we did a couple of tours for Baba. Just as he promised, Baba paid us $20,000 up front at the beginning of the year, and our guarantee every week that we were on tour. All Japan had a stronger tag team division than New Japan, but never seemed to push the idea of a junior heavyweight division. They had given the Tiger Mask gimmick to a young wrestler by the name of Mitsuhara Misawa, in the hope that he would do the same business for them that Sayama had done for New Japan. How did Misawa's Tiger Mask compare to Sayama's? It didn't. Don't get me wrong, Misawa was a great wrestler, but in my opinion, he was too tall and too heavy to be Tiger Mask, and nowhere near as agile as Sayama. He couldn't hope to follow in his footsteps in the ring; no spinkicks, no back somersaults, no moonsaults; but I'll give him credit, he was a hard-worker.

One of the first matches I had with him was a six-man tag, with him on our team. Before the match started I heard him say something to Toshiaki Kawada who was on the other team, maybe complaining a bit, because Kawada said "Dosh tano," or "What's the matter?" I think, even though he had the mask on, Misawa didn't want to be seen in the ring with us – to be honest, I don't think he liked me – and he was having a bit of a sulk. Which was no big deal because he ended up winning that one for us anyway.

We had some singles matches as well, and while I'm sure they were enjoyed by the fans, for me, they were nowhere near as exciting as Sayama's. I wrestled him in Sapporo one night where the stipulation was, if he won, he would move up to the heavyweight division. So I took him from the top rope to the concrete with a side salter, a type of suplex, and the result was a double count out, so he stayed put. I had a lot of matches with Tiger Mask II, in later years some very hard matches, because in a lot of ways, Misawa was like me, when he hit, you had to be ready for it.

Around the same time we made the switch to All Japan, a tide of wrestlers from New Japan did the same, including Ricki Choshu, Animal Haguchi, Isamu Terenishi and Yoshiaki Yatsu. To be honest, Baba had too many wrestlers on his hands, but I know he still paid them even when he couldn't book them. That was what I always liked about Japanese promoters; when it came to money, you could trust them because they were men of their word.

That's not to say Vince McMahon wasn't. But working for the WWF didn't have the same security. Your wage depended entirely on business, and on where you wrestled on the card. For example, if you were in the first match on a spot show, you might get $200. Second match, you get $300, and so on, up to the main event where you could get $2,000. But if you were in the first match at Madison Square Garden, you could get $1,000, while the main-event men like Hogan went home with $10,000, maybe more, for a sold-out arena. But even that could change from one night to the next, so you never knew how much you were going to get paid.

When the WWF really started to expand across the country, they had TV shows going out to just about every town and city in the United States. Once the TV was established and the interest was growing, they ran house shows in every town and city in the United States. But because there were so many venues to cover, they'd often send a couple of teams of wrestlers out on separate tours. As you can imagine, if you were the first match on a spot show in Austin, Texas, or Phoenix, Arizona, where there might have been only 3,000 people in the building, you'd be pissed off knowing that the other tour was doing 10,000 sellouts every night in places like New York, Philadelphia and Baltimore.

But as always in wrestling, success doesn't happen overnight, and you could spend a long, long time getting beaten at the bottom of the card. Ask Bret Hart and Jim Neidhart. They had teamed up to form the Hart Foundation and they spent months getting beaten by the Rougeaus. Rick Rude was the same. When he came into the WWF he thought he was never going to win. He told me. But he stuck at it and look where he ended up – as the Intercontinental Champion. So you had to be patient. The British Bulldogs had a better time of it, because we were babyfaces, and, by comparison, we were a lot smaller than some of the other wrestlers. And it's easier to push the underdogs up the card.

But for the first few months we were with the WWF, because of Japan, it was on a semi-regular basis. But that didn't stop us having some great matches when the right opponents came along, which was what happened when Terry and Dory Funk turned up in the WWF. Terry hadn't changed. He still liked to fool around. We had to catch a plane early one morning to the next venue. Terry got on and he was dragging his rucksack behind him. It looked as if it weighed a ton because he was heaving on the strap, his face was going purple and all the muscles and sinews on his arms were sticking out. So one of the stewardesses walked by and said, "Can I help you?"

Terry was panting and out of breath, but he said, "No, I'll be OK." He finally got the bag to his seat and he started trying to lift it into the luggage compartment. He was struggling again so the stewardess said, "Come on, let me help you." She bent down, lifted it up, and nearly fell over backward because it was empty, there was nothing in it.

But, occasionally, the joke was on Terry. We were in Pittsburgh one night having a drink in the hotel after the match. It got to about 2AM, and although we had an early plane to catch the next day, Terry said, "Oh, come on, we'll have one more."

So I got up and said, "It's OK, I'll get this. What do you want?"

"Thanks Dyno. I'll have a brandy."

While he wasn't looking I slipped a yellow jacket – speed – which a lot of wrestlers used to take to keep themselves awake – into his brandy. I handed him his drink and said, "Cheers Terry."

"Cheers Dyno."

I didn't see Terry again until just before the match the next day. I walked into the dressing room and there was Terry, sitting on a bench with his head down. He looked up at me – he looked bloody awful – and he said, "Dyno, don't do that again."

"What? Don't do what Terry? What are you talking about?"

He said, "I've not been to sleep."

I said, "Terry, I'm being serious. What are you talking about?" I think he believed me in the end, but anyway Terry, yeah, it was me.

Our last match with the Funks was in Buffalo, New York. Terry was having trouble with his knees, and right after the match, he said to his brother, "Dory, tell Dyno I'm going home."

Dory said, "You can't go home, we've got another four weeks yet."

But Terry didn't care. He left, which I didn't blame him for – he never called Vince, never gave them any notice, and buggered off back to Texas. That was when they brought Jesse Barr in as Jimmy Jack Funk, the third Funk brother, and he was rotten; terrible. He thought he was great, but all I can say is, bless him for trying.

As a team, the British Bulldogs were making progress in the WWF, although I felt it wasn't fast enough. We had some great matches against the Moondogs, who at that time were being managed by Mr. Fuji. Rex and Spot weren't the most agile of opponents, in fact, they could be hard work to manoeuvre in the ring. But they were good fun. At one TV taping we had to pretend we were taking tea with the Moondogs; we were being very British, drinking out of posh teacups and saucers and eating little sandwiches and they had to behave like animals. We rehearsed this scene, and I said to Fuji, "Do me a favour. When we've eaten these sandwiches, and Spot starts acting stupid, hit him over the head with a plate."

I didn't think he'd really do it, but he did. He picked up a plate – a real plate – said, "Hey Moondog-san." and then "bang," he smashed it over Spot's head into little pieces. And it went out on TV.

But there were a lot of frustrations as well. In the summer of 1985 Barry Windham and Mike Rotunda beat Nikolai Volkoff and the Iron Sheik to become Tag Team Champions for the second time. They were babyfaces, which meant we couldn't go near the tag team belts. But a couple of months later they dropped the belts to Greg Valentine and Brutus Beefcake. Windham was leaving the WWF, so the team split, which should have made us the top contenders. But it wasn't as easy as that. We were messed around, told we could have title shots, but then told we weren't ready to be champions – even though we were the main event on the B-tour, and we were drawing. So I told Chief Jay Strongbow, one of Vince's road agents, I didn't want the belts anyway, and in November we were back in Japan for the All Japan Tag Tournament.

All Japan was a much stronger promotion now. Jumbo Tsuruta and Genchiro Tenyru were still the top men, but they had a lot of very talented younger wrestlers coming up; Misawa, Kawada and one who I always thought was a fantastic wrestler, Kenta Kobashi. There were some great tag matches with Stan Hansen and Bruiser Brody against Tenyru and Tsuruta, and me and Davey against Misawa and Kobayashi, so standards shot up. A lot of wrestlers were scared of Frank "Bruiser" Brody, and maybe they had good reason to be, because he could use his fists. You may not believe this, but away from the ring, Frank, bless him, was a gentleman, and always very good to me. They were a lot of American wrestlers on the cards, and while most of them did become popular with the Japanese fans, some of them had no idea what wrestling in Japan was all about.

Jerry Lawler and Jimmy Valiant were booked on one tour, just for a week. I imagine it was the only week they ever did in Japan, for a simple reason. Their opponents, the Japanese wrestlers, refused to sell. Jerry would be in the ring with, for example, Killer Khan. Every time Jerry landed a shot, Killer stood there. He didn't move. So then Jimmy, who was on the apron, started shouting, "Mushi, mushi," at the top of his voice. The stupid bastard didn't realize it means "hello" in Japanese, so the crowd started laughing at them.

Back in the dressing room, they were talking to each other, trying to figure out what went wrong. I heard Jerry say to Jimmy, "I've had Killer Khan in Tennessee and he sells all my shots. Tonight he didn't move. I can't understand it."

I thought to myself, "I can. The reason they're not selling is because you're not hitting hard enough, plus, you're in their country. They're not going to be put down in Japan."

Gypsy Joe was another American who we met in Tokyo. One night after the matches we were all going for something to eat. I said, "Gypsy, can you speak Japanese?"

He said, "I speak fluent Japanese. You order and I will tell them what you want."

Bear in mind, we were only in McDonalds in Tokyo, so I asked for a Filet-O-Fish and two Big Macs. Joe said to the young Japanese girl behind the counter, "Two Big Mac-o, one Filet-O-Fish-o."

I thought to myself, that's not Japanese, anybody can say that. So I told Davey Boy Smith to pass me two paper napkins, rolled them up into little balls and stuffed them underneath the straps on the back of his jacket. And while Gypsy Joe was trying to talk to the girl, I got my cigarette lighter out and set the napkins on fire. Now I know this sounds like a bad joke, and it was, but believe me, it was funny at the time. The girl saw the smoke coming up from behind his jacket and started waving and pointing, but he kept saying, "No, no, listen. Two Big Mac-o, one Filet-O-Fish-o." Well, he soon realized that he was on fire, and although he didn't get hurt, he was upset about what we'd done. He went straight back to the hotel and told Tiger Jeet Singh that the Bulldogs had set him on fire.

Tiger Jeet Singh was probably the worst person he could have told, mainly because ever since we'd come into All Japan, he'd been looking to try and push us out. His tag partner for the tournament was Abdullah the Butcher, who was a very good friend of mine and had always treated me well. Tiger on the other hand was a tight bastard, and as a wrestler, a load of shit – kicks, punches – awful. The Japanese people liked his character, the way he ran in the ring with a sword between his teeth – but, marks out of ten for wrestling, I'd give him zero.

Tiger Jeet Singh liked his glory, and didn't like to lose. In a tag match, he made sure he never did. But, Baba had decided that the Bulldogs were ready to be pushed, and Abdullah and Tiger Jeet Singh were our next opponents. When Joe Haguchi told him the finish, Tiger said, "Oh no no no. I do no job for him," as in me, The Dynamite Kid. And on the night, he made sure it was Abdullah who was pinned.

During that match Abdullah opened my head up and I bled all over the place. Tiger Jeet was up on the apron and when he saw all the blood he started calling, "Butcher, Butcher, tag me, tag me." You know why don't you? I was down on my hands and knees, a bit groggy, and he'd come in and kick me in the head. Well, there were photographers all around that ring and he knew it would make a terrific picture for the wrestling magazines – me on the floor covered in blood, and him looking like a million dollars for doing nothing. But he soon tagged Abdullah back in for the finish, because there was no way he was going to let me pin him. The prick.

Anyway, the night that Gypsy Joe grassed me up, I think if he could have done, Tiger Jeet Singh would definitely have got me fired. He reported me to Joe Haguchi, but luckily for me, Gypsy Joe had seen the funny side of it as well and told him it was just a prank. So that was that.

On one tour we were surprised to run into Giant Haystacks again. It was his first time in Japan, and he was probably feeling a little bit nervous, and so I wasn't surprised that he came to me for advice. He said, "Tommy, how do you wrestle these Japanese men?"

I said, "Hard, Haystacks, very hard. When your man goes down, grab hold of his hair and yank him up." He looked at me in surprise. I said, "Really, you have to pull them up by their hair. It has to look good. This is Japan you know."

Haystacks nodded and said, "Right."

I said, "And when you hit him, make sure you hit him."

So Haystacks went off to the ring for his first match in Japan, which was against a wrestler called Kojica. And Haystacks listened to everything I had told him, and he knocked the shit out of Kojica – who weighed about 180 pounds – before beating him with his big elbow drop.

They came back to the dressing room, and Haystacks sat there on a bench, puffing and panting. Kojica walked straight up to him and said, "You want to play monkey business?" and smacked Haystacks straight across the face, a real crack, you could almost feel it yourself. What do you think Haystacks did? Nothing. He just sat there and more or less let him do it.

After two weeks of that tour, Haystacks had had enough. He went to Joe Haguchi and said, "I want to go home." But the All Japan office held his passport, and there was no way he was leaving before the four weeks were up. Haystacks was miserable.

On the last night of the tour, it was Haystacks and Tiger Jeet Singh against Baba and another Japanese wrestler. After 10 or 15 minutes, Haystacks was on the end of Baba's famous chops, and a minute later was pouring with blood. So Haystacks grabbed Baba from behind and held him while Tiger went in his trunks for a knuckle-duster. He went to throw it at Baba's face, but he put his head forward, and Tiger nailed Haystacks instead. When Haystacks hit the mat, Baba crawled over and pinned him, one, two, three. Haystacks had finally got it. Without really trying he made Baba look great that night.

Six-months later, when I was in the UK for a week to see my family, I made it a working holiday and did a couple of matches with Marty Jones. Haystacks was on the same card, and after the match when we were all in the dressing room, I shouted, "Haystacks, what did you think about Japan?"

He looked at me and said, "Fuck off." Then he turned round to the other wrestlers and said, "This little bastard almost got me killed over there by the Mafia." There were rumours that Kojica's family had some connections with the Yakuza, but funnily enough, Haystacks never mentioned the slapping.

It was coming up to the end of the year, and just before we left to go home, I asked Joe Haguchi for our $20,000 guarantee for the following year.

Joe said, "Baba says he will pay you next time you come back."

I thought it seemed a bit funny, but I knew Baba always paid what he said he would. More or less as soon as we got home, the WWF wanted us back again. Which was great – knackering from the travel point of view – but great for the money we were making. We did a couple of weeks; Detroit, Pennsylvania, New York, and some of the smaller towns like Albany and Syracuse. And then one night, we were in the Joe Frazier Stadium in Chicago, when Chief Jay Strongbow told us, again, that we were in line for the title shot against Valentine and Beefcake at Wrestle-Mania II. But only a title shot.

Well, I knew what that meant. And even though WrestleMania was going to be a big show, a pay-per-view event with a big paycheque for us, I said, "No, thank you very much, but when we've finished this tour, we'll be going back to Japan."

Chief Jay couldn't believe I'd said that. He got up and left the dressing room, I think, to make a call to Vince, because a couple of minutes later he was back. He said, "OK. You've got it. But that's it. You finish with Japan."

Which I thought was fair enough; they had to build us up over the next few months to be ready for WrestleMania 11 in April. And I understood why Baba wouldn't give us our money in advance for the next year. He knew we weren't coming back.

CHAPTER NINE

In the space of a year, Vince McMahon had achieved more or less what he set out to do, and the wwf was doing great business right across the United States. A lot of that was down to the wwf World Champion, Hulk Hogan. He had taken the belt from the Iron Sheik, after he'd taken it from Bob Backlund – because Bob would never have lost it to Hogan – and since then, Hulk Hogan, and the wwf, had never looked back.

What did I think of Hulk Hogan? For his opponents – marks out of ten – I would give ten, for making him look good in the ring. For Hogan, I'd give zero, because as a wrestler, he had no ability at all. None. But it didn't matter, because he had a good gimmick, which Vince McMahon had been quick to take advantage of when he spotted Hogan in the awa in 1983. Hulk Hogan had helped a friend of mine, Dave Shults, get in the awa, which at that time was a good promotion – as in, wrestlers were lining up to get in. I know that the two of them, Hogan and Shults, had become good friends, and when Hogan joined the wwf, he made sure that Vince took Dave as well.

To tell you the truth, I never had much to do with Hulk Hogan or his friends. Apart from seeing him in the building just before the matches, our paths never really crossed. Don't get me wrong, if Hogan was in the same room as you, he'd be polite and friendly, he'd shake your hand, buy you a cup of coffee. But he wouldn't really give a shit about you. I can remember getting off the plane with all the other wrestlers, and while we had to go and sort out a car to rent to get to the hotel, Hogan would be chauffeured away in a big limousine, waving to us through the window.

Shults didn't stay in the wwf very long. When the promotion was featured on the 20/20 show on tv, which set out to expose the wrestling business, he got into a bit of trouble.

The reporter, John Stossel, told Dave Shults he thought wrestling was fake. Dave replied, "You think it's fake?," and slapped him and knocked him to the floor. The guy got up and Shults said, "What the hell's wrong with you? That was an open-handed slap – you think it's fake?" And then he slapped the reporter again, even harder.

I know a lot of people thought that was all set up for TV – I mean that was more or less what the show had been about. But it wasn't. It was just Dave Shults being Dave Shults. The TV company filed a lawsuit against the WWF, and soon after that Dave Shults left. I never saw him again.

Whatever you thought about Hulk Hogan, his gimmick was a big draw, no question about it. And it sparked off a whole load of wrestling gimmicks – some good, some awful. Vince McMahon was always coming up with new ones. Some were just plain stupid, for example, Ricky Steamboat, when he became Ricky "The Dragon" Steamboat, and he had to do all that Bruce Lee bullshit on the top rope. And Terry Taylor as the Red Rooster, with his hair painted red, walking round the ring, going, "Cluck, cluck, cluck."

But all of that was just for Vince's own amusement – at least, that was my opinion. I've seen him many times, sniggering and laughing behind the curtain at some of the things he had the wrestlers doing in the ring. And you either did it, or you were fired. So when he walked in the dressing room one night with our gimmick – a pair of real bulldogs – I thought we'd got off lightly.

In fact, the dogs weren't a bad idea. We walked them down to the ring – the people loved them – we wrestled, and after the match we handed them back. A few weeks later, at the next television taping, Vince brought just one bulldog. He handed the lead to Davey Boy Smith and said, "There you go, take her to the ring."

We needed to think of a name for it, and if it had been a male dog, we'd have called it Winston. But it was Vince who came up with the name Matilda. Me and Davey looked at each other a bit blank, shrugged, and set off down the aisle with our new mascot, Matilda. Waltzing fucking Matilda. When we came back to the dressing room, Davey handed her back to Vince, but he said, "No, that dog's yours now. You keep her."

When we were touring, she travelled in the sky kennel, which cost $20 a day, and we flew that dog everywhere; New York, Los Angeles, Detroit, Calgary – you name it, Matilda went with us.

In a way, it was a shame for Matilda, because when we first got her, she was a very quiet, placid dog. We had to make her bad tempered, by provoking her a little bit in the dressing room, so that she'd go for our opponents in the ring. For example, she hated Slick, the manager, because he used to prod her with his stick – not hurting her, but aggravating her, and getting her mad. And it worked. When Davey put her in the ring near Slick, she went for him. Slick panicked, jumped up on the top rope, fell off backward and broke his arm. But as far as the gimmicks went, Matilda the bulldog saved us from a lot worse.

All the kids loved Matilda, and Vince had the idea of using her in an anti-smoking campaign. We taped a sort of public health warning, which was shown during an episode of Saturday Night's Main Event. I put a cigarette in Matilda's mouth, and a load of green smoke started coming out of plastic tubes that they'd taped to her ears. Then I said something like, "Don't smoke kids, it's bad for you," Which was a bit rich coming from me.

Early in 1986, the WWF was building up for WrestleMania II, at that time, the biggest event they'd ever put on. In the run up to our tag team title shot, we had a lot of matches – straight tags, cage matches, and a few six-man tags – with the champions, Greg "The Hammer" Valentine and Brutus Beefcake. The Dream Team.

Greg was a good wrestler – not a flyer, but a hard-hitter, and I got on well with him. But sometimes he complained about our matches. He walked in the dressing room one night and blew up at Rene Goulet, one of the road agents. He was shouting, "Every time I come out of the ring with the Bulldogs I can't get out of bed the next day. I'm being suplexed on the back of my neck, thrown over the top rope, blah, blah, blah, fucking this, motherfucking that." He was really upset, and I don't know why because I thought they were great moves. But anyway, I did like Greg. He was a good, solid wrestler, and he always delivered the goods.

Brutus Beefcake, on the other hand, was, a load of shit, in my opinion. Like one or two other wrestlers, he got into the WWF only through his friendship with Hulk Hogan. In fact, while he was in Portland, working for Don Owen a couple of years earlier, he wrestled as Dizzy Hogan, Hulk Hogan's brother.

WrestleMania II took place at three different venues; Los Angeles, where Hulk Hogan defended the world title against King Kong Bundy, New York, with George "The Animal" Steele wrestling Randy Savage for the Intercontinental title, and Chicago, where the tag team title match was.

Ozzie Ozborne was the special guest ring announcer for our match. It wasn't long, maybe 15 or 20 minutes, but it was a good match. Especially the finish. Davey put a headlock on Greg and shot him off to the ropes, right onto where I was waiting on the middle rope with my head down. I took a fall backward onto the concrete, while Greg fell backward into the ring and was pinned by Davey. That was it; the British Bulldogs were the new WWF World Tag Team Champions. And for that match, for 15 minutes in the ring, we were paid $20,000.

If you remember, we had our manager, Captain Louis Albano, with us that night. A few months earlier, Vince had asked us if we wanted to work on our own or with a manager. I chose the Captain, who I'd met in New York in 1981 when I wrestled Tiger Mask. He had a good character, in the ring, out of the ring, even in the dressing room, and I thought the Captain would be good for our image.

At first Lou and the other managers like Slick and Mr. Fuji were on the road with the wrestlers seven days a week. When the WWF started making cutbacks, they only appeared at the television tapings. But in the run up to WrestleMania II, the Captain joined the Bulldogs for some six-man tag matches against The Dream Team and their manager Jimmy Valiant.

Lou couldn't do much in the ring, so most of the time we had to leave him on the apron. One night, just after I'd tagged Davey Boy Smith in, I stood on the apron next to Lou, and he whispered to me, "How many are in tonight?"

I looked around, casually, and whispered back, "About 5,000."

The next night in Syracuse, he did the same again. This time there were about 8,000 in the building. Bear in mind that we were the main event. Lou said to me, "We'll have done all right then won't we Kid?"

I said, "We have Captain. We'll be all right."

This went on all week, until we got paid at the end of it. Vince gave the Captain his cheque, which was for the same amount that he always got as a manager.

He said to Vince, "Erm, just a minute, how come this is all I get?" He'd been reckoning up the crowds every night and thinking, because he'd taken part in the matches, he'd be on the same percentage as the wrestlers.

Vince said to him, sarcastically, "It's OK Captain. You're family."

But Lou was a good man, a funny man, especially when he went on the pop. Whenever we did a TV taping, which might be three weeks' worth of matches, plus interviews that were shown before the matches, Lou Albano always had a full bottle of vodka plus a full bottle of whisky in his case. Vince McMahon turned up at one taping, when the Captain had already finished one bottle. Vince must have said something because Lou turned round and said to Vince, who is from an Irish-American family, "You fucking Irish bastard, you can't fire me. Nobody can fire the Captain. Your dad said so!"

Anyway Vince fired him.

I thought our schedule might have been a bit easier once we'd finished with All Japan and went working full-time for the WWF. But it wasn't. You were on the road for three weeks – wrestling every day – you had three days off, and then you were back on the road for another three weeks. And in that three weeks, you really had no idea how much you were going to earn. If you were on the same card as Paul Orndorff wrestling Hulk Hogan in Toronto, with 60,000 people in the building, it was great. But if you were wrestling for 500 people in Kansas City Missouri – you'd feel a bit pissed.

For myself, Davey, Bret and Jim Neidhart, most of our three days off were spent travelling home to Calgary, and then travelling back to the start of the next tour.

To be honest, I hardly saw my family at all during the years I was with the WWF. It was the same for all the wrestlers who had wives and kids. But that was your job and you just got on with it. I took good care of my family, even if I wasn't there with them most of the time. When I was at home, I was too tired to be bothered doing anything. Michelle would want to go out, but all I wanted to do was relax, have a couple of beers, watch TV and fall asleep. It was no life for a family, although I suppose the children never knew anything different.

The constant travelling, the jet lag, driving hundreds of miles, then wrestling at night, left you worn out. What kept you going on the road, were the people you hung out with, shared cars with and went drinking after the matches with – your clique. Mine included Davey Boy Smith, Greg Valentine, Ray "Hercules" Hernandes, and "Dangerous" Dan Spivey, plus a few others as they came and went from the promotion. Over the years, Danny became one of my closest friends. We were in Pittsburgh one day when Michelle called from Calgary. She said, "I've found a house. I really want it."

She knew I had some money saved up, and she wanted to buy a new house. What I wanted was to have enough money in the bank, just in case anything happened to me and I couldn't wrestle. With this job, you never knew. You could be injured and out-of-work for months at any time. But she really wanted this house and had a picture of it FedEx-ed to the hotel where I was staying. It looked very nice; an 18-acre ranch, all corralled off, with a great big barn, about 10-miles out of the city. I picked up the phone and said to her, "Do you really want it?"

"Yes please."

So I bought it. It cost $220,000. I let Wayne Hart take over half of the four-plex apartment, and planned to sell the other half later. When he heard what I'd done, Danny Spivey fell about laughing. He said, "You fucking idiot. You've just spent all that money on a photograph."

But Danny was a good friend, and I rated him alongside Bad News Allen, and Billy Jack Haynes as a man who could take care of himself outside the ring. We had one or two close shaves as well. Danny lived in Tampa, Florida, and we had to get to Philadelphia to do a show. I didn't feel like going, and I said, "Danny, let's not go."

He said, "Tommy, we've got responsibilities. We're going."

So we made the flight, rented a car, and set off for the arena in

Philadelphia. I was driving, probably doing around 70mph, when we had to pass a juggernaut. There wasn't really enough room and as I got closer Danny was saying, "Tommy, you won't do it."

I said, "Watch this."

I got right up behind it – I didn't slow down – and took the car up the central reserve and onto two wheels. Danny's face was about two feet off the ground, and he was shouting, "Put it down Tommy." I overtook the juggernaut, put the car back on four wheels, and looked at Danny, whose face was white as a sheet. He said, "Don't do that again." So I did.

I don't know how, but we made it to the show. We came running in, and I remember Gorilla Monsoon looking at us, shaking his head, and saying, "Some things never change."

The Bulldogs were always babyfaces in the WWF, which meant you had to be nice to the fans and behave in the ring. But there was one time when we were wrestling Rick Martel and Tom Zenk in Montreal. It was a championship match – the main event – but because he was French Canadian, Rick had to be the babyface. So Pat Patterson said to us, "Bulldogs, you're in for some stick tonight. I want you to wrestle as heels."

So I said, "OK Pat, if that's what you want. But don't get mad at me when I come back."

For the first few minutes of the match, we behaved. I threw Rick out of the ring, by accident, then sat on the middle rope and held it down for him, like a gentleman, so he could climb back in. The people applauded. I threw him out again, sat on the rope, and as he bent down to climb through, I kicked him hard in the chest. Then we started, using every dirty trick we could think of. So when the match ended with Zenk and Martel somehow getting disqualified, there were 15,000 very angry people in the arena. It was like old times. As we left the ring they were throwing things and shouting and probably swearing at us, but in French, so I didn't understand a word of it anyway.

Given the choice, I would always wrestle as the heel. The heels lead and do the creative stuff, while the babyfaces have to follow and react to it. Plus, the babyfaces have to be nice to the fans. Don't get me wrong, the people who paid for tickets were paying my wages. I never forgot that, which was why I always made sure they got their money's worth. No matter whether the building had 100 people or 10,000 people, they all paid the same money. But, being the babyface meant you were expected to give autographs and pose for pictures.

In Japan, where I was always the heel, I had none of that bullshit. I never signed autographs in Japan – I didn't need to. I was the foreigner, the bad person, and being ignorant with the fans was what they expected.

In the WWF I did sign autographs once in a while. But I figured if you signed one, you ended up signing 100, so most of the time I'd just walk away and let Davey Boy Smith do the signing.

But even as babyfaces, we managed to have some fun in the ring. We were in Albany, in upstate New York, in a small arena – a spot show – and we were wrestling Nikolai Volkoff and the Iron Sheik. Just before the match, I'd noticed the referee in the dressing room – a nice enough man, probably in his 60s, did no harm to anybody – but I could see, as he was fixing his hair, he was wearing a wig.

So we went out, had a good match – at least as far as the people were concerned. As far as I was concerned it was so-so, because of the, erm, talent we had to deal with. Nikolai, I liked. He was a good man; a big strong man, but his ability in the ring... well it was maybe a little bit better than The Junkyard Dog. And he was very nervous in the ring; terrified of being suplexed or bodyslammed. The Sheik, who had been an Olympic-style wrestler, was pathetic. I didn't rate him in the ring and had no time for him out of the ring.

Anyway, the match had been going about 15 minutes when Nikolai threw me into the ropes and caught me in a sleeper. I was losing it. The referee lifted my arm up, and it dropped.

I whispered to Nikolai, "Tell him to get a bit closer."

So he did. He lifted my arm a second time. It dropped again. This was a title match, and I could hear the people getting excited, going, "Oooh." So the third time the referee lifted my arm, I reached up and pulled his wig off. The crowd started laughing, we started laughing, and that more or less ended the match; a match without a finish. The referee put his wig back on, but he had it on sideways, with the sideburns over his eyes, which made the people laugh even more.

We had a lot of laughs on the road, with the pranks and everything, but a lot of the time, I'll be honest, I didn't feel good at all. Some days I struggled to get out of bed, I felt so terrible. I knew what it was. The injuries I'd had over the years that never healed properly, and the drugs – steroids, painkillers, speed, cocaine. I was taking a lot of stuff, mainly just to get me through one day to the next.

I was having a lot of trouble with a shoulder injury I had in Japan a couple of years earlier. I'd slammed my opponent in the middle of the ring – or at least I thought I had. But when I got to the top turnbuckle for the finish, the flying head-butt, I realized he was too far away. Well, as I've already told you, you can't back out of a move like that. So I bent my knees and launched myself as hard as I could to reach him, but I missed. I landed awkwardly on my shoulder and tore all the ligaments. I had surgery on it, which took a few weeks to heal, but it never felt right after that, and a year or so later it began to give me some real pain. So I started using cortisone; injecting it myself, straight into my shoulder, just before a match. The effects lasted about half an hour, but when they wore off after the match, oh I felt it.

Years later, I found out that you weren't supposed to take cortisone more than a few times a year, because it causes deterioration of your tendons and ligaments, and bones. But I didn't know. It probably wouldn't have mattered if I did. The reason why I was doing so well at that time, especially in Japan, was because I would do things that other wrestlers wouldn't dream of doing.

My back had been aching and sore for a long time as well. I know that was partly the crazy things I'd done over the years in the ring, high-risk moves, night after night. And taking steroids didn't help. Really, that pain was a warning sign. But I never thought about slowing down, or taking things a bit easier in the ring. And if anybody else had told me, I probably would have ignored the advice anyway.

Steroids became a way of life – not just for me, but for more or less all the wrestlers; the majority. In fact it's easier to say how many weren't taking steroids at that time.

Steroids didn't just affect you physically, they affected your mind as well. At times I became so aggressive, somebody only had to look at me the wrong way for me to turn really nasty. I couldn't control it. I was in the toilets one night after a match, when this other guy, who I didn't know, came in, stood at the urinal and put one leg right up on the wall.

I looked. I said, "Are you all right?"

He said, "Yeah, Goddam, I'm all right. I do karate." In other words he was posing.

I said, "Oh, very good." And for no reason, I turned round smashed him in the face. It was what they call 'roid rage, and it happened a few times over the years.

While you were on the road you had to sort out your hotel and your own transport arrangements to and from the airports. After a while, you got to know the best places to stay, usually close to the airport, and the cheapest places to eat. We shared the cars and split the rental. And you had to find yourself a gym where you could train, because no amount of steroid would give you a good physique unless you worked out as well.

While the WWF turned a blind eye to wrestlers using steroids, they took a tougher line on cocaine and other recreational drugs. They tested us for cocaine every few weeks – you never knew when you'd be tested, but when it was your turn, you had to give a urine sample. If you tested positive the first time, you'd be suspended, and made to go into rehab. If you tested positive a second time, you were fired. That was OK until Arnold Skaaland, who was in charge of the testing, found out that the wrestlers were swapping urine samples with each other. So then he would stand at the side of the urinal to make sure you pissed in your own jar.

I told a couple of wrestlers one day, who I know for a fact had been taking that shit, that I'd overheard Arnold Skaaland saying they were going to be tested that night. But nobody was supposed to know. Anyway, later that day, they came down to the restaurant with bright red faces. They were like beet roots.

I said, "Have you two been under a sunbed?"

They looked at each other and said, "No, why, what's wrong?"

I said, "Well what have you been taking then?"

The silly pricks had been drinking vinegar – jugfuls of it – because it was supposed to disguise cocaine in the urine. Anyway, it turned out I'd made a bit of a mistake. There wasn't really a drug test that day.

Drug testing made people more careful, but it didn't stop it. You could get a gram of cocaine for about $200, and many times after the matches, a few wrestlers would get together to share three or four grams of cocaine. In the end, it was like smoking; cocaine became a habit. I can still remember the very first time I tried it. We were in a hotel right next to the airport in Miami, Florida – me, my brother-in-law Bret Hart, and a good friend of mine, The Junkyard Dog.

Junkyard said, "Hey man, try this." And he got a pipe and a block of coke and gave it to me. I had a smoke, and straight away – bump – I was high. That was it, we spent all night smoking crack. Some wrestlers preferred to smoke marijuana, but whatever you were taking, if you got caught, you paid the price. Getting fired or suspended was the punishment for serious offences like taking drugs or damaging hotel property, but for minor things, you would be fined.

The British Bulldogs had been asked to appear in a TV commercial for Hostess Potato Chips, so Vince made all the arrangements and told us to be at the studios, somewhere on the outskirts of Chicago, at a certain time. And we had to bring Matilda with us. So we rented a car at the airport and set off for the studios, but we got there 45-minutes late. Vince was waiting for us, with that serious look on his face.

He said, "Where have you two been?"

I said, "Well, erm, we got a bit lost."

Vince said, "Even if you were Hulk Hogan, I would do exactly the same thing that I'm going to do now. You, Tom will pay a fine of $1,000 and you, Davey will also pay a fine of $1,000."

I said, "What for?"

"For making me look stupid. The cameras and crew are ready and you are late."

Anyway, we got changed and the director gave us our lines. All we had say was, "We're the British Bulldogs and this is Matilda. She loves Hostess Potato Chips," and then give the dog some chips to eat. That was it. We got paid $20,000 each for that. Vince had some arrangement with the potato chip company because all the bags had WWF wrestling stickers inside for kids to collect. The year after, Hostess wanted us back to do another commercial, but Vince said we were too expensive. He got Strike Force – Tito Santana and Rick Martel to do it instead, but those two suckers only got $10,000 each.

True to his word, Vince docked the $1,000 fine from our wages. And we weren't the only ones he did that to. Haku, who later became King Tonga, was fined after an incident in a bar in Cleveland Ohio. He was chatting up this woman, just being sociable, when Jesse Barr, or Jimmy Jack Funk, who'd had a couple too many, started calling the woman names like, "a slut," and "a bitch."

Haku said to Jesse, "Hey, hey take it easy." But he ignored him and carried on being abusive. I left the bar soon after that and didn't see Jesse until the next morning at the airport. He had a big patch on one eye, a bandage across his head and he was holding his ribs as if he was in pain.

I said, "What happened to you?"

Jesse said, "Well last night, King Tonga turned into King Kong. He did all this." And for that, Tonga was fined.

After WrestleMania II, we carried on wrestling The Dream Team for a few weeks. We beat them more or less all round the circuit, apart from the non-title matches, when they often got the win. Later on during the summer and fall of that year, we had some matches with the Hart Foundation, which in my opinion, were probably some of the best tag matches the wwf had ever seen, at that time. I always enjoyed wrestling Bret anyway, Jim was a great character in the ring, and our styles were well matched. In between matches with them, we wrestled Nikolai Volkoff and The Iron Sheik, Don Muraco and "Cowboy" Bob Orton, and occasionally, Demolition.

I wasn't sorry when the Sheik got fired. He failed a drug test, after he'd got somebody else, who he thought was clean, to provide a urine sample for him. Only they weren't, and the stupid bastard didn't even realize he'd been done. Not even when Vince McMahon called him to his office and told him he had tested positive.

He said, "Oh thank you very much." He thought it meant it was OK.

One of the last times we wrestled Volkoff and The Sheik, before he left, was the night I was shamed in front of 20,000 people. The trouble with having animals at ringside was that you never knew what they might do. With Matilda, we had to make sure she didn't have anything to eat or drink just before we went to the ring, in case she did anything in it.

We were in the Nassau Coliseum in New York getting ready to wrestle Volkoff and the Sheik. Matilda was in the dressing room, and without me or Davey Boy Smith knowing it, Nikolai decided to feed her and give her a big bucket of water to drink. We got to the ring – it was a sold-out crowd – and Davey put Matilda in the ring so that she would chase The Sheik out the other side, just like she always did that. But on this night, she stood in the middle of the ring and wouldn't move. Me and Davey looked at each other, wondering what was wrong with her. Then she squatted and did the biggest piss I have ever seen in my life; it was running over the edge of the apron. I didn't know where to look.

The State Athletic Commission called Vince McMahon and told him that the dog was barred from ever coming in the building again. And after the match Nikolai admitted to us, a bit sheepishly, that he'd given her the water, because he felt sorry for her. Can you imagine what we felt like? Bloody shamed. All the people were laughing – even Vince thought it was funny. We had to get the ring boys in with brushes to sweep the piss off the mat so we could wrestle. The only people who weren't laughing were the wrestlers who hadn't had their matches because that mat was wet through, and it stunk. But, thinking about it, it could have been a lot worse.

In December that year, I brought Ted Betley, my former trainer, over to Canada from the Isle of Man, to stay for a few weeks. He had a great time, mainly because all the wrestlers treated him like royalty. He had to fly to Edmonton without me one day, and he went with Demolition, which was Bill Eadie and Barry Darsow, instead. He was having the time of his life. But his biggest ambition had always been to go to Madison Square Garden. Vince McMahon had promised me, a few weeks before Ted came over, that he would fix everything up for him in New York. And I'll say this for Vince, he kept his promise. He put Ted in a VIP box in Madison Square Garden, and had him treated him like a king.

Ted had brought a video camera, and as I was driving through the middle of Manhattan – well you know what the traffic is like there – he kept shouting, "Tommy, stop! I want to film this." He wanted to film everything, even a tramp living in a cardboard box. But he thought New York was great.

Ted was in Calgary when the WWF ran a big show at the Saddledome; a sell-out, with 14,000 people in the building. Ted was going round getting the wrestlers to sign his autograph book, and they did: Bret "The Hitman," Jim "The Anvil," Greg "The Hammer," Jake "The Snake," even André the Giant, who could be funny with you at the best of times. He was playing cards with some of the wrestlers when I said to him, "This is Ted Betley, who used to be my coach in England. Would you give him an autograph?"

Well André had been trained in England many years ago, by Tony and Roy Sinclair, so I think he had a bit of respect for Englishmen. Anyway he said, "Sure Boss. I'll sign for Ted." He called everybody Boss, even the midget wrestlers. Well, Ted was made up. He had everybody's autograph, apart from one: Brutus Beefcake.

Beefcake didn't know who Ted was, and definitely didn't know he was my trainer, but, the fact that he was in the dressing room meant that Ted must have been known to one of the wrestlers. Put it this way, in the same position, I would have signed for him. But when Ted asked him, Brutus said, "I've got no time for fucking autographs. I'm going in the ring."

When Ted told me what Beefcake had said to him, I was so mad, I could have done him there and then. I told Greg Valentine, but he more or less begged me not to hurt him. So, on that night, I didn't. But I knew, in a couple of days time, we had a cage match against The Dream Team. And once I had him in that cage, Beefcake had no chance of getting away. I never let on to Beefcake that there was anything wrong, but I had it in mind, on December 14, inside that cage, I was going to mess him up big time, for the simple reason that he was ignorant to Ted. Anyway, I didn't. Because what happened on December 13, in my opinion, made Brutus Beefcake the luckiest man on Earth.

CHAPTER TEN

December 13 1986 was one night I'll never forget. We flew to Toronto and drove down to Hamilton, Ontario, to the Copps Coliseum where I'd wrestled many times before. Our opponents that night were Don Muraco and Bob Orton, but to tell you the truth, I wasn't thinking too much about that match; my mind was on the cage match that I knew was scheduled for the following night. There was a good crowd in the Coliseum, and when it was time for our match, Bob and Don went to the ring first, as the challengers usually do. I was standing behind the curtain with Davey Boy Smith, having a quick smoke and waiting for Rule Britannia to come on, when Nikolai Volkoff came up to me and said, "Tommy, will you crack my back for me?"

I knew that any second I'd have to go out, in fact I heard the music start playing, but I said, "ok, but you'll have to be quick." I got behind him, crossed his arms, held his elbows and raised him up; you know to stretch his spine out. As I lifted him, I felt a twinge in my back; nothing bad, probably a pulled muscle or something. Davey was telling me to hurry up, so off we went.

I got to the ring, felt ok, and for the first five or ten minutes the British Bulldogs were looking fantastic. Whatever we did, we did right. Then it came round to that time in the match when we were about to get a good hiding. Davey tagged me in, I grabbed Don Muraco in a side headlock, and he shot me off to the ropes. I came back, gave him a big tackle, but he came back up like a monster. I did the same again, headlock, off to the ropes, ran back; only this time he dropped, flat on his belly, so I had to jump over him to get to the other ropes. I don't know what I'd planned to do after that, because, as I jumped, literally in mid-stride, I felt something go in my back. I can't really describe the feeling, except that I felt this terrible sharp pain and crumpled to the mat. I couldn't get up – I couldn't move my legs – I just lay there in agony, wondering what had happened.

Tom with John Foley, Stampede 1978

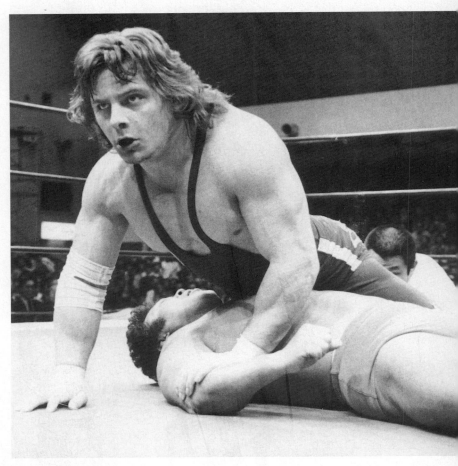

Tom pinning Hoshino, NJPW 1981

Tom with Mr. T, Cincinnati 1987

Tom pinning Bobby Fulton, Montana 1980

Tom with Rip Oliver and The Assassin (Dave Patterson), Portland 1983

Tom backstage with (top) Chris Benoit and (bottom) Eddie Guerrero at WWF PPV Rebellion, Sheffield, England 2000

Tom with Mick Foley, at WWF PPV Rebellion, Sheffield, England 2000

Tom Billington, December 2000

The people in the arena started booing and chanting "Bull-shit," and "Phon-ey," and to be honest, that's what it must have looked like. I lay there, not moving; the pain was so bad, I couldn't think straight. Then I saw Don get up. He didn't seem to realize there was anything wrong, and started laying in to me with his boots. I was trying to say, "Don, don't kick me for fuck's sake," but I don't think any words came out. Somehow, I managed to haul myself – just using my arms – to the edge of the apron and over the side. I know I was counted out because Davey Boy Smith was still on the apron holding his little tag rope. He must have seen me go down, but for some reason, he stood there watching, probably wondering why I'd been counted out.

Once I was out of the ring, I thought somebody would help me. But the next thing I saw was Mr. Fuji standing over me with a folded chair in his hands. He hadn't realized there was anything wrong either, and started hitting my leg with the chair. I lay there on the concrete, in so much pain, saying, "No, Fuji, please, no." Eventually, when he saw that I wasn't moving, he stopped, and that's when they all realized I was hurt. They brought a stretcher out to ringside and got me back to the dressing room. I was nearly passing out with the pain.

As they carried the stretcher out to the ambulance, my left leg started twitching violently, and the paramedics cut my wrestling tights off with scissors and strapped it down to keep it still. I found out later it was nerve damage in my back that was causing it, but at that point, I had no idea what was wrong. They took me to a hospital in Hamilton, but there were no empty beds. So they gave me a painkiller, an injection of Demerol or morphine, and left me in the corridor on the stretcher. I thought to myself, "These bastards don't believe I'm hurt because I'm a wrestler."

King Tonga came with me in the ambulance, and stayed with me all that night. Davey Boy Smith just got changed and went back to the hotel. Eventually an ambulance came from Toronto to take me to the airport, and somebody called Vince McMahon to tell him what had happened. When they got me on the plane, they had to put three seats down for the stretcher, but Vince sorted all that out, and paid for the seats. When we landed in Calgary, another ambulance was waiting to take me straight to Holy Cross Hospital, where I hoped they were going to find out what had happened to me. I knew it must have been bad, from the way I went down and lost control of my legs. I also knew I wouldn't be wrestling any cage matches for a while. This was Brutus Beefcake's lucky day – and he didn't even know it.

I had to wait hours, first to see a doctor, then to be x-rayed, and then to see another doctor. Then they took me for another test, which they said would show up in more detail the damage in my back. I was strapped to a table, and a nurse gave me an injection in my leg. Then the doctor appeared holding the longest needle I'd ever seen.

I said, "Erm, excuse me, but what's that?"

He told me he was going to put the needle into my spine and draw off the spinal fluid, from my neck right down to my tailbone, and inject some dye that would show up on the monitor.

The tests showed that I'd ruptured two discs, next to the fourth and fifth lumbar vertebrae, and I needed surgery straight away. The doctor also told me there could be some nerve damage, which was why I was having trouble with my left leg. I went into surgery a couple of days later, and the operation took about six hours. But when I came round from the anaesthetic, what worried me more than anything was my left leg, the one that had kept twitching when I was on the stretcher. Now it was paralyzed; I couldn't move it and I couldn't feel it. The surgeon who did the operation came to see me, and he told me that it was caused by pieces of the damaged discs getting lodged between the nerves, but he also told me that the loss of feeling was only temporary.

So there I was, lying in a hospital bed, trying to come to terms with what had happened. One minute I'd been running across the ring to nail Don Muraco, and the next, I couldn't even stand on my own two feet. I knew it hadn't really happened just like that. Not on that night. I'd been storing up trouble for myself – for my body – for years. I knew what had caused it as well; those crazy matches I used to have with Sayama. In the space of one match we'd give each other more piledrivers, back suplexes, body drops, than most wrestlers would tolerate in a week. In my mind, it was like hammering a car till the shock absorbers go; and that was what had more or less happened to my back.

A few days after the surgery, three back specialists came to see me. They explained to me again what the injury was, and about the nerves being affected. I told them I was worried about my leg, but they said the feeling would eventually come back, a bit at a time. And they were right, to a point, after a few weeks the feeling did start to come back in my leg, but it never came back properly in my foot. Never. Then I heard the words I really didn't want to hear. "Mr. Billington, we really think it would be in your best interest to find another line of work."

I just wasn't prepared for that. I was only 28. So, to myself, under my breath, I said, "Bollocks to that. I'm too young." But to the doctor I said, "I'm sorry, but no, I'm going back in that ring." And even though at that point I couldn't walk, never mind wrestle, I meant it. I never told anybody what the doctors had said; not Michelle, who was already worrying about me being away from work for a long time, and not my dad, who came out with my mum to stay at my house in Calgary for a few weeks.

Funnily enough, I had already tried to get injury insurance. I went to an insurance company in Calgary, and at first they said "No problem," until I told them what I did for a living. Then they said it was out of the question. "You are in a high-risk occupation Mr. Billington, and we can't insure you against injury."

Now I would bet that like everyone else, these people thought professional wrestling was easy, that nobody ever gets hurt, and we all know exactly how to land – in other words, there was no risk to it at all. But they wouldn't insure me. I know some wrestlers did get injury insurance with one of the big companies – Curt Hennig for example – but for me, there was no chance. The savings I'd had had gone toward the deposit for my house. As far as I could see, I had no choice. I had to go back to work. And wrestling was the only job I knew.

I heard from a couple of the wrestlers while I was in hospital and I remember Roddy Piper calling me to ask if I needed anything, money-wise. But I said I was OK. Piper, I always liked. He wasn't what you would call a wrestler, more of a brawler – but what a talker. He was fantastic with a microphone. I went on Piper's Pit once, on my own, and he was shouting his mouth off about how hard he was. I was on steroids then, and I said, "Mr. Piper, do me a favour. Put your mike down and get your ass in that ring with me, right now." Anyway, he threw the microphone down on the floor and just walked off the set and back to the dressing room. But yeah, Piper was a good man. And at least he thought to call me.

Davey Boy Smith who I hadn't seen or heard from since the night I got injured, finally showed up at the hospital, with his wife, Diana Hart-Smith, and a press photographer. And those two pricks posed at the side of my bed, had their picture taken, and went. They never came to see me again. The next day that picture made the front page of the Calgary Sun newspaper.

Bret rang me, and came to see me, a couple of times while I was in the hospital. The first time he came was maybe a week or so after the operation. He said, "Tom, you're looking all right."

I said, "Yeah, on the outside maybe, but not inside. I'm not being funny Bret, but I'm fucked."

A few days later he was back, and this time he told me he'd been talking to Vince. He said, "Vince asked me to get the tag team belt off you and take it back to Stamford."

I said, "Oh. Right." Bret looked at me, a bit hopefully, like he wasn't sure he'd heard me right. Then I said, "Tell Vince he can fuck off."

Bret's face dropped – well I'm sure Bret had ideas in his own mind about those tag team belts. And although he was my brother-in-law and I did like him, business was still business. He said, "Look Tom, Vince needs those belts, and he doesn't want to run a tournament because it will take too long."

I said, "I'm sorry Bret, but no means no." That was it.

A couple of days after that I signed myself out of hospital – against the advice of the doctors – because I couldn't stand being in the place any longer. It probably was a mistake, because I was still in a lot of pain. Anyway, I signed out, went home, and was lying on the couch one day when the phone rang. It was Vince. He was being polite and asked me how I was doing, and then he said, "Tom, I don't blame you for keeping the belt. You were right to say no Bret."

I said, "What do you mean?" I knew it was Vince who'd sent Bret to get the belt back in the first place. Plus, at that moment in time, it was my belt to keep anyway.

Vince said, "I'm glad you kept it." Which I thought was very diplomatic of him. He'd have had that belt off me in a second if he could. But when he couldn't, he acted like he never intended to. "The trouble is," he said, "I am going to need you and Davey to defend them pretty soon."

I said, "I'm sorry Vince, but I'm not ready. I mean, really, I can't walk."

A week later he called again. "Tom, I know you're not well, but I need those belts back."

I gave him the same reply as before: the truth. I couldn't even get up off the couch. He called, maybe two or three more times over the next week. I think they only had a couple of TV matches left, which we'd taped just before that night in the Copps Coliseum. They'd kept the news about me being injured from the fans, so really, they were trying to carry on as if nothing had happened. On the spot shows, Davey Boy Smith was either wrestling singles or tagging with nobodies. But I knew, sooner or later we would lose those belts because of my condition.

What Vince really wanted was for Nikolai Volkoff and the Iron Sheik to be the champions, but I told him, "No chance." The only team I would lose the belts against was the Hart Foundation, which he agreed to. He told me the next TV taping was at the Sun Dome in Tampa, Florida on January 26. It was still too early for me – I couldn't walk five paces without help, but I said to Vince, "OK, I'll do it, but I'll need somebody to help me. I can't do this on my own."

Arnold Skaaland's son, George, was a wrestler in Calgary, and Vince agreed to pay for his plane ticket so that he could come with me to Florida and then take me home afterward. We made it to the Sun Dome, and I think – I'm sure – some of the wrestlers were shocked at seeing me, The Dynamite Kid, in a wheelchair, plus without the steroids and the workouts, I'd lost all that weight. I'd already taken some painkillers, but the only way I could walk down the aisle to the ring was by linking arms with Davey Boy Smith. He was practically carrying me, because I didn't have the strength to walk on my own. We set off, and the fans were shouting, "Dynamite, go Dynamite, come on." But I knew I must have looked bloody awful. Just before we got in the ring, Bret and Jim jumped us from behind. One of them cracked me on the back of the head, I hit the floor and I stayed there. Davey got in the ring, where they double-teamed him, on and off, for the next few minutes. And that few minutes was all it took to end our reign as the WWF World Tag Team Champions.

Over the next few weeks all I could think about was getting back in shape. A couple of times the pain became so bad I had to go back into the hospital, but slowly, it did start to ease just a little bit, and as soon as I could, I started training again. Just light stuff, maybe one day and then two days a week. But within a few weeks, I was working out in the gym every day, and I started taking my steroids again, building myself back up. I needed to get back to work, not just because I'd put my mind to doing it, but because I needed the money, badly. A regular job which paid maybe $300 or $400 per week was no use to me, not when I could get $20,000 just for one WrestleMania.

WrestleMania III was coming up at the end of March, and I was planning to be ready for that event. Deep down I knew I wasn't really up to it, but I needed the money. After WrestleMania II, Vince had to come up with something special. And he did; he filled the Silverdome in Pontiac, Michigan, with 93,000 fans, which was an incredible sight. Not long after that, Pope John Paul came to the Silverdome, and only about 35,000 people came to see him – which was great, the WWF out-drew the Pope.

Hulk Hogan defended his title against André, Ricky Steamboat took the Intercontinental title from Randy Savage, and Harley Race was wrestling The Junkyard Dog, which, in my opinion, was a bit of a an insult for an eight-time NWA Champion. To be honest, I was surprised that Harley came into the WWF at all. He'd been promoting the Kansas City and St. Louis NWA territory with his partner Bob Geigel, but when the WWF moved in, Harley had made life difficult for them, threatening them with buckets of acid, and locking the arena doors so they couldn't get the ring up. He was just looking after his own business, but he was never going to win.

And then one day, when we'd just arrived in Toronto and were checking into the Howard Johnson hotel, who did I see checking in at the same time but Harley Race. I didn't know he was coming into the WWF, so I said, "What are you doing here?"

He said, "Tommy," – in that laid-back way that he talked – "If you can't beat them... join them."

And he did. I don't know whether it was for Vince's own amusement, or as punishment for all the trouble he'd caused the WWF down in St. Louis, but Harley ended up wrestling The Junkyard Dog all around the circuit, right into WrestleMania III. But he never complained, he'd just get down on his hands and knees with Junkyard, Junkyard would head-butt him, and Harley would roll out of the ring. After every match I'd say to him, "Great match that, Harley."

But apart from that, at WrestleMania III the Hart Foundation were still the tag champions, although that was mainly down to the fact that they had help from the heel referee, Danny Davis. Vince decided to run a six-man tag match; The Hart Foundation plus Danny Davis against the British Bulldogs and... Tito Santana.

I don't remember too much about that match, except that it was short, and to tell you the truth, I felt awful all the way through it. I felt terrible. I was in a lot of pain, and probably shouldn't have been there at all.

Once I'd come back to wrestling, things seemed different between myself and Davey Boy Smith. We didn't fall out, or have words; well, he wouldn't have had the nerve anyway. I did lose my temper with him one time, I think, after I asked him to do me a favour and he said he couldn't. So I blew up at him. "I brought you to Canada, took you to Japan, got you in the WWF; you are nothing but a selfish bastard."

And all Davey could say was, "Yeah, Tommy. You're right. I'm sorry. You have done a lot for me."

Davey was a follower, never a leader, and he'd always been happy with my decisions, and usually, I decided right. For example, jumping to All Japan, and for example, not signing a contract with the WWF. And those first few years as a tag team, we'd got along great. Now, though, things seemed a little bit different.

For example, one night we were in Calgary at the Saddledome. Stu had taken Stampede back, probably about a year after he'd sold it to Vince, and what with the name and the television, we always did fantastic business when the WWF went back to Calgary. Once or twice, on our rest days, we might do the odd match for Stu, you know as a favour to him, because we didn't get paid for it. But when Vince found out, as you can imagine, he wasn't happy. He told us, "I don't care whether it's your day off or not, while you are with the WWF, you don't work for anybody else."

Anyway, this night was a WWF show and we were supposed to wrestle the Islanders, Haku and Samu, only Samu no-showed. Chief Jay Strongbow, whose real name was Joe Scarpa decided that Davey Boy Smith could wrestle Haku in a singles match. I thought, "Great. I'm getting paid anyway. I'll take the rest of the night off and go home."

But Chief Jay had other ideas. He said, "Tom, you can go in with Davey and just walk around the ring."

I said to him, "Well, I can't do that, because I haven't got my Union Jack cape with me. I left it at home." Davey Boy Smith was sitting next to me, listening to all this, and the next thing was, somebody turned up at the dressing-room door with my wrestling cape. So I rang Michelle at home. It turned out that Davey had rung his wife Diana, who had called another friend and sent him round to my house to say that I wanted my cape. So, as you can imagine, I was annoyed, because I can't stand people being underhanded. But that wasn't the end of it. After the match, Chief Jay came to the dressing room.

He said; "I need a favour Tom. Can you get some steroids for my son?"

I said, "I've got 20 bottles, what do you want?"

He said "I'll buy ten off you."

I said, "No you won't." And I gave him ten.

Then he stood up and said, "By the way, you're fined $200."

I looked at him, because I couldn't believe what he'd said. "What for?"

"For being late."

Which was true, I had got there a few minutes late. But I said, "But I wasn't wrestling tonight."

"You were still late."

So I said, "Right. OK." I picked up my stuff, walked out of the dressing room, and went home. When I got home the phone rang at least half a dozen times, but I told Michelle not to answer. And I didn't answer it for three days.

Eventually Vince McMahon called and Michelle answered. He was very polite, and just said. "Would you tell Tom to come to the Capitol Centre in Washington DC for a show tomorrow?"

The Capitol Centre was an afternoon show, which I had forgotten, so when I walked into the hotel late in the afternoon, all the wrestlers were in the bar drinking. I said, "It's a bit early for this isn't it?" Then one of them told me they'd wrestled at 2PM. Meanwhile, Vince had called home again to find out where I was. Michelle told him I'd left Calgary early that afternoon.

The next day, we were in Hershey Park, Pennsylvania, and when we arrived at the arena, Vince was already there, waiting for me. He said, "Tom, can I have a word?"

We went in one of the little offices in the building and sat down. Bear in mind, with missing the Washington card, I'd been away for four days in total, so I was more or less expecting a bollocking. Vince said, "Why did you walk out of the building in Calgary?"

I didn't want to drop Chief Jay, or his son, in the shit so I said, "I don't know Vince. Things just got me down and I suppose I went a bit haywire."

He looked at me for a minute, and then he pointed to my face, which I hadn't shaved for four days, and said, "What's that? You know I like my babyfaces to be clean shaven."

I said, "Well, I'm not being funny Vince, but what about Hulk?"

"Tom. Do me a favour. Shave it off." That was the end of that, and the little matter of me going AWOL was forgotten. But I didn't forget who was at the bottom of it.

Hershey Park, Pennsylvania was where a lot of the wrestlers picked up their steroids. They were easy to get hold of more or less anywhere, as long as you knew the right people. When I ran out in Poughkeepsie one time, Roddy Piper gave me ten vials of the stuff, because he'd decided to give steroids up.

But in Hershey Park, we got them from a doctor, George Zahorian. We were supposed to be seeing him to have our blood pressure checked before we went in the ring, but what we were really doing was picking up our supply of drugs. We'd all come out of the examination room – not that we'd had an examination – with our little brown bags – lucky bags – and that was our valium, halcyon and steroids – but not cocaine. And bear in mind, I'm talking about the majority of wrestlers in the wwf at that time.

There were different kinds of steroids, and sometimes you'd change from one to the other. There were water-based steroids, like Winstrol V, and oil-based steroids, like testosterone and decadurabolin. Most of the time I used testosterone. The first few months I was taking massive amounts, like 1200mg every day. But once I'd got the bulk and strength that I needed, I'd inject maybe every other day, 200mg per one cc each time, it into alternate arse cheeks. If I wanted to change, I'd do testosterone on my left side, but on the other side I would inject decadurabolin, which was only 50mg per one cc. Winstrol, you could take every day, because it cleared through your system very quickly. With the oil-based steroids, like testosterone, you might inject two or three times a week, because it stayed in your system a lot longer. And you had to use a bigger needle, 22 gauge, which is about 1 ½ inches long, and you had to stick it all the way in to get the stuff deep into your muscle.

You'd take the steroids for four weeks or six weeks and then break off for a week. But during that week you had to take another drug called gonadatrophin (growth hormone). Bear in mind, when you took steroids for a long time, your body would eventually stop making its own testosterone. So when you came of that stuff for a week, you had to take the gonadatrophin to make you start producing your own and maintain the weight and bulk while you were off the steroid.

There were steroid pills that you could take as well, but I was told they were more dangerous, because they could damage your liver and your kidneys. For example, Anadrol 50 was a white 50mg pill. You took one a day and it made you very strong. But if you go too many days or weeks on Anadrol, you'd end up with no kidneys, because it is so toxic, so most of the time the wrestlers used injectable steroids.

Bear in mind you were working out every day as well. For the likes of myself and Davey Boy Smith, who have a naturally small build, we had to take more steroids and work out harder than the wrestlers who were naturally bigger. Some of those bigger guys took steroids to cut back. For example, Ray Hernandez. He was a big fat bastard, until he started using Winstrol every day, and working out in the gym. He ended up looking like Billy Jack Haynes, who was in great shape. I saw a picture of Billy Jack a couple of years after he left the WWF and went to Japan, and I'll be honest, he looked like a pregnant woman with a big belly; with good food, working out, but I would guess, no steroids. But at Wrestle-Mania III, as you could see, Ray and Billy looked terrific.

Physically, I was anything but right. I couldn't wrestle without taking painkillers, and I was on Percocets, which are very strong, narcotic painkillers. I took them more or less every night before a match. And when they wore off later in the evening, my back would be screaming out with pain. But during the match, they did their job, and let me do mine. For example, we had a series of matches against the Hart Foundation while they were the tag team champions, and I don't think those matches were any less exciting than the ones we'd had with them before my back went. I still took the big falls, and still made the suplexes, but I paid for them after the match.

The Hart Foundation had Jimmy Hart as their manager. Like Dave Shults, and like Brutus Beefcake, Jimmy Hart had got into the WWF for one simple reason, he was a friend of Hulk Hogan. At one point, he had words with Mr. Fuji, who at that time was the manager of Demolition. Most people were scared of Fuji – don't get me wrong, he couldn't fight or anything, but he could do a lot worse. In fact he was well known for being one of the best – or worst – pranksters in the business.

Anyway, the night after this little disagreement, we were wrestling in the Nassau Coliseum in New York. Fuji was getting ready to go to the ring, and went next door to Demolition's dressing room. But he left his bowler hat and jacket in our dressing room. So I picked up the bowler hat and put my fist through it, and put it back down next to his clothes. Then I rushed to the door, just in time to see Fuji coming back to get his stuff.

I stopped him at the door and said, "Fuj, you know what I'm like don't you?

But I'm not being blamed for this one."

He said, "Boy-san, what's wrong?"

"I don't know what's happened here Fuj, but you know Jimmy Hart? You know your bowler hat?"

"What about my hat?"

I said, "I'm just telling you before you think it was me. Jimmy Hart has jumped all over your bowler hat."

"You're joking."

I said, "No, I watched him do it."

So he walked in the dressing room, picked up his bowler hat, pushed me out of the way and went storming up to Jimmy Hart. He said, "What do you call this you motherfucker?"

Jimmy had no idea what Fuji was going on about, but then he saw me and Davey grinning behind Fuji, saw the bowler hat, and said, "Fucking Bulldogs." Then he started trying to explain to Fuji what he knew had happened, but Fuji wouldn't let him get a word in. I never found out what Fuji did back to him, but I would imagine it was good.

I'll be honest, the Bulldogs did do some terrible things – not terrible in a vicious way, more in a humorous way. Well, they made us laugh.

Funnily enough, in spite of all the pranks that the Bulldogs played on other wrestlers, nobody ever played them back on either me or Davey. In the dressing room I used to say, out loud so everybody could hear, "Right, I'm going to the ring now. My bag's there. If you want to do something to it, do it. I don't care." And to be honest, I didn't. But nobody ever touched my stuff; they were too scared. They knew I'd stuff one of my M80s down their shoes or in their cases and light it, or I'd cut their pants in half with scissors. So, yes I was a terrible joker – or ribber, as the other wrestlers would say – but I never hurt anybody, and most of the time the people I was ribbing deserved it anyway. In my opinion. Vince was always trying out new talent; some of it was very good, and some of it was terrible. I remember a tag team called The Midnight Rockers when they first arrived in 1987; a very young looking Shawn Michaels, and his partner, Marty Jannetty. The first couple of days they were there, they were like two little mice. They sat in a corner of the dressing room and wouldn't speak to anybody. The first time I saw them was when we were in Nashville, Tennessee. I'd been told about them not speaking, and this day, I was feeling in a bad mood anyway, so I walked up to them and said, "What's up with you two, you pair of pricks? Why won't you speak to the other wrestlers?"

Michaels said, "Vince McMahon and Pat Patterson told us to keep to ourselves and stay out of trouble."

I said, "Well, you'd better smarten up then and start talking." And as I said it, I held a fist up. After that, they did become a bit more sociable, but not for very long. About a week later we were in Buffalo, New York, and after the matches we all went to the nightclub that was part of the hotel where we were staying. By the end of the night, Shawn Michaels and Marty Jannetty had had a few too many beers and started throwing glasses and smashing the optics behind the bar. And like I told you before, the punishment for damaging property was getting fired. Which they were – more or less on the spot. But for a lot of wrestlers, for example the Iron Sheik, it didn't seem to matter because within a few weeks they'd be back. Which was what happened with the Midnight Rockers. I'll be honest, they were good wrestlers. I especially rated Shawn Michaels because he was so good for the fans; a great entertainer, and I wasn't surprised that he went all the way to the top with the WWF.

One of the biggest shows on TV at that time – in America and in the UK – was "The A Team." And one of the stars of that show was Mr. T. He'd been involved in a few WWF shows, for example, WrestleMania I when he teamed up with Hulk Hogan, and WrestleMania II when he boxed Roddy Piper. Anyway Hulk Hogan and a few other wrestlers were asked to appear in an episode of "The A Team," including myself and Davey Boy Smith. We only had what you would call a bit-part, that lasted all of about 30 seconds right at the end of the show, and we filmed it in Gold's Gym in Los Angeles. The director gave us our instructions and then he said, "I need somebody to do a head-butt."

Straight away I said, "I'll do it."

All I had to do was grab this guy – the villain – by the jacket and head-butt him, only I wasn't supposed to actually connect with him. Well, I think I must have got over-excited, because I nearly knocked him out cold. But that one take was all it took.

Some of the matches that I enjoyed most that year were the ones we had against Harley Race and "Hercules" Ray Hernandez. Harley Race was now "King" Harley Race, after wining a tournament for the King's Crown the year before. A couple of weeks after that event, they'd held the crowning ceremony, which was shown on TV. Like I've said before, "King" Harley liked his drink, whatever the occasion. On the night of the ceremony, they'd put a big throne in the middle of the ring, which Harley had to sit in while he was crowned. He was wearing a long purple robe, and Vince had booked the midgets especially for that night, to carry it for him.

After the ceremony, with the music and the speech, which was all very solemn, Harley stood up, and Lord Littlebrook, who was the head midget, stood behind him and picked up his robe to carry it. So, The King, being a bit drunk, got through the middle and the top rope, but as he stepped through, he missed the apron. He went over the edge, and landed on his head. As he started to fall, Lord Littlebrook tried to hold him back with his robe – he was heaving back and pulling it tight, but the force of Harley's fall catapulted the midget straight through the ropes, right on top of Harley. I'm sure it was meant to be a very serious occasion, but as you can imagine, all the fans were laughing. Anyway, Harley and Littlebrook picked themselves up and carried on walking back to the dressing room. But that was even funnier because Harley was trying to keep a serious look on his face, but his crown was crushed and hanging off the side of his head.

He was great fun in the ring as well as out of it. I remember a dark match we had with Harley and Hercules in Hershey Park, Pennsylvania. After Davey had tagged me in, I came off the ropes at Harley, and he leapfrogged over me. I hit the other rope, ran back and he caught me with a scoop slam. Then he stood up and dropped his head on me. So I got up on my knees and started mocking him, as in "What was that supposed to be?" So then I slammed him, took two steps back and dropped my head on his. He got up and started mocking me. Nobody else would get away with doing that in the ring, to either me or Harley, but that was how much respect we had for each other.

"Hercules" Ray Hernandez was another good friend of mine, and he could be very funny at times. I remember one time when he'd unpacked his bags in the hotel in a rush and arrived at the arena with only one wrestling boot. He was setting off for the ring when Vince stopped him and said, "Hold on a minute, what do you think you're doing?" like he couldn't believe what he was seeing.

Ray just said, very casually, "Oh, I'm sorry Vince, I've left my other boot in the hotel," as if it was something you did every day. And he went off to the ring with one wrestling boot on, like there was nothing wrong.

Towards the end of the summer of that year, I'd managed to stay out of the hospital long enough to get back to wrestling a full schedule with the WWF. I was still having a lot of problems with my back, and there was no doubt that wrestling was only aggravating it. But I hadn't changed anything in my style. I still dived off the top rope, still did the snap suplexes, and still took the brunt of the landing from a superplex. And all of it was only possible because of the painkillers; I was addicted to them.

A normal working day for me was: speed to wake me up in the morning to catch an early flight, valium to make me sleep on the plane, Percoset just before the match, then we'd wrestle, hit the beer, and the cocaine, until the early hours, before taking another valium to put me to sleep at night.

I was in good company, because the majority of wrestlers all shared more or less the same lifestyle. And I enjoyed that lifestyle. I can't lie about that, I did. Once you got used to it and you were making good money. Now I see it for what it was. We were living life in the fast lane – some of us faster than others.

CHAPTER ELEVEN

Before I joined the WWF in 1985, I'd already seen a lot of the world, but when I started touring full-time, I should have seen a lot more. I must have been to just about every big town and city in the America, but I can't say I really saw any of them. You'd fly, or drive, in and out so fast, you never had the time. Which was a shame because I know I missed out on seeing a lot of nice places. But one that I do remember and which always stuck in my mind, was New Orleans, Louisiana, and the Bourbon Street parade.

After the matches that night, Davey and me headed for the French Quarter of New Orleans, to Bourbon Street, where they held the big Dixieland jazz parades. There was music, people playing trumpets, people dressed in colourful costumes, dancing and singing. Hundreds of people were lining the street to watch, and the atmosphere was fantastic. And behind the crowds were all these old-fashioned buildings, like you see in the films; there were bars, strip-clubs, whorehouses, sex shops – not that I went in any of them – but Bourbon Street was an experience.

So that was New Orleans. I did the guided tour of Graceland and the Lisa Marie (the aeroplane that Elvis named after his daughter) when we were in Memphis. Las Vegas, I only saw the one time. We were wrestling in a place called Notre Dame College, only in America they pronounce the Dame as in same. As we drove into Vegas, Davey spotted the sign for the college and shouted, "Tommy. This is it, Notre Dame." As I tried to find a parking space, he said, "Tommy, is this where the Hunchback came from?"

We'd been challenging the Hart Foundation for the tag belts, on and off, throughout that summer, and came up with some great matches. Whenever the four of us were in the ring, the people knew they were going to get some real excitement and see some genuine heat. Then, in

October, Bret and Jim dropped the belts to Strike Force; Rick Martel and Tito Santana, which meant that for the time being, the British Bulldogs could forget about a title shot.

To be honest, we weren't really being pushed, which I could understand earlier in the year, when I was still having to take time off with my back. But unless you were six-foot-six and built like a brick shithouse, you had to work very hard to keep yourself in a good position on the card. It didn't always come down to hard work or having the ability. If the promotion wanted you at the top, you went to the top. And when they wanted you to go down, you went down.

You might be pushed for three or four months in the run up to a main event on a pay-per-view like WrestleMania, which was something the WWF did very well. For example, early in 1986, perhaps even before that, King Kong Bundy was being pushed as the monster heel that nobody could beat. In the run up to the event, he beat every single opponent to a pulp. And it worked, because, by the time WrestleMania II and that championship match with Hulk Hogan came around, the fans really believed he could kick the shit out of Hogan.

Not long after he lost that match, he was wrestling in a tag match with Big John Studd against the Bulldogs. I don't know what had happened, I don't know who he'd upset, but halfway through the match Davey tripped him, I pinned him, and in the space of a three count, King Kong Bundy was made to look like a load of shit. A year later, when WrestleMania III came around, King Kong Bundy found himself wrestling Hillbilly Jim in a six-man tag match with the midgets. That was how easily you could go up and come down.

Vince had come up with a new pay-per-view event, The Survivor Series, which was going to take place around American Thanksgiving at the end of November. We had to wrestle in teams, and ours included the Rougeaus, Strike Force, the Killer Bees, and the Young Stallions. The Rougeaus, Jacques and Ray, I'll be honest, I never liked them. They were French Canadian and they spoke French to each other, even when you were sitting right next to them. One would say something to the other, which you didn't understand, unless you could speak French, and then they'd both snigger. In other words, you weren't in on the joke.

The Young Stallions, Paul Roma and Jim Powers, in my opinion, they were a tag team that was never going to work, for the simple reason that they didn't like each other, and were jealous of each other. So every time a tag was made, one would try to outdo the other. When the heel hit, they wouldn't make any attempt to sell – they'd just go straight to the corner and tag. Whether they were winning or losing, they both wanted to look the best. And in the end when they did split, it didn't surprise me.

One of the nights in Chicago I met a fellow countryman of mine, Billy Robinson. He was in the same hotel, but working for another promoter. I'd heard a lot of things about Billy, and I don't think anybody would argue that he was a top-class shooter, which was no surprise because he was trained at the Snake Pit, Riley's Gym in Wigan, many years ago. Anyway we got talking about different wrestlers and at one point he mentioned the Iron Sheik, who, in his amateur days, was supposed to have been a good wrestler.

I said, "Billy, was the Iron Sheik really any good?"

He said, "Tommy, the Iron Sheik can be done any time." And then I looked at Billy's hands. They were all bent and twisted, as if he had rheumatism or something. That was from all the years of shooting, and all those painful submission holds that I could still remember from my time at Riley's Gym.

But apart from that, I thought the first Survivor Series in Richfield, Ohio, went down well with the fans. Although the Bulldogs and the Rougeaus were eliminated, the rest of our team survived. We were starting to make some extra money from merchandise sales, which was something Vince went into in a big way. They had some little plastic figures made of us – the British Bulldogs and Matilda – and with the money from that and from video sales, we were earning an extra $10,000 a quarter in royalties.

A big factor in the success of the WWF pay-per-view events, in my opinion, was the commentary team. And probably the best commentator that I ever saw in the WWF was Jesse "The Body" Ventura. He was a great talker, and he could brainwash the fans into believing anything he said. And from the wrestlers' point of view, it didn't matter what you did in that ring, Jesse could make you or break you. That's how good he was.

One night we were in the Sports Arena in Los Angeles, supposedly to wrestle Don Muraco and Bob Orton, only Bob hadn't turned up. So Chief Jay Strongbow said to Jesse, "Get your ring gear on, you're wrestling the Bulldogs."

Although Jesse had more or less finished wrestling when I came to the wwf, he always carried his wrestling gear with him, just in case they were a man short. I remember Jesse coming to me in the dressing room – he was a big man, still in good shape – and saying, "Kid, you know how when I commentate, I always make the Bulldogs look fantastic?"

I looked at him, a bit surprised, and said, "No intention Jesse." In fact, I was going to make him look like a million dollars without him having to lift a finger. Because I was already thinking, "If I touch this man tonight, next week, on commentary, he's going to wipe the floor with the Bulldogs."

So Jesse got changed into his wrestling gear, and he was very nervous – he must have still had it in mind that the Bulldogs might mess him up. Anyway, about five-minutes before our match Bob Orton turned up, completely wrecked, and started getting changed.

Chief Jay said, "Bob, you're too late. They're going in now."

He swayed around a bit, mumbled, "Oh, fuck it," and started getting ready anyway.

We got in the ring. Jesse and Don got in the ring. And about a minute behind them, Bob got in the ring. He walked over to Jesse, started pointing his finger, and said, "We're wrestling the Bulldogs tonight – me and Muraco." That was all Jesse needed to hear. He went straight back to the dressing room.

A similar thing happened when Bobby Heenan had to stand in for Big John Studd when he no-showed at a tag match with King Kong Bundy against the Bulldogs. Bobby, "The Weasel" Heenan came to our dressing room about half an hour before our match, saying he had a bad back. "Take it easy with me, will you Dynamite?"

There was a regular turnover in the wwf. One man got fired and another one would come in and replace him. Some of them lasted a week or a month, some did six months, some went on to become big stars. When Vince brought Jim Hellwig in, and made him into the Ultimate Warrior, I didn't think it would work, because he had no talent for wrestling. None.

Jim came in from Texas where he'd been wrestling for Fritz Von Erich as the Dingo Warrior; for running to the ring, getting in the ring and shaking the ropes, I'd give him ten marks out of ten. Plus he looked good. But once they rang the bell and he started wrestling, he was absolutely pathetic. It turned out, though, that I was wrong about the Ultimate Warrior. His wrestling was the shits, but his gimmick went down a treat with the fans, just like Hulk Hogan. So then he started getting the big push.

Sometimes it worked the other way, and the gimmick overshadowed a person's ability in the ring. For example, with "Hacksaw" Jim Duggan, Jim knew his job, but before he became a pro wrestler, he played American football. And that football gimmick that they had him doing – the three-point stance and the tackle – disguised the fact that he could actually wrestle. I'd give the man six out of ten, which is a lot. But they gave him such a stupid character, he never had a chance to show that he could wrestle. But, as I'm sure a lot of wrestlers were starting to think, did it really matter really as long as they paid you?

I had a lot of good friends in the wwf, people I went drinking with or shared a rental car with, but you had to be careful who you were seen with. If you were caught socializing or driving with a wrestler who you were meant to be feuding with, you could be fired. That was because the Sheik, and his opponent at that time, Jim Duggan, got pulled over by the cops on a drink and drugs charge; Duggan with marijuana and the Sheik with marijuana and cocaine. They were both charged and the story hit the press. But it wasn't the drugs that upset Vince, it was the fact that two wrestlers, who were supposed to knocking the shit out of each other every night in the ring, had been caught in the same car. Well, it was bad for the business. We'd all done it. I'd driven Larry Latham – Moondog Spot – many times when we were wrestling each other. But after that incident with Duggan and the Sheik, Vince told us all, "If it happens again, you will be fired on the spot." And he meant it.

By early 1988 I would say the wwf was doing great business, with sell-out house shows and good buy rates for the pay-per-views. WrestleMania iv was coming around, and this year it was at the Trump Plaza in Atlantic City, New Jersey. For once Hulk Hogan wasn't the main event, because for once he wasn't the champion. In fact the title was vacant, so that entire event was built around an elimination tournament to decide the new World Champion.

Most of us flew into the main airport in Atlantic City, and had a ticket for another flight, just a short one, which took you closer to the arena. As I was walking through the airport, I heard a familiar voice shout, "Tommy, come on with me." It was Harley. He'd hired himself a car and wanted me to share it with him.

I said, "King, I've got a ticket for another flight." It would have only taken me about ten minutes, but Harley insisted I went with him. He was driving, and I said to him, "Do you know this place?"

"Like the back of my hand Tommy." Well, there were some roadworks straight ahead, and a lot of signs saying "Slow 20mph." But Harley ignored them and carried on doing 50 or 60mph. So when a sudden sharp bend came up, he missed it completely and ploughed straight through the barriers and landed nose-first in a ditch. He was cursing, I was holding my head because I'd banged it hard on the windscreen.

I said, "King, I'm not being funny, but I thought you knew this airport like the back of your hand?"

He said, "Frig Tommy, I've not been here for a long time. The bastards have changed the roads."

Harley always made me laugh. One of the funniest things I ever saw was his performance at The Slammy Awards in the Trump Plaza. It was a big occasion, and Vince had hired tuxedos for all the wrestlers. We all looked very smart. Then Vince made us act out little scenes, for example, Randy Savage was playing a trumpet, somebody else was on the drums; all stupid stuff, but intended to build up for the pay-per-view.

At this time Harley Race was feuding with Jim Duggan. Mean Gene Okerland, the MC, was standing in front of a giant movie screen, and when he said a certain line, Harley and Jim were supposed to come crashing through the screen, and start fighting in the arena. But Harley, who had already been drinking, got it completely wrong and burst through the screen on the wrong line. The director or somebody shouted, "Cut! We'll have to do that again." So everybody went back to their places, except Harley. He was staggering around, crashed into Hillbilly Jim's farmyard scene – where they had some little farm animals, like pigs and sheep and chickens – and started trying to grab hold of a chicken. The man who owned the animals was shouting, telling Harley to get out of the farmyard, and as you can imagine, the rest of us couldn't stop laughing.

So they put a new screen up, and did the scene again. This time Harley got it right. He came through the screen with Jim, on cue, they had their fight, and everybody was happy. But right at the end of the taping, the "King" had to walk off the stage, and down a flight of about ten stairs. He had his crown and robe on, and although he was well-gone by this point, he was trying very hard not to show it; maybe too hard, because he missed the first step, and fell straight down the other nine. We all cracked up again, because when Harley got up, his crown was nearly flat, and he had blood all over his face. He wandered over to the audience, to the front row where his wife was sitting, leaned over the barrier and said to her, "How did I do?" She didn't say a word, just got up and walked out.

At WrestleMania iv we wrestled another six-man tag; this time with Koko B. Ware as our third man. Our opponents were the Islanders, Haku and Samu, with Bobby Heenan. The match was ok, on the short side, but they needed more time for the main event. When it finished, Bobby Heenan was supposed to run off up the stairs, with Matilda chasing after him. He'd even put on a special dog-proof jacket like a police-dog handler would wear, and showed it to the fans saying, "See, I'll be ok." But on this night, Matilda would not perform. She just sat there. So we had to run after Bobby, dragging Matilda along the floor behind us.

That was the night Randy Savage beat Ted Dibiase to become the World Champion. Ted was a good wrestler, and a big mouth on the microphone, but for me, that Million Dollar Man gimmick wasn't right for him. What he was then, and what they would still say now, is that

Ted was a wrestling heel. He wasn't aggressive enough. He stuck to the wrestling manual, as in, arm-drag, hip toss, whatever; very methodical, and technically, very good, but he'd no fire inside him, for example, to crack another wrestler in the ring for no reason.

A couple of months after WrestleMania, my son Marek was born, and as you can imagine, I was very proud of him. I still am. But things hadn't been going so well at home between Michelle and me. That was nobody's fault, and I know it was hard for all the wrestlers' wives because we were away so much of the time. But I was away too much. Occasionally, when the WWF came to Toronto or Montreal, or California, it was near enough for me to bring Michelle and the children to see the show, and get to spend some time with them that way. And I always enjoyed wrestling when they were in the building watching me, even though the children were too young to really know. But, over the last three years, we'd almost become strangers and were more or less living our own lives.

During that summer, we had matches with the Hart Foundation, until they turned babyface, the Bolsheviks, the Islanders, and the New Dream Team, which was Greg Valentine and the Honky Tonk Man. Brutus Beefcake was now Brutus "The Barber" Beefcake, and he looked an even bigger prick strutting round the ring with those garden shears. But they were all hard matches. I was still doing the top-rope stuff and the high-impact moves, and those matches really took it out of me, but as a team, we seemed to have lost direction. I thought maybe it was time the British Bulldogs had a change of heart. So we went to see Vince.

As usual I did the talking. I told Vince we weren't happy with the way things were going and said, "I was thinking maybe we should turn."

Then Davey chimed in. "Yeah. We could shave our heads and get some bulldogs tattooed on the side of them."

I turned round and looked at him, and I said, "I'll tell you what Dave – you shave your head and get a bulldog tattooed on each side, and then I'll do mine."

Which I wouldn't, but it didn't matter anyway because Vince didn't want us wrestling as heels. He told us to just carry on as we were. I know why. The wrestlers that were being brought in or pushed to the top were big men, a lot bigger than us, and as heels, we would be too small. We were still taking steroids, still doing the weights and working out more or less everyday, and if ever there was a time when I should have stopped to stop and think about what I was doing it was the time I ran out of my usual steroids and took some horse steroid instead.

I got it from a vet who lived close to my home in Calgary. He told me it was for horses. The label even read, "For intra-muscular use with horses only" and there was a picture of a horse on the front. But I didn't care, I was desperate. I'd run out of my usual stuff and I knew I had to take something, so I shot it. I woke up about 2AM freezing cold and sweating at the same time, and feeling terrible. I got up, turned all the heating on, I even turned on the burners on the stove and sat over them to try and get warm. When I look back to what I did that day, I know it could have killed me. But at the time, you didn't think about it.

What did give me a shock, was an incident that happened in the summer of that year. We'd just landed in San Francisco to do a show at the Cow Palace. A few of us went off to sort out a rental car, and I was sharing with Jim Hellwig, the Ultimate Warrior. I remember picking up the keys and suddenly not feeling too well. I felt warm and light-headed. I said to Jim, "I don't feel too good."

He said, "Go outside and get some fresh air. You'll be all right."

As I was going up the escalator, about halfway up, I started seeing dots in front of my eyes. I shook my head to try and clear it, but couldn't. Next thing, I fell backwards down the escalator, right to the bottom. At least that was what they told me when I woke up in hospital. I couldn't remember any of it. I was on an intravenous drip, aching from head to foot, and feeling completely wiped out. According to the doctors, I'd just had my first seizure. I convinced myself that it was a one-off, and that it probably wouldn't happen again. I never stopped to think about why it had happened – I didn't want to know – and once I was back on my feet, it was back to work.

CHAPTER TWELVE

However bad my troubles were, they weren't as bad as Harley Race's. Earlier in the year he'd been taken ill with some kind of stomach problem. I don't know exactly what the problem was, only that he had to have major surgery, and a big chunk of his gut taken out. He was in hospital for quite a long time, and that operation left him with a great big scar right across his belly. I knew what it felt like to be laid up in bed, not getting paid, and not knowing when you would again. So you can imagine how mad I was when The Honky Tonk Man decided to poke fun at the "King" and his predicament.

I'd never had a problem with Wayne Ferris, which was his real name and the name he wrestled under when he'd arrived in Calgary a few years earlier. Bruce Hart, who loved changing wrestlers' names, came up with the Honky Tonk Man. And to be honest, it suited Ferris. His wrestling stunk – marks out of ten, none – but he was a good talker; a fantastic talker.

After he left Stampede, he made his way into the WWF and became the Intercontinental Champion, which was no big surprise, because he was a very good friend of Hulk Hogan, and in that respect, no different to Jimmy Hart and Brutus Beefcake. The main man could swing favours for anybody. But I'd always gotten along with him, until this one particular night in Boston, Massachusetts. I wasn't wrestling that night, but after the show, Honky was in a car with three or four other wrestlers, and he started waving his paycheque around, saying, "I bet the King wishes he had my cheque now." I'm sure it was a nice cheque too. So he was sniggering and laughing about it. Randy Savage was in the car with him, and the next day in Detroit, it was Randy who told me what he'd said. I thought, "Right." As soon as Honky walked into the dressing room, I said, "Can I have a word?"

He was all smiles, he had no idea there was anything wrong, and he said, "Sure Tommy, what do you want?"

I said, "Can I see you in this room next door?" Well, I wasn't really giving him any choice, so he followed me in. But before he got through the door, I had him by the throat and pinned against the wall. I told him I knew what he'd been saying about Harley. I said, "If you had that cheque on you now, I'd take it off you and give it to the King myself."

He slid down the wall and was more or less on his knees, crying. I didn't hit him, but I twisted his shirt tight against his throat and used my voice – which, because of the steroids, was very loud and very aggressive. I said, "Don't you ever say anything about the King again." Everybody in the dressing room next door had gone quiet. I knew they were all listening.

He looked up at me and said, "Tommy, I thought you and me were friends."

"The King's a friend, you're nothing but a piece of shit." Then I walked out and left him on the floor. Funnily enough, Honky was always nice to me after that. He talked to me, smiled at me, brought me cups of coffee. And he never mentioned Harley Race again.

Eventually, he recovered from his stomach operation and came back to the WWF. But he didn't stay long. They offered him a road agent's job, doing the same thing as Pat Patterson and Chief Jay, which was promotion in a way. But first, he had to wrestle Haku for the title of "King." Well, he lost that match, which was no big deal, because he had his new job lined up and waiting for him. Vince told him to go home, take a couple of weeks off, and they would be in touch to tell him when to start.

So Harley went home to Kansas City, and waited, and waited, but no phone call came. So he called Vince. "It's been two weeks, I haven't heard from you." Vince told him he was sorry but times had changed – in two weeks – and they already had a new agent. So that was that, Harley had finished with the WWF. A couple of years after that, when he'd put some of the weight back on that he'd lost through being ill, he went to WCW and became a manager for Big Van Vader.

I'll be honest with you, a sense of humour was the only thing Davey

Boy Smith and myself had in common. We got along as friends, but not close friends. We never discussed family life or anything personal; and when we did talk it was more or less just to have a laugh, mainly at the expense of other wrestlers. When it came to playing tricks, we thought along exactly the same lines. If an opportunity to play a joke came along, I'd look, he'd look, we'd look at each other, and that was all it took. So at that level, and professionally, when we were in the ring, we got along very well. But I would never describe him as a close friend – as far as I was concerned he was family. That was why I brought him to Calgary, and saw him right in Japan and in the wwf, although I must admit, I also believed we were a good tag team.

But even then, I took a lot of the bangs and the kicks and the suplexes, before I made that final tag and he saved the day. I didn't need to do that either, but I knew Davey was scared of getting hurt in the ring. That's a true fact. If you ever watched his clotheslines, he'd touch and lift his arm away, clear.

I'd say to him, "What did you do that for? Why don't you follow through?"

He said, "I'm not following through Tommy, I might rip my pecs."

I said, "What are you talking about? You don't clothesline and put your arm up in the air like a soft arse. The worst thing that can happen is you'll knock your opponent's head off his shoulders." But he wouldn't go through with it because he was frightened of getting hurt. So, yes, I did get along with Davey, I did my best to look after him because he was my cousin, and when it came to looking good in the ring, I made him look better than me. But it was all one way. For example, when I was in hospital all those weeks, he never came to see me, apart from when there was a photo opportunity. He couldn't even be bothered to call me. But he did call his family – who were also my aunt and uncle – at home in Golborne in Lancashire, and told them that I was so messed-up with drugs I was probably going to die soon. Of course "their David" was Mr. Clean. I didn't find out about all this until a few years later, so I let a lot of things that bothered me about Davey Boy Smith go unmentioned.

There was one tour that we did when we had to wrestle in a cage match every night. Every night for four weeks. At that time, you could be certain that at least one of the wrestlers would get busted open during a cage match. And because Davey didn't like the idea of getting hurt, that wrestler was usually me.

It was the Bulldogs versus Volkoff and the Iron Sheik, or Bulldogs versus the New Dream Team, and every night I ended up covered in blood. Some nights I just opened up the same wound from the night before, because it hadn't had time to close. By the end of that four weeks, my head was swollen and sore. So you can imagine how I felt when, on the very last night, Gorilla Monsoon came to the dressing room, and told us we had to a stop. There was too much risk of contamination from all the blood. At that time, AIDS was making the headlines, and so as a safety precaution, Vince decided to put a stop to wrestlers bleeding in the ring. I said, "Thanks Gorilla. I wish Vince had decided that a month ago."

When Demolition became the WWF Tag Team Champions, the British Bulldogs had a long run of matches with them over the summer months. "Ax" and "Smash" (Bill Eadie and Barry Darsow) were always good for a match, and as heels they took themselves very seriously. Mr. Fuji was their manager and he used to follow them down to the ring, wearing his bowler hat and carrying a walking stick.

One of the referee's sons used to help out at night, taking the wrestlers' jackets back to the dressing room and helping out with the ring crew. One night we gave him Mr. Fuji's bowler hat and stick and told him to follow Demolition to the ring. He thought it was great. They came out, strutting down the aisle with their music playing, looking the part, mean and dangerous, and then this young kid came out, smiling at the people and waving Fuji's stick around. The crowd started laughing. Demolition could see they were laughing, but didn't know why, until they turned round and saw what was going on.

Wrecking your opponent's entrance was a great way of upsetting him before a match. I can remember wrestling for Stu Hart one time, when the German wrestler, Moose Morowski was on the card. He was a big man and a good heel. When he went to the ring, it was to the sound of this loud thundering drumbeat, "boom, boom, boom, boom." That was his music and it matched his character. But on this particular night, he'd got halfway down the aisle when the drums suddenly stopped, and Neil Diamond singing "Love Is In The Air" started playing. The fans were laughing, but all Moose could do was carry on walking to the ring. It turned out that Smith Hart was on the PA system that night.

Stu Hart always used to book the women wrestlers for Stampede Week. And as a novelty for the fans, they were OK, but in my opinion, those women could not hold a candle to the women wrestlers in Japan. Now they really could wrestle – and probably beat some of the men. But Moolah was in charge of the American women wrestlers, and if a promoter wanted to book a women's match, he had to do it through her.

By the late eighties, the novelty value was fading and women's matches weren't as popular, mainly because all the women were getting on a bit. So Vince put women at ringside to add a bit of interest to the matches. For example, "Sensational" Sherri Martel, who didn't really wrestle, but worked as a manager for a few different wrestlers like Randy Savage and Ted Dibiase. I'll give her credit, she got stuck in and didn't mind doing the daft stuff. When they had a cage match and her man was in trouble, she'd climb up the cage and to distract everybody, including the referee, while Savage or whoever she was managing, pulled a foreign object out of his trunks, or did some illegal move.

Sherri did whatever Vince McMahon told her to do, as in, going out to the ring in a little miniskirt, or a tight, low-cut blouse, and she nearly always ended up slipping on her backside, or the opponent would do something to her and she'd end up getting a kicking.

Elizabeth was another ringside interest and a non-wrestler. In fact she didn't do much apart from stand by the apron and look nice for her man, who at that time was her real life husband, "The Macho Man," Randy Savage. In all the years that I was with the WWF I never had more than a couple of words with her. Nobody did. They never got near enough. At regular house shows, Randy would have a car, just for himself and Elizabeth. When they got to the arena, he would take Elizabeth to a dressing room, on her own, leave her there and lock the door. When it was time for his match, he'd get all his stuff on, the hat and the glasses, he'd go and unlock the door, and take Elizabeth to the ring.

After the match, he'd take her straight back to that room and lock the door again until it was time to go home.

Like Hulk Hogan, Randy Savage was one of those wrestlers that I never socialized with. He stuck with his own circle of friends, his clique, the same as us, so outside of the arenas, our paths didn't cross very often. But I did wrestle Randy, just once, during a tournament in Chicago back in 1985. It was the very first WWF pay-per-view, the Wrestling Classic. At the end of the night, Vince was going to give away a Silver Edition Rolls Royce, a real beauty, to the winner of a lottery draw.

There was a single elimination tournament that night, and in the first round I wrestled Nikolai Volkoff and beat him in six-seconds flat. In the second round, or the quarter final, I wrestled Adrian Adonis. Just before we went to the ring, Adrian said to me, "Tommy, you just follow me in the ring and we'll be OK."

I turned round and said to him, "Look, if you want to piledrive me, backdrop me, suplex me, whatever, that's OK, but you do not tell me what to do and how to do it in that ring. Nobody does. You do what you want, and I'll do what I want." All this was only because he'd messed Danny Spivey around, telling him to do this and telling him to do that. And Danny did it.

So we got in the ring, and he did certain things to me, which, as I'd said, was OK. And I knocked the shit out of him – in a working fashion – which was also OK. The match finished when Jimmy Hart, who was his manager at that time, took the apron and held his megaphone up. Adrian threw me right at it, but I reversed it and ended up throwing Adrian, smack into the megaphone. I pinned him, one, two, three.

Somewhere in between the tournament matches, Davey Boy Smith wrestled Ricky Steamboat. The match went for about ten minutes until something went wrong, Davey got hurt, and Ricky had his arm raised.

The next match, the semi-final, was the Dynamite Kid against Randy Savage, who I'd never wrestled before. We had a good match, although Randy was not the easiest person to move around the ring, as in, not as agile as some of the other wrestlers. But I think the people enjoyed it. At one point I had Randy right up on the top rope, suplexed him off the turnbuckle – which was my finish then – and we both went down hard on our backs. As I rolled over to cover him, he got his legs up and small-packaged me, one, two, three. He walked back to the dressing room holding his back as if he was in pain. Which he probably was. In the final match, he had to wrestle The Junkyard Dog. Well Junkyard was useless anyway, wrestling-wise, so Randy went back to the ring for that one, still holding his back, which was a good excuse before he started. And he needed it because Junkyard won.

A few years later, I think Randy really did have some problems with his back. A lot of wrestlers did. But as far as injuries in the ring went, I can't really recall many that were more serious than mine. About the same time that I hurt my back, Paul Orndorff, "Mr. Wonderful," suffered a serious shoulder injury, which left him in a bad way. He was wrestling Hulk Hogan on a big card in Toronto, and it was the main event. Hogan did some sort of leapfrog and Paul ran underneath. Then Hogan rolled onto his back and put his feet up to give him a backdrop, but as Paul went over, he came down on his shoulder.

I don't know what the injury was exactly, but I think it affected all the nerves in his arm. Paul was always in good shape – that was his gimmick – but after that injury, his arm went from a good 19 inches to a good 16 inches. Like I said, this was around the same time I was laid up with my back problems, and I know that comments were made in the gym, or in the arenas, like Dynamite and Orndorff were the "Incredible Shrinking Men." Which was fair enough. We had lost weight, because we'd stopped the steroids, and we had surgery, or at least I had. Paul was too scared of the surgery to get his arm fixed.

Vince had always sent Paul out to the ring before the start of his matches, telling him to pose for a few minutes and look cocky. In fact he looked great. But after he hurt his arm, and he wasn't looking so great, Vince still made him go out and pose in the ring. That was Vince. He did a lot of things that I believed were for his own entertainment rather than the fans. Having said that, the wrestlers weren't in a position to complain about it. When you come into the wwf, you're on a good number. And if you deliver the goods, whatever they happen to be, you know you'll make well.

But going back to Randy Savage, like I said, outside the ring, I'd probably never had more than a few words with him. Then one night, out of the blue, he turned up at my hotel room door asking for my help. The WWF had been at the Spectrum in Philadelphia that night, and by coincidence, Jim Crockett Promotions, or the NWA as it was known, had run a card at another venue in the city. Which was a pretty big deal. There was rivalry between the two promotions even then, and there were always some talk about who could outdraw who. On this night, the WWF came out on top, because they were in a bigger building, but I think the other promotion sold-out as well.

By coincidence, the wrestlers from both promotions were staying at the same hotel that night. That was the only time I'd ever known that to happen, and it was the reason why Randy Savage, the WWF Heavy-weight Champion, was knocking at my door.

What Randy wanted was somebody to watch his back in the bar, just in case a wrestler from the other promotion decided to have a go at the WWF champion. So I said I'd do it. I followed him down to the bar, keeping a slight distance – but staying just close enough. In return for that, he bought me beer all night.

As it turned out, Randy Savage had nothing to worry about. Wrestlers from the WWF, like myself and Davey, Harley Race, and Randy Savage, mixed with wrestlers from WCW, like Ric Flair, Barry Windham, and Lex Luger, and Sting. Well, when I say mixed, we more or less plonked our backsides down at their table. I said to Ric Flair, "All right Ric, how are you doing?"

He said, "I'm doing fine Dynamite. I've been hearing a lot about you." I wasn't sure what he meant by that, but we had a few beers, a few laughs, and the atmosphere was great. After a couple of hours, I went up to the WWF champion who seemed to be having a good time, and said, "How's it going Randy?"

He said, "Oh Yeaahh, I feel good."

I said, "In that case Randy, do me a favour and go to bed."

He said, "Why?"

I said, "You feel good don't you. If you start feeling too good, you might end up getting one – if you see what I mean." And I looked around the bar at all the other wrestlers.

He said, "Dynamite, I didn't think about that." And off he went to bed.

Randy Savage did all right for himself; he worked hard in the ring, with his wrestling and his gimmick, and I would say he deserved to be the champion. Anybody who pulled their weight did. But if you wrestled a really bad match, or kept messing up your spots, you could expect a bollocking from the road agent straight afterward. At least if they had any special plans for you. For example, Jim Hellwig, when he first became the Ultimate Warrior, was the first match on the card. He was wrestling Steve Lombardi, the Brooklyn Brawler, in Calgary one night. Chief Jay Strongbow was in charge, and Jim went to the ring, did maybe two or three minutes, beat Lombardi and came back. That was it. Jim can't wrestle anyway, but the match was so bad, and so short, when he got back Chief Jay pulled him and put him straight. Having said that, I've seen a lot of bad matches where nothing was said; not by Vince or any of the agents. You just never saw the wrestler again.

Bigger wrestlers always did better in the wwf than the smaller wrestlers, regardless of whether they had talent or not. A lot of them had no talent, but one big man who I did rate was Bam Bam Bigelow. For such a big man, he was a great wrestler; very quick, very agile, and a very convincing heel. But outside of the ring, he was big clumsy bugger. We were in a long queue for the airport check-in one time, and Bam Bam, who I knew had been drinking, was standing right behind me. He stumbled and fell backwards over his own case, knocked the person behind him down, and then the next; it was like watching dominoes fall, as one by one, all the people in the queue went down.

It's surprising who you can run into at the airport. I was in the airport in Philadelphia one day when I heard a familiar voice. "Fackin' 'ell Rocket, what are you doin' 'ere?" It was Butch, one of the Bushwhackers, and I hadn't seen him in years. The first time I met Luke and Butch was in Calgary, not long after I'd arrived. They'd come over from New Zealand, and in Calgary they wrestled as the Kiwis. After that, they went down to Portland, Oregon, where they became the Sheepherders, but after that I lost touch with them. I think they went down to Florida or North Carolina with Jim Crockett's promotion. And they got themselves a manager, Brian Adams, who later became Crush, the third member of Demolition when he joined the WWF.

I did a lot of six-man tag matches with the Kiwis against three of the Hart brothers, and Luke and Butch always called me Rocket, as in, "Fackin' 'ell Rocket, are you gonna start this match?"

So when I heard that familiar voice, I was really glad to see them again. Butch said to me, "What's the chances of us getting into the WWF Rocket?"

I said, "I'll ask, but I can't promise." That same night, I spoke to Pat Patterson. I told him I'd seen the Sheepherders and that they wanted a job.

He said, "Dynamite, tell them to send me some pictures."

I said, "I'm not being funny Pat, they asked me as a favour, and I've asked you. But don't tell them to send pictures when you already know them."

Anyway, a few months later, they were in. But when they spoke to Pat or whoever it was that booked them, they were told not to bother bringing Brian Adams, because they didn't need a manager. Luke and Butch were renamed the Bushwhackers, and I know they took a lot of stick for their gimmick, pulling stupid faces and licking people, but they worked very hard, and for the fans, they were good entertainment.

Vince announced another pay-per-view event that year, Summer-Slam, which was going out at the end of August. A short time before that, the Rougeaus, Jacques and Raymond, had turned heel, and when the line up for SummerSlam was announced, the first match was to be the British Bulldogs versus the Rougeaus. I'll be honest, I never liked the Rougeaus. Because we were both babyface tag teams, we'd never wrestled them before. I'd seen a lot of their matches against the Hart Foundation, which the Rougeaus won more or less all the time. They were arrogant and ignorant, and by the time we arrived at Madison Square Garden, Davey and me had agreed there was no way either of those two pricks were going to beat us. I told Pat Patterson the same thing. Bear in mind, Pat is French Canadian, but he said, "OK. You've got 20 minutes."

And we gave the Rougeaus a fantastic 20 minutes. In spite of a lot of pain in my back, I wrestled hard that night, made them look great, and went to a time-limit draw. The Hart Foundation, who had also turned, got the title shot against Demolition that night.

Big Boss Man, who beat Koko B. Ware on the same card, was another new gimmick, which belonged to Ray Traylor. He wrestled in Japan as Big Bubbah, but as Big Boss Man, he took to wearing a law enforcement officer's uniform and carrying a night-stick. Just before Bossman made his debut, Ray spent a lot of time practicing with his nightstick, so he could swing it about like a real police officer. On his first appearance at a TV taping, he was very nervous. He stood behind the curtain, the music started playing, and he walked out, looking like he meant business, and twirling his nightstick around in his hand only he made a mistake and the nightstick flew off into the air. To make things worse, he went running after it, so that part of the tape had to be cut out.

One gimmick that I did think was good, and definitely suited the wrestler concerned, was Curt Hennig's Mr. Perfect. I hadn't seen Curt for about four years, and I remembered him from our Portland days as a skinny kid who weighed no more than 180 pounds. When he turned up in the WWF in 1988, he'd grown, to maybe 250 pounds. But it was great to see him again. The one thing I always liked about Curt was that he was straight – to your face and behind your back. But in the ring he was a cocky bastard and a great heel. I rated his wrestling as well. And he had the Mr. Perfect gimmick off to, well, perfection.

They had him doing videotapes of Mr. Perfect playing golf or basketball or pool, whatever. He'd stand, say, in front of the pool table in a bar and the director would tell him "I want this ball in one pocket, one ball in another, and another in another etc." And Curt would hit the balls, miss all the pockets and the director would shout, "Cut! Re-rack them." This might happen 20, 30, even 50 times; Curt might be there eight hours, and then finally, he'd make the shot, pocket all the balls, spit out his gum, swipe it away and say, "I am perfect." And on the television, it looked perfect, even though he might never have played pool in his life.

But I got along great with Curt – like me, he enjoyed a good prank. But when he played one on the Rougeaus, it backfired on me and turned into something a lot more serious.

We were in Miami, Florida for a house show, and as I've already told you, leaving your clothes unattended while you were in the ring could be risky when certain people were about. A lot of wrestlers had got wise to this and had somebody watch out for their stuff while they were wrestling. And that was what the Rougeaus did. They asked Curt Hennig to keep an eye on their clothes. While they were gone, Curt found a pair of scissors and cut their shirts and pants to ribbons. It had Bulldog stamped all over it, so just before they got back, Curt shot off into the toilet. They walked in, saw their clothes and shouted for Curt. He called back that he was on the toilet. So straight away, they put two and two together and made five, they decided that it was me and Davey Boy Smith. Bear in mind, I knew nothing about this because I wasn't even in the same dressing room.

They started cursing us and saying things about what they were going to do to us, and sure enough, word soon got back to us that our names were mud with the Rougeaus. I still didn't know why at this point, so I thought, "Right." I walked next door into their dressing room, where they all sat playing cards. And I admit, Jacques had his back to me, but all I did was give him a flat-hander, straight across his ear.

He jumped up and shouted, "What are you fucking playing at Dynamite?" Then he turned and tried to dive at me, low, for a double leg, but as he went down, I got on top of him, turned him over and banged him twice in the face. Then Raymond came over and tried to interfere. He put his hand across, saying, "Dynamite, stop, Jacques has had enough."

I said, "Move your hand, this has nothing to do with you." He wouldn't move. So I knocked Raymond out. I'd laid the Rougeaus flat out on the floor. That should have been the end of it. By mistake, they thought I'd cut their clothes up, which was no big deal because I'd done it to a lot of wrestlers, but Curt Hennig later admitted it was him. So as far as I was concerned we were straight.

Two weeks later we were in Fort Wayne, Indiana, to do a TV taping. I'd seen the Rougeaus a few times since Miami, but they'd never said a word to me, or Davey. Anyway, this day, in between taping their interviews, they were both quiet, reading a book, not talking but reading.

Which I thought was a bit funny. TV tapings sometimes took all day and all night. You could be taping interviews to go with matches for up to a month ahead. We broke for lunch, had something to eat, and then one by one the wrestlers were called back for the next interviews. As usual, I was the last one out of the canteen – Davey went back ahead of me.

I grabbed a cup of coffee, lit a cigarette, and started walking back down the corridor to the studio. Ahead of me I could see the Rougeaus talking to Pat Patterson in the corridor. Jacques was leaning against one wall, Raymond was on the other, doing the talking. I had the cigarette in one hand, cup of coffee in the other, and as I got nearer, I remember thinking to myself, "No, they're not going to do me here," because Pat, who was the foreman, was there.

Don't get me wrong, if Pat hadn't been there, I would have approached them in a totally different manner. But I thought, "No, I'll be all right here," and stepped through, when – bang – Jacques smashed me in the mouth with a knuckle-duster. I heard the crunch as four teeth went there and then. My mouth was ripped to shreds, inside and out, and there was blood mixed with pieces of gum, just pouring down the front of me. That first shot had knocked me dizzy, but I still managed to think. Instinctively, I knew I couldn't go down and I needed to back myself against the wall. Everything was a blur, and somewhere in the background I could hear Pat shouting, "Stop, stop," and then Jacques hit me again, maybe two or three times. I was ready to blast him back, when I saw Ray out of the corner of my eye, about to blind side me. For that split second, I thought that was it, I'd had it. I couldn't take the two of them. Then I heard Bad News Brown shout, "What's going on?" He'd heard the commotion and come out of the dressing room into the corridor. Bad News Brown saved my life, because if he hadn't appeared when he did, I think they would have killed me. The Rougeaus didn't hang about. When they saw Bad News, they took off like sprinters, down the corridor and out of the building.

Somebody else, I don't know who, was shouting, "Dynamite's been done." I had too. I was in a mess. Apparently the Rougeaus had left the building, probably for the airport, and gone straight back to Montreal.

I started cleaning myself up. Pat Patterson came in the dressing room with some money. He said, "Here, go to the hospital and get yourself stitched up. But just tell them you've been in an accident."

Somebody drove me to the hospital; I can't even remember who.

At the hospital, the doctor said, "What happened to you?" It must have looked bad. I still had my wrestling gear on, so I told him that I'd been in the studio taping interviews for the wrestling and I'd tripped over a cable and gone face first into some equipment. But I don't think he believed me because he said, "You look as if you've been run over by a train."

Then he started stitching my mouth – I'd never had pain like that, my lips were torn open, and the inside of my mouth was in shreds. Four teeth had gone. Smashed right out.

I got back to the studio and straight away Pat Patterson said, "Vince wants to see you in his office." This was maybe an hour or so after the incident, so I went in, and I think he really was shocked when he saw the state I was in. But the first thing he said to me was, "Goddam Tom. I can't believe you didn't go down."

I said, "No I didn't." Then I told Vince I was going to sort those two pricks out.

He said, "No, don't do that. They might call somebody." He was being serious; they knew people in Montreal who could see me off. But he said, "Leave this with me and I'll sort something out." Well, I knew my teeth were going to cost something to fix.

I came out of Vince's office and went to get changed – he told me I couldn't wrestle that night – but it was only later that I thought about what he'd said. He hadn't been there, he hadn't seen it, but he knew I hadn't gone down. In fact, he couldn't believe I hadn't gone down. That was when I thought, "Was I supposed to have done?"

But at that point, I didn't give it much thought. And I didn't get much of a rest because the next day we had to fly up to La Guardia airport in New York to catch the "Red Eye" special to France. The WWF had a ten-day tour of France and Italy. That next morning was the first time I'd seen Davey since the incident with the Rougeaus. He told me he'd called his family in Golborne, in Lancashire, I imagined, to tell them what had happened. But what he actually told them was, "Only for me, the Rougeaus would have killed Tommy."

So this went all around our home town, "Thomas got a good hiding and David saved him." He was the hero, I was the piece of shit. He was clean, I was taking drugs, and was probably going to die soon anyway. Bear in mind, it was only later that I found all this out. But that was my cousin. In my opinion, you always look after your family, no matter what. That was something I'd always believed. I still do. I couldn't understand why Davey Boy Smith didn't feel the same way.

CHAPTER THIRTEEN

By rights, the Rougeaus should have been fired there and then. All the wrestlers who went on the European tour seemed certain they would be, and I knew wrestlers who'd been fired for less. But the next morning, after I'd had time to think about it, I was having my doubts. In fact, I was convinced that Pat Patterson knew, or at least had an idea that something was going down. Why else would Jacques jump me right in front of the foreman? And because of what he'd said I wasn't even sure about Vince. To this day I still wonder if he knew I'd been set up. So as you can imagine, I was feeling pretty bad, mentally as well as physically. Oh, I was sore. But in one way I was glad to be on that European tour, because it meant at the end of it I could stop off at home for a week to see my dad.

We flew to France, myself and Davey, Demolition, The Junkyard Dog, Don Muraco, Andre and Tito Santana. Lanny Poffo, the brother of Randy Savage, was also there. He was very good at poetry and talking on the microphone, but as a wrestler – well when you picked him up, he was like a lump of concrete. While we took the long route, the 747, Lanny's brother Randy, and of course Elizabeth, were flown out from New York by Concorde. But they were only joining the tour for a couple of nights and then they flew back.

wwf television was being broadcast in France and Italy on one of the satellite channels, and had become very popular. So every night of that tour was a sell-out. For the first few days I still felt rough. Well, as you can imagine, losing four teeth like that, and then all the stitches, I couldn't even eat properly. But in the ring, I knew I'd be ok with Demolition. They treated me like a baby – although the fans would never have known any difference – we wrestled exactly as we would normally wrestle, except, with me, there were no shots above the neck.

We had the same referee for the whole of that tour, a cocky little bastard who thought he was running the show. Towards the end of the tour I wrestled Greg Valentine in a singles match, and I beat him, one, two, three, but I knew I had at least another ten minutes of stuff to do before I was going to nail him with the flying head-butt. In other words, the referee cut the match short with a very fast count. I got up and more or less said, "What are you playing at?"

As he raised my hand he said, under his breath, "I'm the referee. You pinned him, and you got the three count."

I said, "That wasn't the finish, you daft bastard." You see, it was the people who were really cheated, not me.

He did this with a few different wrestlers on the tour; and he really thought he was somebody. So, a couple of nights before we finished in Italy, we were all in the hotel bar for a reception. And the referee was there, strutting round in his nice white tuxedo. Davey leaned over to me and said, "Tommy, shall we do him?"

I said, "Dave, I'm not really concerned. I know he's a prick anyway." Anyway, later on that night, somebody spilled – or maybe threw – a big, tall glass of red wine all over the back of his white tuxedo. But the referee didn't know and he carried on walking round with that "Everybody look at me" attitude.

On the final night before we left, we were sat around having a few beers, and sure enough, that little prick was there again. I looked at him, looked at Davey, and said, "Was that it then, or what?"

So Davey went up to his hotel room, which was next door but one to the referee's. Mine was in the middle. All the rooms had little balconies, which were close enough to jump to from one to the other. And that's what Davey did. He jumped from his balcony onto mine, and then to the referee's, and as luck would have it, he'd left his balcony door wide open. Davey went in the bedroom and found the referee's suitcases all packed neat and tidy and ready for the early-morning flight back to New York. I wasn't there, and I didn't see, but when Davey came back, he told me he'd made a few alterations to the referee's clothes. Which was fair enough, seeing the referee was cutting everybody else's matches short.

Nick Bockwinkel, who at one time had been the AWA World Heavyweight Champion, was the road agent in charge of that tour. Don Muraco had recently turned babyface and gone from wearing black wrestling trunks to blue, so we called him Big Blue. We were standing around waiting to do some interviews, myself and Davey, Don Muraco, Demolition, and a few others, when I spotted Nick Bockwinkel coming towards us. I leaned over to Don and said, "Blue, why don't you do your impression of Bockwinkel for us."

Don hadn't seen Nick, so he did. "Ahaw, ahaw, ahaw, my boy," which was exactly how Nick Bockwinkel laughs and talks. Nick was standing right behind him, listening, and although he didn't say anything at the time, I could tell he was mad. Muraco made things even worse when we had to do a press conference. We had to sit at a long table in front of the TV cameras and the reporters, but I must admit, some of us had had a couple of drinks. Don Muraco included. Nick Bockwinkel stood watching what was going on, and for some reason he said something about the AWA title which was wrong. He made a mistake. But Muraco, who was drunk, shouted, "What the fuck would you know? I've drawn more people than you ever could." You see, when Muraco had a few, he thought he was the man who sold everything out for all those years.

The next night, The Junkyard Dog got himself into trouble when he decided to relieve himself on the back of the coach driver's seat. The coach had already stopped outside our hotel, so really, there was no need.

That tour finished, and while everybody else went back to America or to Canada, I flew back to England and spent a week at home in Golborne with my dad, who I still missed, in spite of being away all those years. But, when I arrived back in New York ready for the start of the next tour, the Rougeaus were still on my mind. It turned out they hadn't been fired, or suspended. They hadn't even been fined. Instead, it was Don Muraco and The Junkyard Dog who were fired for their behaviour on tour. They'd both been reported to Vince, who called them to his office in Stamford. He asked Don, who had no idea what was coming, how the tour had gone.

Don said "Fine." Then Vince told him he was fired. Don said, "What for?"

Vince replied, "I can't have wrestlers talking to my agents like that, because if one starts, they'll all start." Which I thought made us all sound like little kids.

But Vince wanted to set an example, so Don was fired. And because we'd been partly involved in the incident with Nick Bockwinkel, I thought the British Bulldogs might have been next. But for once, as far as Vince was concerned, the Bulldogs had done nothing wrong. To tell you the truth, the way I was feeling at that time, I wouldn't have cared less if Vince had fired us.

But there was still the matter of myself and the Rougeaus to sort out. About a week after I'd come back from England, Vince called to say he'd arranged a meeting for me, himself, and the Rougeaus. It was in a private room at a hotel in California. I think Vince, and maybe the Rougeaus, were hoping to resolve it by leaving things as they were. But not me. I said to Vince, "I'm leaving fuck all. They can pay for these teeth to be fixed. Then I'll leave it."

Jacques started getting angry and said he wasn't going to pay. But Ray cut in. He told Jacques to "Shut the fuck up," he turned round to me, and said, "Get the bill for your teeth from your dentist and let us have it. We'll pay it. That's the end of it." So I did. I got a dentist's bill for about $1,800 and gave it to them. And the Rougeaus paid. But it wasn't my bill. I had my teeth fixed for nothing.

It was as well that things were settled between us, because the next thing we knew, we were wrestling each other at the Survivor Series, which was coming up at the end of November. They were jostling for room at the top of the card now; Hulk Hogan, Randy Savage, who was the champion, and the Ultimate Warrior, they all wanted to be the main man. There were a few new faces in the wwf as well, one of which was Bret Hart's younger brother, Owen. Since the age of 12 or 13, Owen had been working hard in Stu's gym in Calgary. For the last year or so, he'd been wrestling for Stampede, and for a couple of months that year, he'd been the iwgp Junior Heavyweight Champion for New Japan. So he was ready for the big time. I don't know for sure, but I would imagine Bret put a word in for him with the office. And I wasn't surprised when they hired him. Owen was a good wrestler, very agile, and a hard-worker. But when they first brought him in Vince told him he would be wrestling in a mask. He said to him, "Think of a name for yourself."

So Owen, trying to make himself look great before he was even working, came up with the American Eagle. He told Vince. "I want to be the American Eagle."

But Vince said that was no good, and told him he was going to be the Blue Blazer. He had the blue mask, the cape, and the feathers – well he looked like a bloody parrot going to the ring. But he looked good as a wrestler, as in, the aerial moves; the back somersaults off the top rope. And later on, when he got rid of the mask and wrestled as plain Owen Hart, he formed a tag team with Koko B. Ware.

Vince had a thing about big men that was for sure, whether they were big well-muscled men or just big fat buggers. Which, I imagine, was how John Tenta found his way into the promotion as Earthquake, before he teamed up with Typhoon and formed the Natural Disasters. But the last time I'd seen John was on a ferry in Japan, on our way to Hokkaido. This was back in the early eighties. John was Canadian, from Vancouver, in British Columbia, but he had trained seriously as a Sumo wrestler. The trouble was, he couldn't stick to it; he said it was too hard. He'd certainly developed the physique, but he wasn't dedicated enough, so he'd decided to become a pro wrestler instead. Anyway, there we were on this ferry, when John, who used to talk like a little kid, said, "Tom, how can I open Vancouver?" This was back in the days when Al Tomko was running his Vancouver promotion into the ground.

I said, "John, you'll need a bit of money."

He said, "Oh. Well how much will I need?"

"A lot. You've got to pay to bring the talent in and get the television on. And you have to do it right."

So he said, "I don't really understand. I've only ever been a Sumo wrestler."

I said, "Well, you're in the professional ring now John. Things are different." He hadn't a clue. He did move back to Vancouver for a while, but ended up back in Japan. So when I saw him as Earthquake in the wwf, I said, "John, what are you doing here?" more or less meaning, what happened to Vancouver, what happened to promoting?

He said, "Well, I'm Earthquake now." And he was. He was a big man and he could make that ring shake. But that was about all.

Vince had brought a new tag team in that month, the Brainbusters: Arn Anderson and Tully Blanchard, managed by Bobby Heenan. They were a good team, and they'd done OK for themselves in the NWA as the Tag Team Champions. But in my opinion, most of their success was down to Arn Anderson. He was a good solid wrestler and he was a great heel. Tully, in my opinion, was full of shit. But apart from that, I think Vince had plans for the Brainbusters, and somewhere along the way, they involved the British Bulldogs. Or they would have done if it wasn't for something that happened in early November.

The WWF tag team ranks were strong, business was great – I couldn't say for certain, but I probably earned more money that year than any other year, with the pay-per-views, the house shows and the royalties and everything. But, like most people, I still had my principles. We were in Chicago one night, the last night of a three-week tour. As usual, right after the matches, Chief Jay was handing out the plane tickets for the flight to Syracuse and then the connecting flight home. The WWF always paid for the air tickets; the wrestlers paid for cars and hotels. When I went to get mine and Davey's tickets, Chief Jay told me there were none left.

I said, "Why's that?"

He said he didn't know, and I think he was telling the truth. I also think the reason why we didn't have any plane tickets might have been a punishment, a slap on the wrist, for something we'd done. But at that point, there was nothing the Chief could do, which left us with a 200-mile drive to Syracuse before we could get back to Calgary.

I was mad – well, we both were – because we were the only ones who didn't have a ticket. In fact I was mad enough to have quit – just walked out, there and then – which I knew would have been a stupid thing to do. But, by the time we got back to the hotel to pick our stuff up, my mind was made up. I picked up the phone and put in an overseas call to Tokyo.

Shohei Baba's wife, Motoko, answered the phone and sounded very surprised to hear from me. But, before I had chance to explain why I was calling, she told me to put the phone down because someone would call me back. I waited. And waited. Then the phone did ring and as I expected, it was Lord Blears, a former wrestler who now lived in Hawaii and acted as Baba's agent. Baba was a very private man, and didn't really speak to any of the wrestlers. If you wanted to speak to Baba, you more or less had to do it through Lord Blears. So he said, "What can we do for you Dynamite?" I told him I wanted a job for myself and Davey Boy Smith.

Straight away he said, "When can you come?"

It was too close to the start of the next tour to go straight away, so we agreed on the next one, which would be New Year's Day, 1989. The deal was done, as simple as that. I put the phone down, looked at Davey, and said, "Bollocks to all this, we're done." And although you might find it hard to believe, Davey never once argued, complained, or said a word against that decision. He just went along with it. Bear in mind we were giving up a lot: the money, mainstream television exposure, and the celebrity status. But, like I said, I had principles, and once I'd made my mind up, there was no going back.

We handed our notice in a couple of weeks before the Survivor Series, which was to be our last night. I thought we might as well go out on a big show, with a big paycheque. When Vince heard what we'd done, he didn't really say anything. I don't think it was because he didn't care; I'm sure he didn't want us to go. But I think he was confident that within a couple of weeks, we'd be back. For example, on one of the last nights before we finished, we were wrestling the Brainbusters in Columbus, Ohio. Pat told us in the dressing room, that the Brainbusters were going over, via pinfall. I told him they definitely weren't.

Pat said, "What do you mean?"

"Do you really think they are going to beat me, or my partner, one, two, three in that ring?"

Pat said, "That's right Dynamite."

I said, "I'll tell you what will happen. They might count us out, or they might disqualify us, but there is no way those two are going to pin me, or Davey Boy Smith."

So then he got on the phone, complaining about me to Vince.

"Dynamite says he'll do this, Dynamite says he won't do that."

Vince just said, "Tell Tom to do whatever he wants in the ring." Considering we were leaving anyway, plus, Vince was wanting to push the Brainbusters, it wasn't what you would expect him to say. But I think the reason he said it was because he was sure I'd be giving him a call in a couple of weeks saying, "I've made a mistake, can I come back?"

So Pat came back with Vince's message. "Go out and do whatever you feel like doing." And I did. The Bulldogs were disqualified.

The second annual Survivor Series was at the Richfield Coliseum in Ohio again. We teamed up with the Rockers, the Hart Foundation, the Young Stallions and the Powers of Pain, to wrestle the Rougeaus, The Brainbusters, Demolition, Los Conquistadors and the Bolsheviks. Walking down a WWF aisle for the last time as the British Bulldogs, maybe I should have felt a bit sad or emotional. But I didn't. I felt great. I'll be honest, I didn't even need that last match. If Vince had said to us, "Here boys, here's your $20,000. It's your last night, you don't need to work," – not that he would have said that in a million years – I'd have taken the money and gone home.

It was going to be an interesting match, for the simple reason there was the chance we might end up in the ring with the Rougeaus. As it was our last night for the WWF, who knows what could have happened? But it didn't work out like that. Five minutes into the match, Bret Hart let them off the hook by pinning Jacques and eliminating them from the match. And they were out of that ring like a shot.

We stayed in until close to the end of the match when Smash caught me out and eliminated the Bulldogs. When we got back in the dressing room, there was no sign of the Rougeaus. They were long gone. I said to Pat Patterson, "That was a short one wasn't it Pat?" He didn't say a word.

There was just one thing left for us to do before we had a last drink in the hotel bar. We had to give Matilda back to Vince. That dog had flown thousands of miles with us and chased our opponents across more rings than I could remember. I'll be honest, I'd never really cared much for her one way or the other; she was more Davey's dog than mine, but as our mascot, I thought Matilda had done a good job.

Vince shook our hands, saying, "All the best," and "See you soon." In four years, we must have caused enough trouble to have been fired a few times over. But I was pleased that we left on good terms, with no hard feelings.

How did I feel about leaving the WWF? I felt pretty good. My back was sore, which was no big deal. That was more or less permanent now. As we headed for the airport and the flight back to Calgary, I was looking forward to spending more time at home, and going back to Japan, which I had missed. But what I think I was looking forward to more than anything was slowing down the crazy pace of life I'd been living for too long.

Don't get me wrong, you had to work just as hard in Japan – in some ways even harder, but it was only for so many weeks, and then after that you knew you would get a break before the next tour. In the WWF, there was no break. You didn't take a week's holiday like you would in a normal job. If you took time off because you were injured, you didn't get paid. It was one long hard slog. I can remember one of the longest stretches we did, back in 1986 when we were the Tag Team Champions, we did a straight run of thirteen weeks without a break. When I complained to Pat Patterson, all he could say was, "You're the champions, what do you expect?"

So, yeah, I could live without all that. Funnily enough, Michelle didn't seem to think it was such a great idea having me back home. Within a couple of weeks, she was asking when I was going back. I told her I wasn't. I owned all my properties, everything was paid up, and if I wanted to, I could afford to retire for a while and live off the interest. But she kept begging and pleading, and begging and pleading. She said, "You've got to go back, you can't stay at home all the time."

I said, "Michelle, I'm tired and I'm sore. And I don't need to go back. I want to stay at home for a few weeks and rest." But she wouldn't let it go. In other words, she wanted me out of the way. I knew what the reason was. For the last four years she'd got used to having her freedom and living her own life, going out to nightclubs and restaurants. Now that I was back, I think she could see all that was going to change.

Stampede Wrestling had been running for a couple of years after

Vince had given the business back to Stu. But business wasn't very good. There were no big names and the names who were there had been there for years. One face who I wasn't surprised to see was Chris Benoit. That skinny little kid who'd told me he was going to be a wrestler like me, had done exactly that. He was still only young, maybe 20 or 21, but he was looking very good in the ring. He was a nice lad as well. Chris was a good listener and a good learner. He listened to me in the dressing room, and on the one occasion that I wrestled him in the ring. He wasn't a name then, and I know he went through some shit working for Stampede, but he came out of it as somebody I would definitely rate.

Brian Pillman was another new face, although he'd been with the promotion for a year or so, mainly in tag team action with Bruce Hart. He used to play football with the Cincinnati Bengals, and in my opinion, he might have been better staying there. I trained with Brian in Stu's gym and I showed him a few things, but I never really rated him as a pro wrestler. For example, he'd walk to the ring as a babyface, but with the exact same cocky attitude as when he was a heel. No smiling or shaking hands, or "high fives" with the fans. Later when he joined WCW and teamed up with Steve Austin as the Hollywood Blondes, he had exactly the same entrance as when he was a babyface in Stampede. Don't get me wrong, when he was with the right partner, he helped to make a great tag team, and I'll give him credit for being a good talker on the microphone, but the only move he did as a "flyer" was that big splash off the top rope.

But apart from that, with us coming straight from the WWF, and all that television exposure, Stu wanted the British Bulldogs for his main event. And unlike a lot of other wrestlers who left the WWF, he could have us. I had to hand it to Davey Boy Smith; for once, he'd made a good decision. A lot of wrestlers couldn't use their ring names once they'd left the company, because they were the property of the WWF. But when Vince McMahon made us the British Bulldogs in 1985, Davey, or more likely, his wife, had that name trademarked. And at the time, I gave Davey credit for doing that, but even that backfired on me a few years later.

When we went back to Stampede, the promotion was in a bit of a shambles. It wasn't organized, mainly because Stu was only around on television nights, and it seemed to be one or other of the Hart brothers who were running things. So you can imagine how surprised I was when Ross Hart came to me in the dressing room at the Pavilion and said, "Dynamite, we want you to take the book." In other words, he wanted me to be the foreman.

I said, "Why?"

Ross said, "The thing is, some of the other wrestlers are getting a bit out of hand, you know, on the road, and in hotels." I nodded; I knew exactly what he meant. He said, "The thing is Dynamite, the wrestlers respect you."

I thought about this for a minute, and then I said, "What's that got to do with anything?"

So Ross said, "Well, the other thing is, we thought if we put you in charge, you won't act as stupid as you usually do either."

So I said, "OK, yeah, I'll take it." I must admit, I was thinking more about money and maybe a little bonus, which, in fact, I never got. But at the time, I thought being the foreman might be a good move. And one of the first things I did as booker was to bring Big Blue, Don Muraco, into the territory. But first I had to sort things out with Bruce Hart, who I'm sure thought I wasn't suitable as a foreman. Bruce wanted to carry on running the promotion his way, but he had been coming up with some stupid ideas. He liked to go overboard; throwing fire in people's faces, or having wrestlers spraying stuff in each other's eyes. That was Bruce.

Anyway, we had a card in Medicine Hat one night and Don Muraco was wrestling a guy called Biff Wellington. Just before the match, Bruce Hart gave Muraco a bit of a pep talk, and I was standing right behind Bruce, listening to all the bullshit advice he was giving. Muraco looked at me – he knew I was in charge, he knew Bruce was trying to be in charge – and I just stood there shaking my head, as if to say, "Don't take any notice of what he's saying."

So Don said to Bruce, "Yeah, right OK," and Bruce disappeared.

I said to Don, "Look, just go in there, beat the man with whatever you want to beat him with, but have a good match. You don't need any fire-throwing, or being kicked in the balls, or throwing talcum powder in his face. And make him look good before you beat him."

You see in my opinion, if you go in, wipe the floor with a man, make him look like a piece of shit, and then just pin him – who have you beaten? Nobody. So Don went in, he had a good match with Biff, and then pinned him. It was a good match, but Bruce Hart was watching, and he thought otherwise. When he gets angry, he grits his teeth, shakes his head and throws a tantrum. That's true. And that's what he did when Don Muraco came back to the dressing room. He said, "Who the fuck told you to do that?"

Don shrugged and said, "Well, Dynamite is in charge."

Then Bruce came to me. He said, "Tom, I think you and me could be very good partners," as in joint foremen or bookers.

I said, "No Bruce, I'm just doing the job I've been told to do. There's no fire, no bullshit gimmicks, just good solid wrestling, like they do in Japan. The people don't want to see all that shit." In other words, no, I didn't think we'd have made a great booking team.

Within a week or so of being back in Stampede, we were filling the buildings. All round the loop, the same towns that we used to go to, we sold-out there as well. Just before Christmas, we beat Jerry Morrow and the Cuban Assassin to become the Stampede Tag Team Champions. It was only a couple of weeks away from our return visit to All Japan, and I figured, rather than have those belts sitting idle while we were away for a month, we might as well let somebody else have a crack at them. Davey Boy Smith went along with it, although if he thought he was the one who was going to be pinned, it would have been a different story.

We had a match coming up with Makkhan Singh and Vokkan Singh, otherwise know as Mike Shaw and Garry Albright. Mike, who wrestled as a lot of different characters over the years, including Bastion Booger in the wwf, was a good man. But his ability, with being so big, was very, well, marks out of ten, I could only give him two. Outside of the ring, he was a nice man. Garry was fairly new to pro wrestling, but he had a very good, strong Olympic style. Plus he was a big man, he had a mean face, and made a great heel. The day before our match, he came to me and said, "Tommy, you know me. I'm ok you know."

I said, "What do you mean Garry?"

"It's OK, I'll do whatever you want in the ring."

What he meant was, would I take care of him during the match? I said, "Don't worry." And I did take care of him. We wrestled a decent match, considering Mike Shaw's limitations, and 15 or 20 minutes into it, Garry hit me with a terrific belly-to-belly suplex and pinned me, one, two, three. The Singh's were the new Tag Team Champions.

That match didn't need to have ended like that. If we'd wanted to, we could have wiped the floor with them. But unlike the Harts, and unlike an awful lot of other wrestlers, I was never glorified. To me, win, lose or draw, the only thing that matters is having a good match.

The night after that match was New Year's Eve, but for the British Bulldogs, there was no time for celebrations. It had been three years since we'd wrestled in Japan, and as we made the connecting flight to Vancouver and then on to Tokyo, it felt like the old times again.

CHAPTER FOURTEEN

Nothing had really changed in All Japan, at least not in the way the promotion was run. In New Japan, when it was television night, you were always under pressure. The referee Peter Takahashi would be onto you all the time, saying, "You must do this, you must do that; you have to go so long," Always a lot of pressure. With All Japan, there was no pressure. They more or less left us to get on with it.

Some of the younger wrestlers, who were just starting out the last time I was there, had made a lot of progress. Jumbo Tsuruta and Tenryu were still the main event men, most of the time, but other wrestlers like Toshiaki Kawada, Mitsuhara Misawa, who was still wearing the Tiger Mask, had worked themselves into stronger positions on the card. Standards of wrestling were definitely higher in Japan, for the simple reason that good wrestlers were in the majority.

We were just getting back into our stride, when a week into that first tour Emperor Hirohito died and all the wrestling cards were cancelled for the next two days as a mark of respect. We still got paid though, and as you can imagine, we didn't let those two days go to waste. There were a lot of familiar faces on the tour – American wrestlers were always a strong feature of the promotion – and it was good to see some of my old friends like Danny Spivey, Stan Hansen, Abdullah the Butcher, and Terry "Bamm Bamm" Gordy.

The only ones who were missing were the Funk brothers, Terry and Dory Jr. We'd had some great times with them on our first run with All Japan. I remember one night when we'd been out drinking in Tokyo; myself, Terry Funk and Harley Race, and when it got late, we went back to my hotel room and started on the mini-bar. All of a sudden, for no apparent reason, Terry started smashing my room up; he broke the bed, and the lampshades, he more or less wrecked everything. I said, "I'm not being funny Terry, but what are you doing?"

He stopped, looked around at the mess, and said, "Don't worry Dyno. We'll go down to the front desk and report this."

And we did. Terry walked straight up to the receptionist and reported the damage. Then he said to her, "And I know who's done it. I saw the guy breaking the place up." The receptionist called the police, and when they arrived, they asked Terry where this man, who had allegedly caused all the damage, was. Terry said, "He's in Room 509." So the police went up to Room 509 and knocked on the door. It opened, and it was Dory, Terry's own brother. He was half asleep and had absolutely no idea what was going on. Those two were as different as chalk and cheese – Dory was always very serious and straightforward, Terry was like a wild man – but as brothers, they were close.

Terry used to talk a lot about the old days, when he and Dory Jr. took over their dad's promotion in Amarillo, Texas after he died. Business was down, and Terry was trying to think up new ways to bring more people in. He got on the microphone and said, "Ladies and gentlemen, next week we have a surprise for you. I am going to wrestle Terrible Ted the grizzly bear."

As you can imagine, the people were quite excited by the idea, but when the State Athletic Commission found out, they objected. They told Terry there was no way he could wrestle a grizzly bear in that building. Well, Terry thought about this, and the following week, he went to collect Terrible Ted, just as he had planned, and picked him up in his brother Dory's brand new Cadillac. On the way back, he bought a can of white paint, and painted Terrible Ted from head to foot – he got white paint all over Dory's new car – and then drove to the arena. Terry got on the microphone and said, "Ladies and gentlemen. I'm afraid Terrible Ted couldn't make it. But don't worry. I've managed to get a replacement. It's Snowy the polar bear."

Well, all those years later, Terry hadn't changed at all. He was still a little bit crazy. Just like the traffic in Tokyo at night time. We were all standing outside the hotel one night, the Bulldogs, Terry Gordy, Terry Funk and a few others. We'd all had a few beers. All of a sudden Terry Funk shouted, "Watch this." And he threw himself onto the bonnet of a passing car. As it stopped, he rolled off and pretended he was dead, with his arms stretched out wide. Somebody called the police, but even when they arrived, he just lay there, complete havoc all around him, not moving. There was nothing wrong with him, but for a few minutes he had everybody convinced that he was dead.

But the funniest thing I remember about Terry Funk was the day I walked into his hotel room to check if he was awake. The coach was waiting to leave for the next destination, all the other wrestlers were on board, but Terry hadn't shown his face. I went back up to his hotel room, saw that the door wasn't locked, and pushed it open. There was Terry, lying on the floor, fully clothed and covered in sick. His Stetson was all crushed, he had one boot on, and one bare foot propped up on the bed. I leaned over him and said, "Terry, what happened?"

The former NWA champion looked up at me – his eyes were all bloodshot and he could hardly open them – and he said, "Dyno, there's only one way to become a champeen."

I said, "What's that Terry?"

He said, "You've got to be a total fuck up."

It's been quite a few years since I last spoke to Terry, and that was one Christmas. I was in Calgary and I called his house in Texas. When he answered I said, "Hello Terry. It's only Dynamite calling to wish you a happy Christmas."

Terry said, "Oh Dyno, you've just ruined my fucking Christmas."

So yeah, I did like Terry Funk, in and out of the ring, and for me, All Japan wasn't the same without him. But there were a lot of few new faces. One American tag team who we met for the first time in Tokyo were the Nasty Boys, Brian Knobbs and Jerry Saggs. To be honest, the first time I saw them, I didn't think much of them. They were both big men, and Knobbs was always joking and laughing and dancing around, in that loud, obnoxious way that some people do. But they were new faces in Japan – in fact it was probably their first tour – so me and Davey were giving each other looks, as if to say, "Who the fuck do they think they are?"

A few days later, we arrived at the arena, looked on the board – because you never knew who you were wrestling until you got there on the night – and saw it was the British Bulldogs against the Nasty Boys.

We went to the ring. They were already in there with their Mohican haircuts, looking mean and vicious, as if they meant business. Just before the bell rang, I shook everything out, arms and legs, cracked my neck from side to side, like Mike Tyson used to do, and as I brushed my hand across my mouth, I muttered to Davey, "Don't sell anything." In other words, when they hit, don't respond, just crack them back.

The match got underway, and right from the bell, whatever moves they tried, we countered them. We didn't give them a thing. Basically we made them look like a pair of idiots. Don't get me wrong, to the crowd it looked like a great match, at least from the Bulldogs' point of view. Towards the end of the match, Davey made the tag and I got in with Knobbs. I gave him a turnbuckle, and said, "Clothesline. Don't move." I threw him in, and he stayed there. Then I ran at him as fast as I could, and hit him with the clothesline – only I accidentally caught him across his face and split his mouth open. A couple of minutes later, I pinned him, one, two, three. But even after I'd done that to Knobbs, they both came to see us after the match, shook our hands and said "Thank you very much."

About five minutes after we'd got back to the dressing room, the referee, Joe Higuchi walked in with a worried look on his face. He said, "Tom. Baba is very mad."

I said, "Why, what's wrong with Baba?"

"He is mad. You wrestled Nasty Boys, but Nasty Boys didn't do anything to Bulldogs."

I decided to act dumb. "I'm sorry, I'm not with you Joe."

He said, "You wrestled them, but they don't wrestle back."

I said, "Well they could have done if they'd tried. But they didn't try. We did our best Joe."

Well, we weren't to know that Baba had big plans for the Nasty Boys, but yes, we did kick the shit out them that night – in a working fashion. Funnily enough we also ended up becoming good friends; hitting the sushi bars, drinking beers and playing cards on the coach. We only ever had that one match with them, probably because Baba didn't trust us to wrestle them again. But if we had, I'd have been up in the air for them all night. That's true.

That four-week tour finished at the end of January, and we flew back to Vancouver and then on to Calgary. Davey had been quieter than usual for more or less all that tour, I mean he still had a laugh and a joke, but I had an idea something was bothering him. I didn't give it a lot of thought, because once we were back home, I had Bruce Hart to deal with.

Me and Bruce had our own opinions when it came to wrestling and how to promote it, and they were very different opinions. Because of that, there was always a little bit of tension between us, even going back to 1978 when we first met. Don't get me wrong, I never forgot that it was Bruce that brought me over to Canada in the first place, and I was grateful to him for that, but there was always that bit of friction between us, and just after I got back from Tokyo, it came to a head.

We had to go to Yellowknife, one of the towns on the Stampede loop. The wrestlers were still travelling around in a beaten up old van, with holes in the floor. It was very cramped, and with twelve of us inside, with our cases on our knees, a 700-mile trip was the shits, which was what we had ahead of us this particular day. We all got in the van apart from Bruce, who told us he was getting a lift with a friend and would catch up with us later.

So there we were, like sardines in a tin, driving along the highway, when all of a sudden this very nice Buick overtook us. I looked, and then I looked again. There was Bruce Hart, reclining in the passenger seat, feet up on the dashboard, hands behind his head; in other words, he was posing. He saw us all looking out of the van window, and he smiled and waved to us. I thought to myself, "Right."

When we got to Yellowknife I found Bruce in the dressing room. I said, "How was your trip?"

Bruce said, "Not too bad. A bit long." Then he started grinning like a Cheshire cat. He said, in a sarcastic tone, "Why, how was yours?"

"Mine was all right Bruce, but I'll tell you what you can do for me."

He said, "What's that?"

"You can get on the phone and get me an airplane, or a helicopter, and have me flown back to Calgary."

He said, "I can't do that Tom, but I'll tell you what, you can come back in the car with me."

Bruce was still smirking, as if he didn't really mean it. And I must admit, I'd had a few beers in the van on the way – just like everybody else – so I said, "And you can fuck off. I came here like this, I'll go back like this." He just sniggered, and in that split-second, I lost my temper, and, bang, cracked him one straight in the jaw, and walked out of the dressing room.

I was still mad when I went to the ring with Davey. And when I got there, I realized that the ring announcer was the same person who had been driving the Buick. So during the match, I smacked him one as well. We were the last match on the card, so the fact that he couldn't do any more announcing that night didn't make a lot of difference.

Somebody called the police, and straight after the match, Bruce and his friend made a dash for the Stampede van and locked themselves in while they waited for them to arrive. I went out after them; I was knocking on the window, shouting at Bruce to wind it down, but he wouldn't. To be honest, he looked scared to death. In the middle of all this the police arrived and they physically held me back while those two got out of the van, into their car and drove away.

A week or so after that incident, it was Owen Hart's wedding. He was getting married to Martha, and me and Michelle were on the guest list. But the day before the wedding, I had a call from Ross Hart. He said, "Tom, what time will you be leaving for Edmonton tomorrow?"

I said, "What do you mean Ross?"

He told me, "Look Tom, if you turn up at the wedding, Bruce won't come. And if he doesn't come, Owen will be upset and Martha will be upset."

I got the picture. I said, "I leave at five."

And the next day, which was Saturday, I did leave at five. Do you think I went to Edmonton to wrestle? Course I didn't. I went to the pub instead. When Stu called to ask what had happened, I made some excuse about my car breaking down, and he didn't say any more about it. The following Friday was television night, and it was Bruce who came up to me and held his hand out. He said, "No hard feelings. We're still friends." So we shook hands, and that was the end of it. I don't know whether he really meant it, but we both knew we had to work with each other, and at least on the surface, he was OK with me. So were the rest of the family, apart from Dean.

For some reason, Dean wouldn't let the matter drop. He wasn't that really involved in the wrestling business anyway, but he barged into my dressing room one night, being a bit cocky, and saying things which could have stirred up another load of trouble, which I didn't particularly want. The truth was, Dean Hart was very ill at that time with kidney disease. But it didn't stop him mouthing off and threatening me, so I started shouting back. Ross walked in right in the middle of all this, stood between us, and said, "Tom, don't. You'll kill him." I would never have touched Dean anyway, but it didn't make any difference. A month later, Dean Hart was dead. The kidney disease had killed him.

The British Bulldogs were booked on another tour of All Japan that summer, but the reality was, as a tag team, the Bulldogs were just about through. We'd more or less finished wrestling in tag for Stampede, and Davey spent most of his time in singles matches. But Baba wanted us on that tour as a tag team, and I suppose Davey wasn't ready to give that sort of money up. Not then anyway.

I'll be honest, this time around with All Japan we weren't as strong, name-wise, as we had been back in 1985. For one thing, I'd really started to cut down on the steroids. I still took the odd shot, but nothing like the amount I'd been taking over the years. And even though I was still working out hard every day, I lost quite a bit of weight. If that bothered Baba, he never said anything about it. I think he just wanted me there. I definitely felt better in myself for not taking it, but in the ring, knowing how my body used to look, seeing how some of the Japanese wrestlers' bodies still looked, I didn't feel too good about myself.

So we couldn't get to the top of the card. Where we had been. I can remember the very first time we wrestled Jumbo Tsuruta and Genchiro Tenryu in the Yokohama Arena in 1985, when they were the two top men. I mean, in the annual tag team tournament, the final match would nearly always be Stan Hansen and Bruiser Brody against Tsuruta and Tenryu. And when we wrestled them, just on that one occasion, we went to a 30-minute draw, which, for us, was fantastic. And they were good to wrestle. I know with a lot of other tag teams they could be a bit awkward and single-minded; they liked to do everything their way.

I wrestled Tenryu in a singles match in Osaka one night. At that time, I liked to get my opponent in the corner and finish very fast with a sharp elbow, right in the face. I'm not talking about close to their face, I mean in it. I knew Tenryu liked his matches to be "self, self, self," but I thought to myself, "Tonight, there's going to be a contest first."

And that's what it was. I nailed Tenryu with ten of my sharpest elbows. His chin was opened up, and when I looked, there was a river of blood pouring down over his neck and chest. All the people were going, "Oohhh." The match finished and, fair enough, I did get beat. But when I saw Tenryu afterward, he was over the moon with that match. He smiled and said, "Kid-san. Very sharp elbow tonight."

We also wrestled the Malenko brothers, Joe and Dean, at the Korakuen Hall, and to be honest, when I first saw the bill, I thought it was going to look terrible. We were babyfaces; they were babyfaces, plus, the Malenkos favoured a shooting style of wrestling. I thought, "What are we going to do here?" I went to see Joe, who was the eldest of the two brothers, and asked him what he wanted to do, style-wise.

He said, "Well, what do you think?"

I said, "I don't really care. We can shoot on the floor if you want, or what do you think about maybe mixing it with a bit of professional wrestling?"

They were both happy to do that, and it turned out to be a great match. The submissions looked great, and we kept the pace of the match up with some strong professional wrestling. The crowd loved it. I got along fine with Joe and Dean, and as wrestlers, I rated the both of them. Karl Gotch had trained them, and as usual, boasted to everybody about what a good job he'd done; so good, he reckoned Joe was unbeatable on the floor. And Joe was such a gentleman, very polite and soft-spoken, but he did know the job. Dean and Joe were both quiet, and definitely not jokers. They took their work very seriously.

We'd just finished a match at Budokan Hall in Tokyo one night when there was a knock at the dressing room door. I must admit, when I opened it, the last person I expected to see was Vince McMahon. I had no idea what he was doing in Tokyo – probably a little bit of business with another promoter – but he seemed genuinely pleased to see us. He walked in with a big smile on his face, looked at the pair of us and said, "Bulldogs, you're looking good."

But apart from that, Vince McMahon wasn't at the Budokan Hall on a social visit. He said to me, "I'm surprised I haven't heard from you Tom," meaning, how come we hadn't been in touch asking him for our jobs back.

I said, "Vince, when I said I was finished, I meant it." But I don't think he believed me, because not long after that, he called me again, at home, and asked when I was coming back. I said, "I've already told you Vince, I'm not coming back."

He said, "Look, I want you to do a television in Maple Leaf Gardens with the Brainbusters. They could piledrive you on the stage, we'll air it coast-to-coast, then in six-weeks' time, you come back for the return matches."

I said, "So the Brainbusters piledrive me on national television?"

"That's right."

I said, "Thanks for asking me Vince, but no thanks." I didn't hear from him again.

Apart from the fact that I wouldn't go back to the wwf on principle, I knew that the British Bulldogs were just about through as a team anyway. It wasn't my decision, Davey Boy Smith had already decided that without telling me.

On one flight home from Japan we were playing cards, 100 Yen, maybe £4, a game, which I always won, because I knew how to fix the cards. Things hadn't been going too well between us for a while, we weren't speaking to each other properly, and there was a bad atmosphere. During that flight from Tokyo to Vancouver, I said to him, "Dave, why don't we get our act together and do something good as the Bulldogs?" He never answered me, he just shrugged. A few days after we'd got back a mutual friend called round at my home, which was only a mile or so from Davey's house. He'd just been to see Davey, and I said to him, "How come he never comes here to see me?"

He said, "Well funnily enough Tom, Davey thinks it should be you that goes to see him." Which was what I did most of the time anyway.

But that, for me, was the moment when I realized it was over for the British Bulldogs. There was no argument, no trouble, no big dramatic split, the two of us just went our separate ways.

While I'd been away, Stu had hired a couple of new wrestlers, one of which was a guy called Mitch Snow. Now that was a name I really didn't expect to hear again; not after what had happened in Japan a few years earlier.

Mitch Snow was a big-mouthed prick. He loved to tell you he was from the Carolinas, but he said it a way that implied if you were from anywhere else, you were a piece of shit. So I took a dislike to him more or less straight away. I think everybody on that tour did.

Sometimes we would wrestle six-man tags, where, for example, me and Davey might team up with Misawa. On this night it was Snow and two Japanese wrestlers against Don Muraco and two other Japanese wrestlers. Towards the end of the match, Snow dived across Muraco for a cross body block. When he got up from it, he looked at Don and shook his head, as if to say, "You nearly dropped me you fucking idiot."

Muraco caught the look and said to him, under his breath, "You piece of crap."

Mitch Snow got on everybody's nerves. If the Bulldogs played a bit of a prank on somebody, we would all have a laugh about it, except for Snow who would say, "Hah, you Bulldogs could never catch me out." Anyway this night he stood behind us watching the card game, and he kept chiming in saying, "You played that card wrong, didn't yah?" Everybody more or less ignored him, but me and Davey looked up at each other and nodded.

Three days before the end of that tour, we were wrestling a six-man tag, the Bulldogs and Don Muraco against Snow and two Japanese wrestlers, one of which was Shinji Takano, the brother of George "The Cobra" Takano. I said to Shinji, "I'm going to do him tonight."

He said, "How?"

"When Muraco goes for the piledriver, we, my tag team partner and me, will spike him."

He looked at me in surprise and said, "Kid-san, are you sure?" I nodded.

Sure enough, Muraco went for the big piledriver, and when the time was right, I got on one rope, Davey got on the other, we jumped, grabbed one leg each and spiked him, straight into the mat. After the match, when Snow had cleared his head, Joe Higuchi took him to one side and said, "Tomorrow, you go home, for your own safety and welfare."

But he didn't get away that easily. Later that night, Dan Kroffat took him out to Roppongi, which is the redlight district of Tokyo, for a few beers. While he was gone, we found some scissors and got into his hotel room. And I would say that Mitch Snow definitely lived to regret saying those words, "You Bulldogs will never get me."

So I was surprised when he turned up in Stampede Wrestling, although probably not as surprised as Mitch Snow when he found out I was the foreman. Part of my job was to sort out any trouble and keep the other wrestlers in line. We were in Lethbridge one night when some of the other wrestlers, just for a joke, decided to tie one of the lads up in a blanket from the hotel bed, fasten him to the back of the van and drag him along the road. It was icy, so the road was slippy, and they weren't driving very fast, but I'm sure, from where he was lying, Mitch Snow from the Carolinas didn't see the funny side of it.

I was the foreman. I was supposed to be in charge. Well, you can imagine all the jokes and pranks I'd played on people over the years. So when I found out about this one, I thought, "Tommy, what are you going to do here?" I mean, if the shoe had been on the other foot, I probably would have driven the van myself. But I decided to be responsible, and I said "Whoever's done this, if I find out, they will be fired." Well, it was Brian Pillman, wasn't it, and by rights I should have fired him on the spot, but to tell you the truth, by this point I'd had enough of being in charge. Deep down, I think I'd had enough of Stampede Wrestling.

As for Mitch Snow, he must have thought he would never see the back of the Dynamite Kid, because a year or so later, I got a call from a promoter in Portland, Len Denton, who asked me if I was interested in some work. I told him I was.

"That's great," he said, "but there is one condition."

"What's that?"

He said, "We've a wrestler here by the name of Mitch Snow. If you come down, he wants your assurance that you'll leave him alone."

"I'll tell you what Len. Let's forget it."

Johnny Smith, who, if you remember, was Ted Betley's nephew, John Hindley, was still with Stampede. He'd also worked a couple of tours for New Japan, and was doing OK for himself. Johnny had turned heel in Stampede and was wrestling as Johnny Smith, The British Bruiser. I always preferred wrestling as a heel anyway, plus I would sooner wrestle in tag matches, so we got together and became The British Bruisers. Johnny was a lot quieter than Davey, and was definitely not a prankster – he would never dream of doing half the things that I'd done. But he laughed as much as anybody at the things I did to other wrestlers.

Like the time I nearly caused a fight between Bobby Fulton and Tommy Stanton. Bobby had a habit of brushing his hair and looking at himself in the mirror, while Tommy was always cleaning his glasses. They were very good friends outside the ring, but on this night they were wrestling each other. While they were gone, I put Bobby's brush down the toilet in one dressing room and Tommy's glasses down the toilet in the other. When they came back from their match I went straight up to Tom and said, "I'm not being funny Tom, you know I like a good laugh and a joke."

He laughed and said, "Oh I know that Tom."

I said, "But I'm not being blamed for this one. I just saw Bobby put your glasses down the toilet."

I told Bobby the same thing; that I'd seen Tom throw his brush down the toilet, just for a laugh. I said to him, "It's out of order this Bobby. It's not right." Bear in mind, I was supposed to be the foreman at that time, so I said to Bobby, "And I don't want my name mentioned in this. I'm not being blamed for something I haven't done." The next thing was, the two of them were going at it like crazy, but my name didn't get mentioned.

One wrestler really did try to blame me for something I hadn't done. But he didn't get away with it. Sandy Scott, whose real name was Jim Palmer, came to Calgary from Scotland. In fact, it was me that brought him over to Stampede. He rang Stu up one day and said to him, "Stu, I can't wrestle, I've got diarrhea really bad, and I know for certain that Dynamite's done me."

When I got back to Calgary from wrestling round the loop, Stu called and said, "What have you done to Sandy? He's had the shits all week and couldn't wrestle."

I said, "Look Stu, even if it was me that had done him, I wouldn't tell you anyway. But you'll have to believe me that this time it really wasn't me." Which was absolutely true. "I'll tell you where he's been. At home all week with a woman." Sandy Scott did have a reputation with the ladies.

The next time I saw Sandy was on the Saturday when we were getting ready to go to Edmonton. I went to the back of the van where the cases were, looked for Sandy's, picked it up and threw it right up into a tree. It stuck there. The wrestlers climbed into the van, I sat down opposite Sandy and said to him, "What's this you've been telling everybody that I'm supposed to have done you?" He didn't say a word, just looked at me in an arrogant fashion and then looked away. So I clocked him in the face, not hard, but enough to annoy him.

He jumped up and said, "Right, that's it. I'm not having this." And he got out of the van and went to get his case. I just sat there, acting very casual. A minute later he was back. He climbed back in the van, came up to me and said, "Where's my fucking case?"

I said, "Don't look at me like that when there are 12 other people in this van."

He ignored me. "What have you done with it?"

I said, trying not to laugh, "No. Sorry Sandy. You're barking up the wrong tree altogether." But the truth was, I had become disillusioned with Stampede Wrestling. I'm sure I wasn't the only one.

Chris Benoit was really shaping up and I knew that with his style he would go down well in Japan. He was ready for it. There was a little Japanese guy in Calgary who we used to call Tokyo Joe, and quite a few years ago he'd been involved in a bad road accident. It was winter and the van with all the wrestlers inside had broken down. Everybody climbed out and started trying to push the van from behind. A truck came along, skidded, and ran into the back of the Stampede van. Everybody except Tokyo Joe managed to jump clear, but he took the full brunt of it. In fact he almost lost both his legs, but they lay him down and packed a load of snow around them, and in the end he only lost one, which he had replaced with a wooden leg.

I had a few arguments with Joe about other wrestlers, in particular, about Chris Benoit. Over the years, Joe had sent a lot of wrestlers over to Japan, to IWE and New Japan, but he always kept ten percent of their guarantee. At one point I was trying to get Chris Benoit a deal with All Japan, but not with the intention of making any money out of it for myself. I believed Chris had the style and the ability to go places in Japan. In fact, if it wasn't for the difference in age, I would definitely have had Chris Benoit as a tag partner; that's how high I rated him. Anyway, when Joe heard that I was trying to help Chris get some work in Japan, he accused me of stealing his "boys" from him, I said to him, "Well why do you always take their money?"

Joe said, "If you had any sense, you'd do the same."

I said, "And if I had some gas, I'd throw it over that wooden leg of yours and set the bloody thing on fire."

There had been a few problems with Stampede and things came to a head when Stu paid me a couple of bad cheques. They were way short of what they should have been, so after the matches, I went to see him, told him I was finishing, and handed the cheques back. I said, "Evidently, you need these more than me." Stu didn't say anything, but he took them off me. And at that moment, I believed I was finished with Stampede Wrestling.

I thought about the Brainbusters, Anderson and Blanchard, going into the WWF from what was then Jim Crockett Promotions, and figured it might be worth trying to return the favour. So I called Ric Flair, who was now head booker for the promotion.

He said, "Hello Dynamite. What can I do for you?" When I told him I was looking for some work, the lying bastard said, "Oh we don't do that kind of thing anymore."

I said, "What do you mean?"

He said, "We don't have wrestlers switching promotions anymore.

So I'm sorry. I really can't help you." I didn't believe him for a minute. What he really meant was, he knew I had a reputation and he didn't want me upsetting anybody in his promotion.

As the year came to a close, Stampede Wrestling went down for the count. Business was so bad that Stu had no choice but to wind the promotion up. But he wanted to go out on a high note, which I could understand. I'd just got back from a tag team tournament in Japan, when he called me at home and said, "Kid, we're closing down and I need you to do me a favour. Will you do a Streetfight with Owen for the last night of Stampede?"

I didn't want to let him down, so I said I would. The Streetfight was the main event for a sold-out crowd in the Pavilion, on the very last night of Stampede Wrestling. I'd helped to train Owen when he was a kid, but I'd never wrestled him before. Because it was the last night, I knew Stu would want Owen to win, partly because in Stampede, the Harts always did, and partly, I think, because of what I'd done to Bruce. Anyway, Owen did win; not by pinfall, as Stu expected, but by count out. Which didn't matter anyway, because it was a great match. Better than anyone imagined. A couple of days later, Stu called again. He said, "We did great business on that last night, do you think you could do another one, a Streefight II?"

So, again, I said, "No problem." But before Stu could say anything about the finish – I knew what he wanted – I said, "But I'll do it my way."

The crowd were whipped up into a frenzy that night. After the first Streetfight, they were expecting something good, and I wasn't going to disappoint them. I didn't even wait for Owen to get to the ring. As he walked down the aisle, with all the fans cheering him, I ran up behind him and smashed him over the head with a trash can. Bear in mind, Owen was a lot younger than me, but we still had a good, hard match, physically tough and very violent. We both bled all over the place. Owen backdropped me out of the ring, but the referee didn't see it. I lay there on the concrete, and then Owen came out and hit me with a piledriver, right onto the concrete, which split my head open. Somehow, I managed to get back in the ring, and we really went at it, blasting away at each other.

Johnny Smith was at ringside, and as I caught Owen and held him from behind, I signalled to Johnny to get in the ring and help me out. He ran in, and threw a punch at Owen's face with a knuckle-duster, but somehow, Owen dropped to his knees, and Johnny caught me – bang – straight in the mush instead. Owen stood up, drop kicked Johnny over the top rope and small packaged me for the pin, one, two, three. The Harts had their final moment of glory, the crowd got a fantastic match, and Owen, bless him, proved what a good wrestler he had turned out to be.

But in 1989, that was it for Stampede Wrestling. In all the years I was with the promotion, I worked really hard for Stu, and I know for a fact that I helped to turn business around when the promotion was struggling back in the early eighties. What do you suppose I got at the end of it? Not a "thank you," not a "kiss my arse;" nothing. But that's wrestling.

CHAPTER FIFTEEN

With Stampede closed, and my career with the WWF a whole year behind me, All Japan was all I had left. I wasn't worried. Although we were no longer the British Bulldogs, Baba was still booking The Dynamite Kid and Davey Boy Smith on a regular basis. On a couple of the tours, Johnny Smith joined us for some six-man tag matches. It wasn't easy getting Johnny in there, because he'd been working for New Japan, and things were still a bit sensitive when it came to wrestlers switching promotions.

Riki Choshu and his Army had followed us to All Japan in 1984, but Choshu had since returned to New Japan, along with a lot of the wrestlers who'd originally jumped with him. I don't know whether there was still some bad feelings about the Bulldogs leaving New Japan, but six years on, when I tried to get Johnny released from there, nobody would take me on. I rang a Japanese agent who I knew, who was based out in Kansas City, but who was very well-connected with the wrestling promotions in Japan. I said to him, "Would you please ask Inoki if Johnny Smith can wrestle for Baba?"

Straight away he said no. "Inoki and Baba have an agreement. Nobody switches promotions anymore."

End of story. A couple of days later, I called again and told him I needed this as a favour. I said, "Surely they can make this one exception."

Again, he wouldn't take me on. I called him a third time. Eventually, he said he would call Inoki and ask. But no promises. So I was surprised when he came back to me and said, "Inoki says OK, but definitely this is the last time for switching promotions." So I thanked him for his help, and then he said, "How much do you want?" In other words, what was my cut?

I said, "I don't want anything. Whatever Baba pays will be Johnny's guarantee."

"OK. How much does Johnny Smith want?"

I knew Johnny was earning about $1,000 a week with Inoki, so I said, "He will need $1,800 a week."

He went back to Baba, called me back, and the price was agreed. The deal was done.

If Johnny Smith had any faults, it was that he was always too shy to ask for more money. The trouble is, in wrestling, unless you ask, promoters don't offer.

Early in 1990 I had a call from Big Blue, Don Muraco. He was working for a promotion in New Zealand, of all places, and wanted me and Johnny to go over there to do a ten-day tour. At first I said I would go, but the first few weeks of that year, I was having a lot of trouble with my shoulder. I was in so much pain, I could hardly move it. I rang Johnny Smith and told him.

Johnny said, "Don't cancel Tommy. I really need us to go to New Zealand. I'm broke."

I said, "Well I'm not broke John, but I'm not far off."

And because I didn't want to let him or Don Muraco down, I said I would go. We went to Auckland and Wellington, the two biggest cities in New Zealand, and wrestled a tag team called the American Pitbulls. They looked the part too, a couple of tough, stocky buggers, and decent wrestlers as well. One night they put us on with two of the Guerreros, Hector and Mando. They were part of a very famous wrestling family, and they knew it. So, in the ring that night, I did my usual pre-match shake-out and warm-up – I couldn't crack my neck like I used to, because two of the discs in my neck were now starting to deteriorate. I watched those two across the ring, and said under my breath to Johnny, "Don't give them anything."

We didn't take them on at all. They were only two little short bastards anyway. The Mexican style, as I've told you before, works the opposite way round to the American and Japanese styles. Instead of taking your left arm or left leg, they'd go for your right arm and right leg. And it takes some getting used to. But apart from that, we gave Hector and Mando a hard time in the ring that night. I think we were supposed to go the full week with them, but by the end of that first match, they'd had enough, and we never wrestled them again.

We did our ten days and went back to Calgary, but, I could see that New Zealand promotion was going to struggle. They tried to bring some bigger names in, and I know that Big Blue called Vince and The Bushwhackers went out and did a couple of matches in their home country, but business was never that good, and not long after that, the promotion closed.

There were a couple more tours that the three of us, Davey, Johnny and me, did for All Japan that year, working six-man tags or in different combinations of tag teams. Occasionally we did some singles matches, and one that I remember very well was one that I had against Mick Foley, known to the fans then as Cactus Jack.

For me, Mick was a good wrestler, but he did a lot of dangerous moves, and I'll give him credit for that because he was a big man. I mean, he would slam you outside the ring onto the floor, get up on the apron outside the ropes, run down the apron and drop a big elbow on you. He tried to do it to me, but I moved out of the way, so he took the full brunt of that landing himself. I had a good match with him, but I must admit, with it being Japanese-style, when Mick went in he was white, but when he came out he was a little bit black and blue. We both were.

On this night in Japan, Cactus Jack took a great clothesline. And we had a terrific match. You see, he had the heart for the Japanese-style of wrestling, and his style was perfect for Japan. Over there, the fans love a wrestler who will take risks. When I said he was a dangerous wrestler, he was more dangerous to himself than to his opponent. He impressed the people by messing himself up and by making his opponents look good. But I know he did hurt himself; all those big bangs and hard knocks, win, lose, or draw, just to please the fans and the other wrestlers. He just got it in his head that he was going to go out there and do it, and in that respect, we were very similar. The only difference was that Mick was always a bit more reckless than me. But all credit to him: Mick Foley did great for himself in Japan, and even better with the wwf, and in my opinion, he deserved it.

I don't recall who was the babyface or who was the heel in that match, and to be honest, in Japan, it never really mattered. Not to the fans anyway. I always went to the ring as a heel when I was over there, but in a match, with, for example, Misawa, when I was onto him, the fans would chant, "MI-SA-WA, MI-SA-WA." But when the match swung the other way, they didn't cheer like they would in America. They'd chant, "KI-DO, KI-DO." Good guy or bad guy, in Japan, as long as you wrestled as hard as you could, the people didn't care.

I know that the best of my ability in 1990 was nothing like it had been five years earlier. I could do more or less the same moves as before – even the snap suplex – with smaller men. But with tall men, it was very hard, and I was always worried about doing more damage to my back. For example, the nip-up, which usually followed a drop kick from the top rope, became a struggle, because that move puts all the strain on your lower back.

I was in a tag team one night, myself and Davey Boy Smith against Tsuyoshi Kikuchi and Masa Fuchi. I was on my back in the ring, and Fuchi had me by the wrist. I was about to do a nip-up, but suddenly realized I probably wasn't going to make it. I looked up at Fuchi, and under my breath said, "Fuch. Help." And as I went for the nip-up, he gave me just a little bit of lift.

With somebody the size of Baba, I really struggled. I wrestled him in a tag match one night, myself and Johnny Smith against Baba and André the Giant. I could suplex Baba OK, but when I tried to snap him; with him being so long and tall, I just couldn't do it. But I'll give Baba credit, he'd still take his bumps; even my piledriver, which a lot of Japanese wrestlers didn't like, he took it. When he gave you a chop to the forehead, the fans used to go wild, and a lot of his opponents, well, they'd throw themselves around like fish out of water. But I would never over-sell those chops, because they never looked hard enough, not even to the fans.

I'd known Johnny Smith as a friend and as a wrestler for years, but it took me a while to get used to working with him as a tag team. Don't get me wrong, Johnny was, and still is, a very hard-worker, maybe technically better than Davey Boy Smith. But after all those years together, Davey and me had our routine in the ring down to perfection. I mean we could wrestle with our eyes closed and not miss a spot. I'd run towards him, he'd press slam me and I'd go into a head-butt right onto my opponent. When I tried the same thing with Johnny, he'd get me up, and then start to lose his balance. And that's worrying when you're the one up in the air. So in that respect, Davey Boy Smith was easier to work with. And after spending so long working with somebody, doing the same thing night after night, you would imagine that you got to know them very well. But, in November 1990, after nearly a decade in the ring with Davey, I realized I didn't know him at all.

The annual tag tournament, which is a big event for All Japan, was coming up. It always took place three weeks into December, but just two weeks before we were supposed to go, I heard that my tag team partner for the tournament, Davey Boy Smith, had gone back to the WWF. When I say that I heard, I did – literally. Not from Davey, but from somebody else, because Davey couldn't, or wouldn't, tell me himself. I had no idea how long he'd been planning it, but he had never mentioned that he was thinking about going, or that he'd spoken to Vince McMahon. Which I didn't care about one way or the other. Davey had a wife and kids to look after, he had a mortgage to pay, and he had to earn the money. So he went back to the WWF. No big deal. What hurt me the most was that he didn't tell me he wouldn't be going to Japan for the tag tournament. In other words, he let me down. But I never got the chance to ask him about it, because I never saw or heard from Davey Boy Smith again. That's true.

I suppose I was angry and upset at what he'd done, but I didn't have time to think about it. I needed a tag partner, quick, and was glad when Johnny Smith said he would go instead. But that wasn't the end of it. When I tried to get my visa sorted for the tournament, the agent who usually arranged it for me in California said to me, "Dynamite, are you all right?"

I said, "I'm fine, why?"

He said, "We almost cancelled you from the tour. Somebody called the office in Tokyo and told them you had been in a car crash. A very bad car crash."

In fact, they were about to replace me with somebody else, because they didn't think I was going to make it. I said, "Well I am fine, and I haven't been in a car crash."

The only people who knew I was going to Japan, and who knew how to contact the office in Tokyo were Davey Boy Smith. And his wife. So I figured that somebody, maybe out of spite, decided to call the office to try and wreck my plans. I don't know why they would want to do that, but to this day, I'm convinced that they did.

So now it was the New British Bulldogs who entered the All Japan tag tournament in early December. All Japan was going through a few changes as well. Genricho Tenryu, one of the top men for years, had left the company to set up his own promotion, scs. That had cleared the way for some of the younger wrestlers like Mitsuhara Misawa, who had finally got rid of the Tiger Mask, and Toshiaki Kawada. And behind them were the next generation of wrestlers waiting to take their place on the card.

There was one young Japanese guy who stuck out in my mind as a very talented wrestler. His name was Kenta Kobashi, and he was what I would describe as being completely dedicated to wrestling. He was always watching, always training, always working out. I wrestled him quite a few times in singles matches and he was getting better, and stronger and harder all the time. But he was also a very nice young lad, always very polite and respectful. One night before a match I told him that I thought he was good enough to beat me. He looked at me as though I was mad. He said, "On, no, no, no. I beat Dynamite, the people will cry."

I told him it didn't matter, that I believed he was ready for it. But he wouldn't listen; I don't think he felt ready. Anyway we went out and had a real battle in the ring, bang, bang, corner to corner, until finally, I sent him flying into the rope. As he came back, I caught him in a bear hug, leaned back, as if I was going into a bridge, and dropped his neck across the top rope. As he bounced back from that, I floored him and pinned him, one, two, three. But look at him now, Kobashi looks like a million dollars. Oh yeah, I did rate Kobashi. I knew he was going to be good.

Some wrestlers didn't seem to age at all. Abdullah the Butcher had been in the business for years. He'd been a big draw in Calgary, a fairly big draw in Atlanta for Jim Barnett, and he was definitely a big draw in Japan. I always got along with Abdullah, and he was always very good to me, but if anybody fucked about with him in that ring, he was a bastard. Abdullah wasn't a fighting man, but he could do a lot of damage to you in that ring, as in splitting your head right open. Even the Japanese young boys just sitting round the ring watching the matches – if they got in his way, he'd rip them open as well. I've seen him do it.

Years ago, he was wrestling a Canadian called Angelo Mosca, who was a big heavyweight, and had a reputation for taking liberties – he was a bully with some of the smaller wrestlers. Abdullah, who was a little bit lighter at that time, had an idea that Mosca might try something in the ring this particular night. And he did. He press slammed Abdullah up into the air, ready to throw him to the mat. Abdullah put both hands on Mosca's throat – bear in mind his fingernails were – well – let's just say they were razor sharp – and he said, "Put me down champ," in that quiet little voice of his. Not "throw me down," but "put me down." And as soon as Mosca felt those razors on his neck, he placed him, very carefully, back down on his feet. From then on, Mosca was like a big baby in that ring. In my opinion, Abdullah was one of those wrestlers, if you go with the flow with him, he'd do the same for you. But if you didn't, you'd come out needing quite a few stitches.

Stan Hansen was another American who was getting on a bit, but never lost his popularity with the Japanese fans. That was because he always delivered the goods. Stan was a very hard worker – a hard wrestler – and he kept himself in good condition. He always looked the part in the ring, because when he connected, kicks or punches, you knew about it. You always came out black and blue and aching all over after a match with Stan.

It was during those tours with All Japan that I became a very close friend of Danny Spivey. We'd met in the WWF, got into a few scrapes, and spent a lot of time messing around. But his reputation as a hard man was legendary. I know because I found out the hard way.

I got on the coach one morning just before we set off for Yokohama, and I walked passed Danny who was already in his seat. I said to him, "All right Danny?" Spivey didn't answer. I said, "Maybe you didn't hear me." Still no answer. So I walloped him across the back of his head with my metal case. Without any warning, he sprang up out of his seat and went for me, so I ran as fast as I good to the back of the coach. I shouted at Johnny Smith to move out of the way, and Johnny got up to move, but Danny was nearly on top of me. I was trying to get behind Johnny, but Danny just curled this huge punch right round Johnny's body into my ribs. I crumpled to the seat, all the breath was knocked out of me. Danny never said a word. He turned round and strode back down the coach to his seat. Do you think I left it at that? I waited a few minutes until I'd got my breath back, picked up my case again and crept down the coach. This time I really cracked him, I mean really cracked him right across his head. I said to him, "I said, maybe you didn't hear me." This time, Danny didn't move, and I know to this day, he still has a lump on his head. So I would say we were more than good friends; we developed a mutual respect for each other as well.

Steve "Dr. Death" Williams came to All Japan that year and tagged up with Terry "Bamm Bamm" Gordy. They became a very strong tag team, and although they were bigger than me and Johnny, we had some great tag matches with them. The reason was that although they were names and we were names, nobody was trying to outdo the other, or look better than the other. There was no animosity between us. It was all give and take in the ring, and after the match, we'd come back to the dressing room and everybody was happy.

We spent a lot of time with them socially as well. After, say, the second week of a five-week tour, Steve would stand up, look at the calendar on his watch and shout, "Only three weeks to go." And he had this great big booming voice – worse than mine – that went all around the bar or the restaurant.

Other times we'd hit the sushi bars and restaurants – not the big expensive ones in the main part of the city, but the smaller ones off the beaten track. After all those years, I got to know the place like the back of my hand. In fact, I would say I got to know Tokyo better than I knew Wigan. And probably better than Calgary.

It came as no big surprise when Michelle and I decided to separate. It was sad, because she was expecting our third child, but the truth was, we'd grown so far apart, we couldn't carry on living together any more. At the end of January, 1991, I flew back to Calgary from Japan; back to an empty house. There was an airline ticket waiting for me on the kitchen table; a one-way ticket to England. I packed one little suitcase – I left most of my stuff behind – put all the money I'd made on that tour – at least $30,000 – down on the table, and just kept a few dollars to see me through the flight. Then I left for the airport. I was leaving behind my two children, Bronwyne and Marek, and a third one on the way, but apart from them, I knew there was nothing left for me to stay in Calgary for.

It was almost exactly 13 years since I'd left England for Canada. Back then I was 19 years old, just a kid, with no idea of what was ahead of me. I can still see the look on my dad's face as he waved me off at the airport, and all I had was £20 in my pocket. And now, as the plane touched down in England, I looked at the few dollars I had left in my pocket and smiled. I'd broke even, I'd come back with £20 as well.

CHAPTER SIXTEEN

So there I was, back where I started. I had no money, no job – at least not until the next tour for All Japan – and nowhere to live, and for a while I moved back in with my mum and dad. But not for long. I was feeling a bit depressed, so I called Danny Spivey at his house in Tampa, Florida, and told him I was coming over. He was great about it, and picked me up at the airport, but as he drove us back to his house he told me he was going to Japan for a couple of weeks. He said, "It doesn't matter Tommy. I want you to stay, and while you are here, my house is your house, and my car," – which was a brand new Lincoln Continental – "is your car."

So, while Danny was away I relaxed, lazed around, and did absolutely nothing. To be honest, I couldn't remember the last time I'd been able to that. A couple of days before I was due to fly home to England, Danny arrived back from Japan. He told me before I left that he had something special lined up for me. He said, "Tommy, don't eat a thing today. Have a couple of beers, but don't eat anything."

I don't know what it was that he gave me, this stuff was wrapped in toilet paper and you had to dissolve it. It might have been LSD. So I took it, and ten minutes later I started feeling funny, but I didn't feel good. When I stood up, I knew there was something wrong. I shouted, "Danny, help me." He was laughing – he knew I was a joker – but when I shouted again, "Help me, Danny," he knew I wasn't messing about. I collapsed on the floor, and I must have looked bad because Danny called an ambulance. In fact, my heart had stopped and when the paramedics got there they said I had actually died. Danny told me all this later. One of them said, "This is touch and go," and they had to put the resuscitator paddles on me, twice. I died twice on the floor of Danny's house. A third time, and I think I would have had it. That was what they told me when I woke up in hospital.

When the doctor came to see me, he told me I was lucky to be alive. He said,

"Have you ever taken steroids?"

I said, "Yes, I have. Why?"

He said, "When we x-rayed your chest, we found some black scars on your heart. You see, when you were taking those steroids and working out, it wasn't just your biceps and triceps that got bigger. Your heart got bigger, because that's a muscle as well," which was something I'd never thought about before. He said that the scarring would take a couple of years to heal, and then if I was lucky, my heart would return to normal. "But," he said, "I would advise you not to take steroids again, otherwise you will be putting your life at risk."

I was 32 years old, and definitely not ready for that, so as I lay there in that hospital bed, I made a decision, a promise to myself, that I'd taken the last drugs I was ever going to take. Steroids, cocaine, speed, halcyons; I'd finished with them.

A few weeks later I was back on my feet again, but still feeling terrible. Somehow, I managed another trip to Japan with Johnny Smith. But it was a struggle. In fact, one night, I looked so ill, Baba wouldn't let me wrestle. He made me take the night off, which, apart from when I injured my back, was something I'd never done before. I only just made it through that tour before I went back to England to pick up some work there.

And there was still work in England; Max Crabtree was still around, Brian Dixon and Oric Williams were running their own promotions, but as you can imagine, the standards of wrestling in 1991 were worse than ever. They were terrible. The first thing I noticed were the gimmicks. The WWF was being shown on television in England, and most of the English wrestlers were nothing but poor imitations of the Americans.

I did a few matches for Oric Williams against Dave "Fit" Finlay, who could wrestle, and Skull Murphy. I was the main event, and for that Oric was paying me about £130 a night, plus travel expenses. And because he billed me as the British Bulldog, with the name Dynamite Kid underneath in very small writing, he was selling-out every night.

You see, by this stage, Davey Boy Smith was appearing on TV with the WWF every week as the British Bulldog.

And it caused a bit of trouble with somebody from the Trade Descriptions Office, who turned up at the arena one night asking to speak to me and the promoter. Somebody had reported me for using a wrestling name without permission; according to them, I was an impostor. It was Davey Boy Smith's parents, Sid and Joyce, my aunt and uncle, who had seen me billed as the British Bulldog on a wrestling advertisement. They called Davey in Calgary and he'd got onto the officials to try and stop me using the name.

Oric Williams, the promoter, pointed at me and said, "There's the original Bulldog there."

The man ignored him and said to me, "You can't use that name. If you do, we'll have to take matters further."

I said, "I've been a Bulldog all my life. You sue me, and I'll counter-sue the fuck out of all of you."

The same thing happened at a show in Belfast; two complete strangers telling me I couldn't use my own ring name, telling me I couldn't be a British Bulldog. I replied, "I am a British Bulldog. Furthermore, I have all the evidence – the videotapes, the programmes, the pictures to prove it. And I will use that name tonight. You can either try to stop me or you can take me to court, but I'll sue the bollocks off the lot of you."

So while Davey Boy Smith was making $20,000 for one-night's work on a WWF pay-per-view, I was making £130 – which, by English standards, was great – but for some reason, that bothered him. The stupid thing about it was, that if it hadn't been for me, Davey Boy Smith would never have been a British Bulldog in the first place. Oric Williams said the same thing to Davey's parents when he rang them and told them to back off. He said, "How can you carry on this game with Tommy, when you know for a fact it was Tommy who took him over there?" They never gave him an answer, but the Trades Descriptions people never bothered us again.

Some things hadn't changed at all in English wrestling. I did a few shows for Brian Dixon, who ran All Star Promotions. I did a tag match for him in Bristol one night – I can't even remember who it was against, I'd never seen them before in my life, and they were terrible anyway. When I came out of the ring, Brian Dixon had already left the building, but he had given my envelope with my pay to another wrestler, Drew MacDonald.

As soon as Drew handed me the envelope I said, "This is wrong." Brian always gave me my money in my hand when I came out of the ring. I opened it and it was £30 short. I got in my car – Danny Collins, and Skull Murphy had to come with me because we were sharing cars – and I found Brian Dixon up the road, at a pub called the Windmill, which was a famous picking-up point for the wrestlers. I got out of the car, walked over to his, and asked him to wind the window down. I said: "Brian, you've paid me short, and I know you've done this on purpose."

Brian said, "Dynamite, it's just a mistake."

I said, "Yes, it is a big mistake on your behalf Brian, and I want that £30 now."

He said, "I've got no money."

So I said, "In that case you'd better find some money right now." He was still in his car and couldn't get out of the car park because I had blocked the entrance with my car.

He said, "Er, Tommy, I'll tell you what, I'll send you a cheque."

"You won't send me a cheque, you'll pay me now you sonofabitch." I think that was when he realized I was being serious.

Brian turned to the referee who was sitting in the car with him and said, "Give me £30, quick," which he did, and Brian handed it to me. That was also the last time that he booked me.

But I carried on working for Oric Williams, and for a three or four month spell I was working up to seven days a week. I wrestled Skull Murphy and Dave "Fit" Finlay. I did a few tag matches with Johnny Smith when he came over to England for a few weeks. We did tours of Wales, Ireland, Scotland, all over England, and the crowds were great. We were in a bar one night having a beer after the matches and one Irish lad came up to me. I was just being polite when I said to him, "All right lad?"

He said, "I'm not a fucking lad. And I want my money back." I was wrestling as a babyface on this occasion, so I ignored him. All the other wrestlers were there, and they ignored him as well. Then he said, "This isn't the WWF. I want my money back."

When I came out of the bar, six of this guy's mates were waiting for me outside. That's when I realized their problem was nothing to do with the WWF or the British Bulldog. It was the Union Jack tights I'd been wrestling in. We were in Londonderry and I suppose they took it as an insult. So there were a few verbals out in the car park, but I looked at the six of them, and one of me, and thought, "No way." I got in the car and drove back to the hotel.

But I think that in spite of the rivalry, the promoters in England are really as thick as thieves. And I'm sure that Oric Williams had been talking to Brian Dixon, when he asked me one night if I would take a pay cut.

I said, "I don't think I should," and held out for my £130. I got it too, but that was my last night for Oric Williams, in spite of me drawing all that money for him. A few months later, Oric did call me back, asking me to do a show in Doncaster, Yorkshire. So I said I would. I was wrestling Skull Murphy in the main event, and Skull asked me to pick him up at a service station just north of Manchester. I told him to be there at 6PM, but I never went. And Skull never went because I didn't pick him up. So Oric Williams had no main event that night, which I thought squared things up between us.

At the end of November 1991, Johnny Smith called me from Calgary to make sure I was still on for the end of year tag tournament in Japan. To be honest, I didn't think I could manage it. We'd done a tour about two months before that, and I'd had it in mind that that might have been my last for All Japan. I even told Joe Higuchi, but all he said was, "What you need is a good rest, Tom. A few weeks. Then you'll feel better." So I'd carried on.

But I knew this time would have to be my last time. I just couldn't do it anymore. The day we arrived in Tokyo, I went to see Joe. I said, "I'm sorry, Joe, but this will be my last time in Japan." He just sort of laughed, as in, "Where have I heard that before?" I said, "No, you don't understand. This is the last time. Every time I go in the ring I get bodyslammed or suplexed, take backdrops. My body is in too much pain. So after this tour, I finish. No more."

He said, "What you should do is just take it a bit easier in the ring. Not so hard. You'll be OK, Tom."

But that wasn't it. Injured or not, I've never taken it easy in the ring. When you are there, in a full arena, the fans all shouting your name – you want to do it. You want to provide. And whether I could or I couldn't, I'd still try. I mean, I'd gone to the ring in Japan many times with ripped knee cartilages. I just taped them up and got on with it. And one thing for sure was that your Japanese opponent would never take it easy with you. Joe did his best to change my mind, but I said, "Please tell Baba thank you very much, but the last day of this tournament will be my last day of wrestling in Japan."

Word soon got around that this was going to be my retirement tour. The Japanese wrestler, Fuchi, came to see me. He said, "Kid. Please don't retire. Just take six months off."

I said, "What difference will that make?"

"Tell Baba you will be back in six months, but don't say you are retiring."

In his mind, Fuchi was thinking that maybe Baba would pay me some money if he thought I was coming back. But six months, a year, no amount of time away was going to make any difference now. I knew that for a fact.

December 6 1991, the day after my birthday, was the last night of the tournament, which was won by Steve Williams and Terry Gordy. Me and Johnny Smith wrestled Johnny Ace and Sunny Beach. It wasn't a long match, and it ended when I suplexed Sunny off the top rope and pinned him, one, two, three. At the end of my match, all the Japanese wrestlers climbed into the ring, all wearing track suits. They grabbed hold of me and threw me up in the air and caught me. They did that three times, and the people were all cheering and shouting, "KI-DO, KI-DO," which I must admit made me feel a bit sad, because I knew I'd never hear it again. But they gave me a good send-off. And although I probably did feel a little bit down, maybe even depressed, there was no getting away from the fact that as far as my body was concerned, retirement hadn't come soon enough.

I didn't go away empty-handed either. Back in the dressing room, the wrestlers presented me with a sweatshirt that everybody had signed. From Baba, I had a radio-cassette player, and a few other presents from different people in the promotion. After the matches, we hit the Tokyo nightlife for the last time.

The next morning, we were all at Narita Airport waiting to catch our flights to England or America. Abdullah the Butcher came over to me and handed me a present. He said, "There you go, champ. Something to remember me by." It was a watch.

I said, "Thanks Butch."

Abdullah said, "Go on, fuck off." I think he was ready to cry. That was the last time I saw him. You say to people that you'll keep in touch, give them a call, but as I found out, once you've left the business, that doesn't happen often. Out of sight, out of mind is very true.

In May of that year, I had become a dad again, to my second little girl, Amaris. The following year, the divorce was finalized. I never contested it. I left Michelle everything; the properties, the cars, the lot. All that mattered to me was that my three kids would have everything they needed.

As you can imagine, on English wages, wrestling wasn't the best way to earn a living. So in 1993, when I had a call from Tokyo, telling me that Baba wanted me to come back to Japan, not to wrestle, but to judge some matches, I said I'd go.

They flew me over, just for the one night, and all I had to do was judge the best match between Dan Spivey and Kobashi, Stan Hansen and Kawada, and Misawa and Taue. When I walked into that arena, I got a great reception from the fans, as if they were really pleased to see me again. I sat at ringside next to the commentary table, watched the wrestling, and picked Misawa's match as the best. That was all I had to do. The next day, I was on a plane home to England. And for that one-day's work, Baba paid me a full-week's guarantee: $6,200.

I thought it was funny, the way they flew me in and out like that. But deep down, I knew why. They knew if I was there for a whole week, but only working one day, I'd have six days to get into trouble. A few weeks after that, against my better judgement, I did one more match with Johnny Smith for Baba, but it was a big mistake. It was terrible. If I hadn't needed the money, I would never have gone back.

Not long after that *final*, final match for Baba, I had another unexpected phone call, this time from Bret Hart. He was over on a tour of the UK with the WWF and wanted to come and see me. He turned up with Scarpa, or Chief Jay Strongbow, and Brian Knobbs. We sat and talked for hours, had a few beers, and then Bret said to me, "Tom, do you want to come back to the WWF? I'm the top man now you know."

I said, "No, not really Bret. Even if I wanted to, I'd have to juice up a bit," as in, get back on the steroids. I'd maybe taken half a dozen shots since I had come back from Calgary.

Bret said, "Oh no, you don't need to do any of that."

I said, "Why's that?"

He said, "Nobody's allowed to take steroids any more." Which made me smile because I knew that all the wrestlers had slimmed down a lot and they were saying things like, "Oh, I've lost weight, I'm going for the leaner look," which was bollocks.

Anyway I said, "No I'm in the main event with Dave Finlay at the moment. Thanks for asking me Bret, but I'm doing OK."

He said, "OK, But if you do want to come back…"

And then Chief Jay interrupted him, "…we'll send you a ticket next week."

Which made me feel good, but I still wouldn't change my mind. You see, three years, fours years on, it didn't matter. Once I'd told Vince I was finishing, I did mean it. And physically, I wasn't up to it anyway.

It was around the same time that I heard Davey Boy Smith had left the WWF and joined WCW. But he didn't stay long, and by the end of the year, he'd left the company and was working for independent promoters. I knew that for a fact, because the following year, 1994, he was back in England working for Max Crabtree. When I heard that he was appearing on a card in Howe Bridge, a small village not more than a couple of miles from Wigan where I was living, well, I couldn't resist. I had to go.

You see, the problems that eventually split up the British Bulldogs, had gone beyond just two wrestlers. They had affected both our families as well. My dad and Davey's mum were brother and sister, and a few years ago, had been very close. When my dad found out he was dying of cancer, that was the time when they should have been even closer. The doctors had diagnosed the cancer five years earlier, and his chances looked bad then. But he fought it, and managed five more years, five good years, before it finally took hold. They took him into hospital one weekend when I was away, wrestling in Germany. When I heard, I came home straight away to see him.

I said, "What's wrong, dad?" And he told me the cancer was back. And this time, there was nothing they could do for him. Now, as I told you right at the start of this story, my dad was never a swearing man. Not even when he was working down in the mines (my own excuse is that I spent too long around other wrestlers). Davey's mum, Joyce, knew that he hadn't long to live and she called my mum, to ask if she could visit him.

She told him, "Billy, Joyce wants to know if she can come and see you."

My dad was very weak at this point, very ill. But he turned round to my mum and said, "Tell them to piss off."

Shortly after that, he died. He never did see Sid and Joyce again. When he went, I was devastated. I thought the world of my dad.

So all of this was still fresh in my mind when I turned up at the wrestling hall in Howe Bridge. Davey was wrestling a tag match, and the first thing I saw when I walked in was a table full of his pictures. So I tipped the thing up, and the pictures flew everywhere. Max Crabtree came over, trying to calm things down, but in the middle of all this, somebody opened the doors to let the fans in. Max was shouting, "Close those doors."

Then I saw Davey's dad. My uncle Sid. I said, "All right, where is the fat bastard?"

He said, "He's not here yet."

I said, "If you're here, he's here. Where is he?"

While all this was going on, somebody called the police and eventually about eight of them came. They arrested me, handcuffed me, and led me out of the building. I found out later that Davey Boy Smith had locked himself in a private dressing room.

One of the last shows I did in the UK was in Croydon, in 1996. I did it because I needed the money – believe me, I didn't enjoy it. Anyway, after the matches, this little Japanese guy who had been in the crowd, came to see me. He told me his name was Hiroshi and he was a booking agent for a new promotion in Japan called Michinoku Pro. And the promoter wanted me to go over there and work for him. I'll be honest, at first, I didn't take him too seriously. It had been three years since I'd stepped in a Japanese ring, and I knew then that I was a long way from looking good. Now I looked bloody awful. And I felt awful. I was having trouble with my back, my legs, my shoulder – in fact my whole body seemed to be in pain at some time or another. But I needed the money. Plus, I always liked Japan, and wanted to see it again – just one last time.

Hiroshi asked me how much Baba had paid me when I was with All Japan. So I told him. $6,200 a week guarantee. He rang the promoter in Japan, a wrestler by the name of The Great Sasuke, and eventually Hiroshi came back and told me that Sasuke would pay me the equivalent of £500, about $700.

I said, "How much?" But Hiroshi said that was all Sasuke would pay, which was very poor compared to what I'd been used to earning in Japan, plus, physically, I wasn't even sure whether I was up to the 12-hour flight. But I said I would do it.

The first time I went for Michinoku Pro, they wanted me there as a surprise for one of the wrestlers in the promotion. I was driven by taxi from the hotel to the arena, and I had to wear a mask, which I always hated because they made me feel sick. I walked down to the ring, and stood face to face with a man I hadn't been in the same ring with for 12 years. It was Satoru Sayama, Tiger Mask. When I took my mask off, he looked really shocked. He put his hands up to his face, like he couldn't believe it was me – although I'm sure part of it was the shock of seeing how much I had changed. Don't get me wrong, Sayama had changed as well. He'd gained a bit of weight, and looked chubbier than I remembered him, and he wasn't as agile as he used to be. It was hard to believe how fast those 15 years had gone. I didn't wrestle that night, I just sat and watched the matches. They asked me to say something over the microphone, so I said something like, "Sayama, ichiban," or, Sayama, number-one man.

I watched Sasuke wrestle – and I must admit, he did some very dangerous moves; over the ropes, into the crowd. I mean, he had to have a lot of faith in his opponents who were catching him coming down. When he came into the arena before his match, I thought to myself, "There's something wrong here," because he walked down the aisle with maybe seven or eight girls, all in single file, behind him, each one holding one of his belts up in the air. I thought, "Now that was what I called being glorified." But when Sasuke asked me to come back in October, he came to the ring with one belt, so I thought, fair enough, he doesn't always win.

That second time I went, they wanted me to wrestle in a six-man tag match – myself, Kobayashi and a Mexican wrestler, Dos Caras, against Sasuke, Sayama and Mil Mascaras. I wasn't feeling too good on the flight over, and by the time I got to the building I knew I was very ill. I kept getting that familiar feeling of light-headedness and seeing spots in front of my eyes. I knew what was coming, just like I'd known on half a dozen previous occasions. I stood in the dressing room, trying to shake the feeling off, and saying to myself, "Tommy, just hang on lad. Get the match over and get your money." You see, if anything had happened before the match, I knew I wouldn't get paid. So I drank about a gallon of water and kept shaking my head, saying, "Don't let it happen now. Please don't let it happen now."

All I wanted to do was to get the match over and go home. I made it to the ring, the arena was full, and I'll be honest, the fans were cheering and clapping, like they were genuinely glad to see me, but I'm sure they must have been shocked at the way I looked. Thankfully, the other wrestlers did most of the work in that match, in fact they more or less kept to themselves in the ring. I never felt part of it, and to tell you he truth, it was just big relief when the bell rang and I could get back to the dressing room.

I was due to fly home the next day. I'd made it through the match, Sasuke had paid me, but that horrible feeling was still there in my head; something bad was definitely going to happen. I was feeling a bit down anyway, because I knew, for the first time in my life, I'd been booked for my name instead of my ability. The truth was, I didn't have any ability at that moment. But it was still a terrible feeling.

Hiroshi, the booking agent, picked me up from the hotel and we caught the train to Narita airport. I said to him, "I will check in, while you change my money from Yen to Sterling." He disappeared. I put my case down, and that's when it happened. I suddenly felt warm and light-headed and saw the stars in front of my eyes. I said, "Help," but my voice sounded like it was coming from a long way away. The next thing I knew, I was in hospital, aching from head to foot. I missed three flights home because of that seizure, but I knew I'd been lucky that it hadn't happened in the ring the night before.

I never heard from Sasuke again. Hiroshi rang a couple of times to tell me about another new promotion in Japan called Battlearts. He said, "If you bring some more wrestlers from Wigan, you could be their manager Tommy." But for whatever reason, it never came to anything.

The year after that, just when everything seemed to be as bad as it could possibly get, something good happened. I met my wife, Dot. She didn't know who I was, or what I'd done, never heard of the Dynamite Kid, never watched wrestling, but we hit it off straight away. All those years I was wrestling, I never knew whether people wanted to be around Tommy Billington or the Dynamite Kid. When you're a famous face on television, and you're earning good money and living a good lifestyle, as I did, you find all kinds of people coming out of the wood-work wanting to get close to you and be your friend. But when you're no longer that famous face, and the money and the lifestyle are gone, they crawl back into the woodwork. That's when you find out who your real friends are.

We got married in 1997, and everything was great, until just a few months later, when my past finally caught up with me, big time. I'd noticed my legs and back were aching a lot more then they ever used to, and some days, it was a struggle even to walk or climb the stairs. I tried to ignore it, but I was worried. On a couple of occasions my legs just buckled under me and I collapsed. I'd managed to deal with the pain before, but now it was much more serious. I couldn't walk.

I went to see a specialist at the local hospital, and he sounded hopeful that they could sort me out with surgery. They ran x-rays and tests, including a CT scan, and ten-days later, I went back for the results, and to fix up a date for the operation. All I wanted was to be able to get back on my feet and walk. But as soon as the doctor walked into the room, I could tell straight away from the look on his face that it wasn't good news. He started off. "Mr. Billington..."

I stopped him and said, "My name's Tommy. What's yours?"

He said, "Sam."

"OK Sam, can you just tell me what's wrong with me altogether?"

So he gave it to me straight. "Basically Tommy, the damage to your back is too extensive."

"What do you mean?"

He said, "There's nothing else we can do for you."

I said, "But will I be able to walk again?

He said, "I can't be absolutely certain, but no, probably not." He told me there was nothing more they could do for me surgically, because there were complications from the original operation that I'd had in Calgary in 1986. There was too much scar tissue, and the chances of success were so slim, they weren't prepared to take the risk. I couldn't see what difference that made. If there was only a one-per cent chance of success, for me, it was still worth trying. In my opinion, they couldn't make things any worse. But he said no; he was very sorry, but he couldn't help me. That was it. I wouldn't walk again.

I wasn't prepared at all for that. It was a bombshell. But I wasn't going to show it there in the hospital, so I thanked the doctor, politely, turned round to Dot and said, "Get me out of here."

It was the end of the world and I really couldn't see any point in carrying on.

CHAPTER SEVENTEEN

Without a doubt, that was the worst day of my life, and for the next few months after that I was really down. I'm sure you can understand why; when you think about all the things I used to be able to do in the ring, and now I couldn't even walk across the room. It was too painful to even think about wrestling, never mind watch it on TV.

But in my mind I knew that there was no point crying over spilled milk, and I reached a point, what I would call rock bottom, where I knew I had to change my attitude. And slowly, over the next few months I did. I started coming to terms with it. I even managed to think about the wrestling business again; the people I met, the places I'd been – and the pranks I used to play. As far as wrestling goes, the memories are all I have left.

Thirteen years isn't a long time to be in the wrestling business, not when you see how long some people have lasted. But I packed a lot in to that 13 years; I met, and wrestled, some of the greatest names in the business. Some were already legends, others were definitely heading that way. And I met a lot of men who had no wrestling ability at all, but for me, were great men all the same.

If I had to name a favourite place to wrestle, I'd say Japan. Not just for the quality of the matches, but for the respect that Japanese wrestlers have for the business, and the standards that they set for themselves. They were classy. Everything they did – even presenting you with your championship belt – the Japanese did in a very professional way.

I wrestled so many good men over there, it would be hard to single any one of them out as a favourite opponent, but definitely, some of the best singles matches I ever had were with Satoru Sayama – in my opinion, the best of all the Tiger Masks. And I always had great matches with Tatsumi Fujinami, who was a gentleman and a very talented wrestler.

And Kuniaki Kobayashi. And Riki Choshu, who was one of the hardest hitters in the promotion.

In All Japan, Mitsuhara Misawa, who, I'll admit, I didn't always see eye to eye with, was one of the most solid wrestlers in the ring. The matches between the Bulldogs and Misawa and Kawada, were some of the most intense tag matches I'd ever been in. On the last night of the tour, it was like the Gunfight at the OK Corral – that's how intense they were. And those two worked hard – I mean, sometimes, a little bit too hard. That's when I used to tape my fist up because I thought to myself, "One bad move here, one of them tries it on, and I'll knock his head off." They were incredible matches. Way back in 1985 when I first wrestled Misawa, I thought he would go all the way to the top with All Japan. He did it, and he deserves it.

The late Shohei "Giant" Baba, I will always remember as a great promoter and an even greater man, who kept his word, even when he was mad with me. He knew he wasn't the greatest wrestler in the promotion, and as he got a bit older, took his place a little bit further down the card to make way for the younger men. He wrestled because he enjoyed it, he was never in it for the glory. Antonio Inoki, who I also liked and admired, saw things a different way. He always went last, no matter who his opponent was. He could have a card full of spectacular matches, but he'd still keep that top slot for himself. Don't get me wrong, the people in Japan loved Inoki. He really was a legend, but sometimes, he'd climb in the ring, rip the towel from round his neck – and depending on who his opponent was, that could be the best move of the match.

There were a lot of American wrestlers who I rated – and still do rate – whenever I get chance to see their matches on television. As a tag team, the Bulldogs' matches with the Hart Foundation were as good as any I can remember. Bret was the captain of that team. He did all the work and made the matches. And in singles, I always enjoyed wrestling Bret Hart. Maybe he wasn't the best there ever was, but he was one of the hardest workers and definitely deserved his success.

What do I think about professional wrestling today? It has taken a very different direction to the one I remember, and because of that, a lot of people have asked me, was the style of wrestling better in my day?

Did I have the best of it? I'm sure the likes of Lou Thesz and Bert Assirati thought they had the best of wrestling in their day. And when Steve Austin and The Rock look back, they'll think exactly the same. I'm not sure you can ever pick out one era of wrestling and say that was the best time. The truth is, the best of wrestling is what a wrestler makes it. And I definitely gave it my best shot.

As far as Vince McMahon Jr. goes, like the man or dislike the man, you can't knock success. All said and done, at this moment in time he's got all the big names in wrestling; Rock, Triple H, Kurt Angle, Steve Austin, Chris Jericho, Chris Benoit... the list goes on. You never would have thought it years ago, but some big men have become flyers.

These days I don't know what goes on behind closed doors. All I know is they are doing a good job in the ring at this moment in time. Times do change, but I'm sure there are some pranksters around in the WWF. The world would be boring if everyone was the same.

After quite a few years of being away from the wrestling world, I finally returned to it, last December at the WWF PPV Rebellion in Sheffield, England. I hadn't seen some of the people there for over 12 years, but it was great to meet up again with Vince, Pat Patterson, Jerry Briscow, Earl and Dave Hebner, Tim White, Tony Garea, Chris Benoit, who is a very good friend of mine, Mick Foley, Rikishi, and Dean Malenko. We had a few laughs about the old days and some of the things the Bulldogs got up to.

It was good to see that business was doing so well. I also met quite a few of the newer wrestlers; Chris Jericho, Rock, the Dudleys, Edge and Christian, the Hardyz, Steve Richards, Eddie Guererro, Perry Saturn, Chyna, Lita, Trish Stratus, and quite a few others. They were all very polite and seemed to me like good decent people – all I can say is good luck to them in their careers. All said and done, it is their time right now. I did my time in the seventies and eighties.

I also met Jim Ross at Rebellion, who I would like to thank for mentioning my name a couple of times on the night of WrestleMania 17. It is good to know that you are still remembered so many years after you have left the wrestling world.

I always tried to give the fans their money's worth, and my opponents, their matches' worth. At five-foot-eight inches tall, I must have been the smallest WWF Tag Team Champion ever, if not the one that caused the most trouble. When I remember that match that I had with Sayama, in Madison Square Garden, 1982, I believe, that between us, we showed Vince McMahon – who was commentating at ringside that night – that the smaller guys can do the business just as well, maybe even better, than the big guys. He even told me a few years later. "Tom, that was one of the best matches I ever saw." And I think he meant it.

Danny Spivey still calls me from Florida. His legs are nearly as knackered as mine, but we still make each other laugh. He tried his hand at promoting a couple of years ago, and called to tell me about it soon afterward.

I said, "What's up, Eug?" His middle name was Eugene – plus he really is huge – but nobody else was ever allowed to call him that.

He said, "Tommy, I've just run a show in Tampa. I had the Sheik on"

"Not THE Iron Sheik?"

"No. The other one, Jack Coogan." Well he was a terrible wrestler anyway, but Danny had had to fly him in, along with about ten other wrestlers, but a couple of them no-showed. So Danny, who was the promoter, had to wrestle instead. Bear in mind that his legs had gone and his hips had gone. He had to pay all the airline tickets, all the wrestlers' guarantees, and he only managed to bring about 200 people into the building.

I said, "What happened?"

Danny said, "Tommy, I lost my ass."

"What do you mean?"

"I'm broke. Flat broke." But even as he was telling me, he was laughing.

I was laughing too. I said, "Well, Danny, it was worth a try."

To be honest, I don't hear from too many people in wrestling. As I soon found out, once you've left the business, and the lifestyle, behind, people soon forget about you. It was a lifestyle that I loved, but I paid a price for it; I left behind my three children, Bronwyne, Marek, and Amaris, who I think the world of and will always be very proud of. And when they watch some of their dad's old matches on video, I hope they're proud of me.

A couple of years ago I met up with an old friend, and a former colleague of mine, John Naylor, the Golden Ace, – you remember, who gave Honeyboy Zimba a goat for his Christmas dinner? I hadn't seen John for over 20 years, when he rang me out of the blue and said he was on his way to see me. It turned out we'd been nearly neighbours for years and neither of us knew. He still has his allotments – and his goats – which is where I spend a lot of my time these days, helping him with the livestock, and going to the auctions.

As for my former tag team partner, there isn't much more I can say. I haven't spoken to Davey Boy Smith in over eight years, and probably never will again. But it doesn't make any difference to the way I feel about the British Bulldogs. As far as I'm concerned we were one of the best tag teams in the business, at that time.

I'll be honest, when I started out wrestling as the Dynamite Kid all those years ago, I had no idea things would end up the way they did. But I'd do it all again. I wouldn't change a thing. Which I know sounds strange coming from a guy whose wrestling career put him in a wheelchair, but it's true. Wrestling was my life, and I loved it. No regrets. I had a blast.